THE PHILOSOPHY OF HORROR

The Philosophy of Popular Culture

The books published in the Philosophy of Popular Culture series will illuminate and explore philosophical themes and ideas that occur in popular culture. The goal of this series is to demonstrate how philosophical inquiry has been reinvigorated by increased scholarly interest in the intersection of popular culture and philosophy, as well as to explore through philosophical analysis beloved modes of entertainment, such as movies, TV shows, and music. Philosophical concepts will be made accessible to the general reader through examples in popular culture. This series seeks to publish both established and emerging scholars who will engage a major area of popular culture for philosophical interpretation and examine the philosophical underpinnings of its themes. Eschewing ephemeral trends of philosophical and cultural theory, authors will establish and elaborate on connections between traditional philosophical ideas from important thinkers and the ever-expanding world of popular culture.

SERIES EDITOR

Mark T. Conard, Marymount Manhattan College, NY

BOOKS IN THE SERIES

The Philosophy of Stanley Kubrick, edited by Jerold J. Abrams
Football and Philosophy, edited by Michael W. Austin
The Philosophy of the Coen Brothers, edited by Mark T. Conard
The Philosophy of Film Noir, edited by Mark T. Conard
The Philosophy of Martin Scorsese, edited by Mark T. Conard
The Philosophy of Neo-Noir, edited by Mark T. Conard
The Philosophy of The X-Files, edited by Dean A. Kowalski
Steven Spielberg and Philosophy, edited by Dean A. Kowalski
The Philosophy of Science Fiction Film, edited by Steven M. Sanders
The Philosophy of TV Noir, edited by Steven M. Sanders and Aeon J. Skoble
Basketball and Philosophy, edited by Jerry L. Walls and Gregory Bassham

THE PHILOSOPHY OF HORROR

Edited by Thomas Fahy

THE UNIVERSITY PRESS OF KENTUCKY

Copyright © 2010 by The University Press of Kentucky

Scholarly publisher for the Commonwealth,
serving Bellarmine University, Berea College, Centre
College of Kentucky, Eastern Kentucky University,
The Filson Historical Society, Georgetown College,
Kentucky Historical Society, Kentucky State University,
Morehead State University, Murray State University,
Northern Kentucky University, Transylvania University,
University of Kentucky, University of Louisville,
and Western Kentucky University.
All rights reserved.

Editorial and Sales Offices: The University Press of Kentucky
663 South Limestone Street, Lexington, Kentucky 40508-4008
www.kentuckypress.com

   14 13 12 11 10   5 4 3 2 1

Library of Congress Cataloging-in-Publication Data

The philosophy of horror / edited by Thomas Fahy.
    p.   cm. — (The philosophy of popular culture)
  Includes bibliographical references and index.
  ISBN 978-0-8131-2573-2 (hardcover : alk. paper)
  1. Horror films—History and criticism. 2. Horror television
programs—History and criticism. 3. Horror in literature. 4. Horror
tales, American—History and criticism. 5. Popular culture. I. Fahy,
Thomas Richard.
  PN1995.9.H6P45 2010
  791.43'6164—dc22
                      2009053152

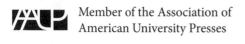

Contents

Acknowledgments

I'd like to thank the contributors for all of their hard work and impressive essays. I am particularly grateful to Anne Dean Watkins and everyone at the University Press of Kentucky for making this book a reality. I am also indebted to Long Island University, Daniel Kurtzman, Susann Cokal, and Pamela L. Ayari for their support. Lastly, for going above and beyond the call of duty in helping with this project, I'd like to thank John Lutz.

This book is dedicated to Tatyana Tsinberg and Nicolai Meir Fahy for their love and inspiration.

Introduction

Thomas Fahy

Not long ago several friends invited me to go skydiving. The prospect of jumping out of a plane made my stomach tighten and my mouth go dry, but reluctantly I agreed. Part of me wanted to be perceived as adventurous and brave. I had always been afraid of heights, and this was an opportunity to confront that fear, to overcome it. The afternoon adventure included a fifteen-minute training course on leaping from the aircraft, arching one's body during the fall, breathing, and, of course, pulling the ripcord. First-timers (all of us) had the added benefit of making a tandem dive—in which an instructor was strapped to our backs to make sure we landed safely.

As the plane took off the dryness in my mouth became more acute. My heart pounded in protest, and I couldn't remember why I had agreed to do something so stupid. While waiting for the jump all of us alternated between making jokes and sitting in silence. Then it was time. As my friends started leaping from the plane, I became more and more nervous. I walked unsteadily to the open door and glanced at the desert ten thousand feet below. I'm not sure if I jumped, fell, or was pushed out of the plane by my instructor. But I can remember moments of the experience vividly. The weightlessness of my body. The air pressing hard against my skin. The strange sensation of falling quickly and slowly at the same time. It was thrilling and terrifying, exciting and awful.

When it was over I felt a profound sense of relief.

But the story of my dive didn't end there. After the jump each of us was encouraged to purchase a video of the event. The dive would be set to music (a song of our choice) and mailed to us a few days later. Now we could watch it again and again, sharing the experience with family and friends.

In many ways the horror genre promises a similar experience: the anticipation of terror, the mixture of fear and exhilaration as events unfold, the opportunity to confront the unpredictable and dangerous, the promise of relative safety (both in the context of a darkened theater and through a narrative structure that lasts for a finite amount of time and/or number of pages), and the feeling of relief and regained control when it's over. As Stephen King notes in *Danse Macabre*, we realize that "the worst has been faced and it wasn't so bad after all."[1] King calls this moment "reintegration," which he compares to the end of a roller coaster ride when one gets off unhurt. We have confronted the threat and survived. These feelings of anxiety, fear, relief, and mastery are certainly an integral part of the pleasure that people derive from the genre, as are the questions that horror typically raises about fear and suffering: Is the world a just place? Does our suffering have meaning? Is there justice and accountability? As these questions suggest, horror not only plays with our desire to encounter the dangerous and horrific in a safe context, but it also wrestles with the complex nature of violence, suffering, and morality.[2]

The pleasure of horror can also come from rewatching and rereading a text. I've enjoyed viewing my skydiving video several times because it allows me to relive the experience, but knowing the outcome certainly changes my relationship to it. Repetition creates a new space for elaborating on a narrative (the stories told about the event) and, in some cases, for finding the humor in it. (One friend vomited during her dive, for example, and when retelling the story, she gleefully points out that the instructor still asked her out on a date when it was over.)

The humor in horror (intentional or not) eases tension, and on a second or third viewing/reading, it often comes from a recognition of the playfulness of the genre. When Freddy Krueger confronts Alice at her restaurant in *A Nightmare on Elm Street 4: The Dream Master* (1988), for example, he orders a pizza with pepperoni and sausages that have the screaming faces of his victims. The image is startling, disgusting, and, of course, completely ridiculous. But as numerous Web sites about Krueger demonstrate, this is exactly the kind of campy humor that many fans enjoy. Horror audiences, as Noël Carroll notes in *The Philosophy of Horror; or, Paradoxes of the Heart*, tend to "desire that the same stories be told again and again," but they also find pleasure in subtle variations of the expected formula.[3] This kind of repetition, both in varying the conventions of the genre and in the form of sequels, disrupts a fixed interpretation of the text. It opens up new possibilities for frightening audiences, for innovation, and for fun.

Critics often acknowledge this aspect of horror, but play doesn't tend to be the focus of most critical discussions. In *Men, Women, and Chain Saws: Gender in the Modern Horror Film*, Carol J. Clover argues that the genre has moments of "great humor, formal brilliance, political intelligence, psychological depth, and above all a kind of kinky creativity," and she also describes it as "the most self-reflexive of cinematic genres."[4] Such a sentiment is echoed by David J. Russell, who insists that any theory of horror needs to account for innovation, including "horror parody and horror comedies or, for that matter, . . . intergeneric hybrids such as combat horror, horror musical, romance horror, and horror westerns."[5] As Russell's list suggests, horror is preoccupied with novelty, variation, hybridity (through monsters that are living and dead, human and animal, and so on), and collapse. It is self-referential and parodic. And it thrives on drawing from a range of genres (suspense, thriller, fantastic, science fiction, mystery, and the like) and themes in provocative and disturbing ways.[6]

This bricolage and constant reproduction (which are evident in titles such as *Abbott and Costello Meet Frankenstein* [1948], *Dracula vs. Frankenstein* [1971], *I Still Know What You Did Last Summer* [1998], and *Alien vs. Predator* [2004]) are also integral to the genre's ability to speak to/comment on contemporary issues. In Eli Roth's *Cabin Fever* (2002), for example, five college friends take a vacation to a remote mountain cabin for a weekend of sex and drinking. As this description suggests, the film immediately invokes numerous slasher movie clichés. But instead of a predatory serial killer who punishes libidinous teens, the young protagonists of *Cabin Fever* become victims of a flesh-eating contagion. Roth uses horror here to explore modern-day fears about biological terrorism in post-9/11 America.[7] This film illustrates the ways in which the genre can raise philosophical and social questions about our longing to find meaning in a chaotic, fragmented, and often violent world.

The versatility of horror is mirrored in this collection as well. In many ways, *The Philosophy of Horror* is about play. It explores some of the most current variations on the genre. It interrogates our desire to find justice amid the dangers and violence of the natural world. And it considers the crucial role of reproduction, adaptation, and humor in horror today. The title of this collection pays homage, in part, to Carroll's influential study. His exploration of the genre has been the touchstone for philosophical analyses of this topic ever since, and this collection is part of an ongoing discussion that continues to be in dialogue with his work.[8] Specifically, Carroll focuses on the emotional effect that horror is designed to have on audiences, analyzing the genre in terms of recurring structures, narratives, images, and figures with a particular emphasis on the monster. He labels this emotion "art-horror" to distinguish it from natural horror (the terrible things that happen in the everyday world).[9]

Art-horror can be found in various media such as novels, films, and television programs. People watch cable channels dedicated to horror, such as Chiller and Monsters HD, rent horror films, and read books by Stephen King all in the same week. They seek out adaptations of their favorite books and enjoy the seemingly endless variations on vampire and zombie myths. They laugh at the parodies found in *Scream* and *Scary Movie*, and they consume many of these over and over again. *The Philosophy of Horror* puts discussions of horror in literature, film, and television side by side to reflect the ways in which audiences consume the genre. Such an approach cannot be comprehensive, of course, but arguably no study of horror can be. The genre has become too expansive and diversified for that. Instead, this collection attempts to balance classic horror "texts," such as Mary Shelley's *Frankenstein* (1818), some of the horror films of the 1930s, Stephen King's novels, Stanley Kubrick's adaptation of *The Shining*, and Alfred Hitchcock's *Psycho* (1960), with works that have largely been ignored in philosophical circles. In addition to essays about Truman Capote's *In Cold Blood* (1965), Patrick Süskind's *Perfume* (1985), and James Purdy's *Narrow Rooms* (2005), several contributors examine some of the most popular horror and torture-horror films of the twenty-first century, including *Saw* (2004), *Hostel* (2005), *The Devil's Rejects* (2005), and *The Hills Have Eyes* (1977, 2006). Likewise, the essays on television acknowledge the ongoing popularity of horror on the small screen, including the newest hybrid of horror: reality-horror television.

In many respects, only the first two essays of this collection are about the "philosophy of horror." The topic of the rest of the book might best be described as "philosophy and horror," offering aesthetic, cultural, and post-structuralist interpretations of the genre. Nevertheless, these opening essays raise crucial questions and provide an important jumping-off point for the interdisciplinary philosophical interpretations that follow. Many contributors draw on feminist, postcolonial, queer, Marxist, and/or psychoanalytic criticism, and this range of critical approaches mirrors the fluidity and hybridity of horror as well. Overall, these essays celebrate the rich, strange, compelling, and disturbing elements of this genre. They invite us to think about its various manifestations and transformations since the late 1700s, probing its social, cultural, and political functions. And they continue an ongoing discussion about the popular need for and interest in horror.

Overview

In keeping with this emphasis on play, each essay uses horror texts not only to animate philosophical and cultural discussions about the genre but also to demonstrate how horror "plays with" philosophy—bending or twisting our notions of rationality and "nature." Accordingly, the volume is organized around several philosophical concepts: morality (Philip J. Nickel, Philip Tallon, Jeremy Morris, Thomas Fahy), identity (Jessica O'Hara, Amy Kind, Lorena Russell), cultural history (John Lutz, Paul A. Cantor), and aesthetics/medium (Susann Cokal, Robert F. Gross, Ann C. Hall, and David MacGregor Johnston).

In "Horror and the Idea of Everyday Life: On Skeptical Threats in *Psycho* and *The Birds*," Philip J. Nickel takes up the first topic of the volume, morality, by posing two questions: What is horror? and What is good about it? Most criticism has focused on why the genre is pleasurable, often demonizing the most violent examples as promoting corruption, but Nickel considers its moral value. He argues that the good of horror comes from its ability to challenge our commonplace assumptions about safety and security: "The idea of security in the everyday is based on an intellectually dubious but pragmatically attractive construction. We can hardly resist relying on the world not to annihilate us, and we can hardly resist trusting others not to do so." Using Alfred Hitchcock's *The Birds* and *Psycho* as examples, Nickel argues that horror's power comes from a "*malicious* ripping-away of this intellectual trust, exposing our vulnerabilities in relying on the world and on other people." So what is good about this experience? Nickel concludes that the value of horror comes from reminding us of this vulnerability, demonstrating the importance of acting in the presence of fear, and making us aware of the ways in which we have constructed a safe worldview in order to function.

Philip Tallon's "Through a Mirror, Darkly: Art-Horror as a Medium for Moral Reflection" also investigates the ways that horror disrupts and challenges our perceptions. The value of art-horror, Tallon argues, comes from "reminding us of our inner moral frailty and . . . forcing us to take seriously the moral reality of evil." Mary Shelley's *Frankenstein* offers a portrait of this frailty through Victor Frankenstein. She uses his hubris to expose the dangers of scientific rationalism and exploration in the Enlightenment era. Tallon juxtaposes Victor's moral weakness here with postmodern horror. Just as the Romantic era questioned Enlightenment attitudes about progress, postmodernism has attacked similar assumptions about progress in contemporary society. Even though the postmodern era has given rise to moral relativism, it has not removed a longing and desire for order. This is what makes horror so effective today: it offers audiences "a sense of moral, social, and aesthetic stability." As Tallon explains through Stephen King's *'Salem's Lot*, "it seems, then, that horror not only provides a critique of our optimism about the world, but also expresses our pessimism about any sense of order: horror helps to illuminate aspects of our commonly held, if explicitly denied, underlying objective view of morality."

The extreme violence of torture-horror films, however, makes it difficult for many viewers to find the kind of moral value that Nickel and Tallon propose. But Jeremy Morris argues that understanding the moral issues at play in works like *Saw, Hostel,* and *The Devil's Rejects* is essential for appreciating them. Like other works of horror, these types of films strive to elicit fear in the audience, but they do so through torture. Some of the essential features of torture-horror include a role reversal between torturer and victim, realism, retributivist elements, narratives that seek an appropriate code of punishment, and sadism. These aspects ultimately raise questions about justification and pleasure: Is torture justified? Is the audience's enjoyment of torture justified? Putting these questions in dialogue with Kant's ideas about autonomy as they relate to retribution and sadism, Morris concludes that the audience's pleasure comes from the ways in which the torturer's pleasure is infectious. "Here is the genius of sadistic torture-horror: it transforms the source of fear from a distant other to something familiar in ourselves. The terror of the victim is supplanted by the delight of the torturer, which is being consciously shared by the audience: *that* is the source of horror." Torture-horror, therefore, requires an audience both to empathize with the victim and to share in some of the unsavory joy of the torturer/killer. This response is not a way of condoning torture; it merely acknowledges that an empathetic person can share in the pleasure of both moral and immoral acts.

Just as torture-horror films collapse this distance between self and other, Truman Capote suggests that violent crime can make us interrogate our own capacity for brutality as well. My essay, "Hobbes, Human Nature, and the Culture of American Violence in Truman Capote's *In Cold Blood*," explores some of the disturbing questions raised by this novel: How and why were Dick and Perry capable of such brutality? Could you or I do such things? These questions resonate with Thomas Hobbes's philosophy about the innate aggression and brutality of human beings. His pessimistic outlook can provide some insight into the source of terror in Capote's work—that such violence, resentment, and anger are in all of us. Before discussing this connection, I argue that *In Cold Blood* taps into the conventions of the horror genre by focusing on its use of a horrific event and the imagined encounter with the monstrous. I then discuss Hobbes's notion of human nature and the sovereign—a figure that promises to provide moral justice and prevent mankind from being in a perpetual state of war. But what happens if this source of moral authority (the sovereign) is absent? If the veneer of civilization is removed? Capote's answer, like the one offered by Hobbes, is clear: we will all act in cold blood.

Jessica O' Hara turns our attention to the concept of identity (how individuals perceive themselves and the world) through the recent phenomenon of horror reality television. In "Making Their Presence Known: TV's Ghost-Hunter Phenomenon in a 'Post-' World," O' Hara considers both the philosophical implications of these shows and their cultural significance right now. Since these programs are about the ways in which people perceive and experience the world, they often investigate whether or not familial dysfunction alters perception (causing people to see the normal as supernatural), or if this dysfunctionality actually invites in a supernatural presence. This raises concerns about the nature of perception, about whether or not one can prove the "real" existence of ghosts, and about the problem of evil more broadly. As O' Hara explains, horror reality television tends to approach such phenomenological and metaphysical issues from a postmodern perspective. Noting the ways in which these shows lack resolution and a consistent view of the supernatural, she writes: "In these senses, ghost-hunter shows take a distinctively postmodern approach to discourse and narrative in their preference for micro-narratives over grand narratives and their practice of bricolage." The play here comes from these micro-narratives and from the variety of perspectives and discourses they employ. Ultimately, O'Hara argues that the current popularity of horror reality television stems from our interest in evil, our need to mourn the dead as a way of seeking justice, and our focus on the sanctity of domestic spaces after the trauma of 9/11. "On September 11, public space had shown itself to be dangerous indeed. Thus, the idea of retreating from the public into the private sphere became all the more appealing." Ghost hunting is therefore about mourning and remembering.

Amy Kind continues this discussion of television by looking at the innovative use of the vampire myth in Joss Whedon's work. What if a vampire felt remorse for his actions? What if he had a conscience? In "The Vampire with a Soul: *Angel* and the Quest for Identity," Kind discusses the ways in which the television series *Buffy the Vampire Slayer* and *Angel* explore identity and moral responsibility. Once a gypsy curse restores a soul to Angelus, he becomes Angel, a vampire with a conscience; subsequently he must deal with the guilt, shame, and remorse of his past actions. Kind ponders the extent to which we should hold Angel morally accountable for the actions of Angelus, since they can be considered separate individuals. As Kind notes, "There has been considerable philosophical discussion about the problem of personal identity—the question of what makes an individual the same individual over time. This is often referred to as the problem of *reidentification*." Citing Derek Parfit's psychological theory of personal identity (inspired by John Locke), Kind argues that Angel is responsible for some of his actions, but not necessarily for all of them.

Lorena Russell moves the discussion from individual to familial identity. Specifically, her reading of two versions of *The Hills Have Eyes* considers the complex and often contradictory ideologies surrounding family and "family values" in America. By presenting the family under siege theme, both films question these culturally constructed ideologies and explore the repercussions of state-sponsored violence. Using the post-structuralist theories of Althusser and Foucault, Russell first argues for the importance of cultural criticism in film studies (a claim that some philosophers reject) because it challenges us to recognize the sociopolitical significance of a work like *The Hills Have Eyes*. It also invites us to consider the ambiguities surrounding the production of meaning and the power that operates through ideological formations. In these ways, "film can at once further and challenge ideological struggles around complex political concepts like 'family values.'" The critique of government-sponsored violence and deception in *The Hills Have Eyes*, for example, comes from the ways in which the film invites us to sympathize with the murderous outlaw family and, through Doug, Bobby, and Brenda's transformation into warriors, to see our own capacity for violence. The inversion of self/other and "civilized"/"savage" suggests an ambivalence about family that Russell sees as in line with the complexities found in the horror genre. "While on the surface *The Hills Have Eyes* rehearses the time-worn theme of a family under siege, thus seemingly reiterating American family values, on another level the films radically revise assumptions about the legacy of the 'nuclear family' and its uneasy place in American history."

Russell's use of cultural criticism provides an effective segue for the next three essays, which focus on cultural history. In "Zombies of the World, Unite: Class Struggle and Alienation in *Land of the Dead*," John Lutz explores the similarities between the economic system in George Romero's *Land of the Dead* and Karl Marx's view of capitalist society, arguing that the film is an allegory for "America and its relationship to the underdeveloped, exploited nations on the periphery of empire." He begins with a discussion of the African American gas station attendant "Big Daddy." Romero uses this figure to link issues of race and class in his critique of capitalism in the United States, as the character "[points] to the disproportionate number of African Americans in impoverished conditions and the role of violence in enforcing this condition." Lutz also argues that the allegory of the film functions as an indictment of America's central place in global economic imperialism—a place that is maintained by violence and exploitation. This violence not only operates on a global scale, but domestically it also protects those of wealth and privilege. Ultimately, the living dead become metaphors for the working classes, who have been dehumanized by brutal working conditions, hunger, and poverty. And Romero's film uses the zombie revolt as an image for socialist revolution; it even presents a revolutionary consciousness as essential for the working class (zombies) to regain their humanity. "In an interesting parallel to Marx's description of class consciousness as a product of revolutionary struggle," Lutz points out, "the zombies begin to regain their humanity only when they revolt against the wealthy denizens of Pittsburgh who have been appropriating and consuming the commodities taken from their territory."

Turning our attention to the golden age of Hollywood horror, Paul A. Cantor discusses the influence of German expressionism on American films in the 1930s. In "The Fall of the House of Ulmer: Europe vs. America in the Gothic Vision of *The Black Cat*," Cantor examines the European and American aspects of Ulmer's masterpiece. Ulmer's idea, as Cantor explains, was to situate the film in the Gothic tradition, using its conventions to depict the horrific aftermath of World War I in Europe. In this way, "*The Black Cat* is a fascinating case study of how Europeans looked to Americans at one moment of cultural history and how Americans looked to Europeans—all in a film created by a man who, as an émigré filmmaker, was moving between the two worlds himself." This dual function is somewhat paradoxical. On one hand, the tension between European sophistication and American innocence in the film suggests that Americans fail to understand the depth of the tragedy of World War I in Europe. On the other hand, this tension portrays American innocence as essential for building a better future. Cantor concludes that the film "is a kind of elegy to a European high culture that seemed to have killed itself off in the cataclysm of World War I and its aftermath. But it is also a tribute to Ulmer's new homeland, the United States, with all its optimism and moral decency."

The impact of past violence on the present is also examined in the novel and film versions of *The Shining*. John Lutz's essay "From Domestic Nightmares to the Nightmare of History: Uncanny Eruptions of Violence in King's and Kubrick's Versions of *The Shining*" pinpoints in these works three interrelated elements of what Freud called the "uncanny"—the domestic abuse story, "the postcolonial narrative of American expansion at the expense of nonwhite victims, and the desire for power and control that underlies commodification and the social hierarchies that reinforce it." Specifically, Kubrick draws on a crucial moment in King's novel when Danny compares his own feelings of vulnerability to a picture that challenges viewers to "find the Indians." This image, Lutz argues, becomes the visual puzzle that Kubrick uses in his adaptation of the book to critique "the inability of America to acknowledge or come to terms with the genocide of Native Americans." While King's novel focuses on domestic abuse, Kubrick gives the film a broader historical scope. The film "maintains the core elements of domestic violence but widens the scope of the past to incorporate European and American history."

The uncanny also operates in Patrick Süskind's *Perfume* through the protagonist, Grenouille. As Susann Cokal explains in "'Hot with Rapture and Cold with Fear': Grotesque, Sublime, and Postmodern Transformations in Patrick Süskind's *Perfume*," Grenouille is a quintessential figure of horror—a malevolent, deformed, ugly, and odorless monster who is associated with the grotesque and the sublime. Cokal argues that his quest for identity, which leads him to "destroy and deconstruct beauty in order to create something sublime, is part of the book's ultimate horror, as *Perfume*'s readers (or moviegoers) hover between feelings of revulsion and the hope inspired by beauty." In this way, Süskind invokes different aspects of the sublime—contrasting its understanding in the eighteenth century (as influenced by Kant) with that of the postmodern era—to contemplate the plight of the artist. The tragedy and horror for Grenouille, as well as for the eighteenth-century philosopher and for artists in general, are that he can recognize the sublime, can reproduce and even communicate it in his work, but he always remains aware of his own limitations. As a result, he can never experience his creation as others do.

Robert F. Gross continues Cokal's examination of the aesthetics of horror in "Shock Value: A Deleuzean Encounter with James Purdy's *Narrow Rooms*." Gross navigates the slippery terrain of "interpreting" art through the works of Félix Guattari and Gilles Deleuze. These French philosophers rejected the practice of such interpretation, arguing that most critical schools tend to be reductive. It is in this spirit of rejecting such reductions that Gross uses Deleuze and Guattari to explore the multiplicity of meaning in Purdy's novel. The multiplicities of *Narrow Rooms* challenge our understanding of the horror genre, society, and the nature of homosexual love. They yoke together opposites and combine the horrific with the beautiful, inviting us to embrace the former: "While horror is often configured or understood in our culture as an impulse that turns us away from encounters, Purdy constructs an acceptance of horror as an expansion of our possibilities." It ultimately "strengthens our ability to live creatively" and gives us insight into certain experiences without having to go through them ourselves.

Ann C. Hall takes up the problem of production and reproduction in the horror medium. In "Making Monsters: The Philosophy of Reproduction in Mary Shelley's *Frankenstein* and the Universal Films *Frankenstein* and *The Bride of Frankenstein*," she considers some of the cultural anxieties about reproduction in Shelley's novel and some of its filmic adaptations in the 1930s. Using the writings of Luce Iragaray, Hall argues that male attempts to usurp female reproduction in the Frankenstein myth suggest profound fears about women's roles in a patriarchal society: "Shelley communicates her own views about reproduction, views that challenge the patriarchal construct of motherhood . . . in a language that highlights the multiplicity of the female experience." Just as Shelley resists patriarchal interpretations of femininity, the bride's refusal of her bridegroom in *The Bride of Frankenstein* is also a statement of power and resistance.

Finally, in "Kitsch and Camp and Things That Go Bump in the Night; or, Sontag and Adorno at the (Horror) Movies," David MacGregor Johnston considers the importance of kitsch and goofy moments in the horror genre. Using the works of Clement Greenberg, Theodor Adorno, and Max Horkheimer, Johnston begins with an examination of the culture industry surrounding kitsch, which has traditionally been viewed as antithetical to avant-garde art, high culture, and good taste because of its sentimentality. Kitsch also relies on repetition, lending itself effectively to the horror genre: "Instead of appealing to sappy sentimentality, horror films are frightening, but generally they are frightening in ways that do not challenge us to question these films, our responses to them, or the worlds they represent." These works scare us in familiar ways. Johnston sides with critics who take issue with the more negative assessments of kitsch, reminding us of the need to distinguish between good and bad kitsch. One way to do this is through a camp sensibility. Camp, "a refined aesthetic taste for the vulgar," embraces excess. Its excessiveness and artifice can help us appreciate kitsch, and Johnston concludes by discussing these elements in *Scream* (1996), *I Know What You Did Last Summer* (1997), and *Scary Movie* (2000).

As the essays in this collection suggest, horror is just as comfortable with the mundane as it is with social, political, and cultural critique. It can slide between highbrow and lowbrow, incorporating a range of genres and tones. It can be serious or kitschy, terrifying or ridiculous, and it can raise profound questions about fear, safety, justice, and suffering. Just as audiences crave the fear it elicits, they also take pleasure in its predictability. It is this safety net of predictability—of closing a book, of leaving the theater when the lights go back on, or of knowing that a professional skydiver will pull the cord to your parachute—that enables us to enjoy the thrilling, horrifying journey. It is this safety net that makes horror so much fun.

Notes

1. Stephen King, *Danse Macabre* (New York: Everest House, 1981), 27.

2. Cynthia Freeland makes a similar argument in her essay "Horror and Art-Dread," in *The Horror Film*, ed. Stephen Prince (New Brunswick, NJ: Rutgers University Press, 2004). She defines the latter as an emotional response to art that confronts us with something terrible and obscure. For Freeland, films of art-dread "sustain interest by showing how human beings, whether sympathetic or good or not, cope or fail to cope in their encounters with deep and profound evil, or with a fear of life's arbitrariness and meaninglessness" (203).

3. Noël Carroll, *The Philosophy of Horror; or, Paradoxes of the Heart* (New York: Routledge, 1990), 98.

4. Carol J. Clover, *Men, Women, and Chain Saws: Gender in the Modern Horror Film* (Princeton, NJ: Princeton University Press, 1992), 20, 166.

5. David J. Russell, "Monster Roundup: Reintegrating the Horror Genre," in *Refiguring American Film Genres: History and Theory*, ed. Nick Browne (Berkeley: University of California Press, 1998), 236.

6. This analysis also resonates with Isabel Pinero's reading of horror as postmodern in *Recreational Terror: Women and the Pleasure of Horror Film Viewing* (New York: State University of New York Press, 1997). Specifically, she argues that the postmodern horror film (which she situates between the 1960s and the 1980s) explores the blurring of boundaries while retaining enough "features of the classical genre . . . [to] appreciate the transgression" (14).

7. This reading resonates with some of the studies that Mary Beth Oliver and Meghan Sanders survey in "The Appeal of Horror and Suspense," in *The Horror Film*, ed. Stephen Prince (New Brunswick, NJ: Rutgers University Press, 2004). When discussing some of the social approaches that psychologists have examined in regard to horror films, several studies have noted a correlation between violent entertainment and those who "experience or witness a great deal of violence in their everyday lives" (249).

8. This allusion is not meant to minimize the important scholarship of Robin Wood, Andrew Tudor, James Twitchell, and others, whose work preceded Carroll's; it merely acknowledges the significance of Carroll's book in the field of philosophy while inviting readers to consider the ways in which this volume elaborates on, develops, and challenges some of his ideas.

9. Many scholars have debated Carroll's insistence that supernatural monsters are

the defining feature of the genre, arguing that this prerequisite excludes works that most people consider to be horror, such as Alfred Hitchcock's *Psycho*. For example, Russell agrees with Carroll's entity-based reading of horror (the notion that monsters are central to the genre), but he notes that Carroll's theory leaves out the "psychokiller horror film" ("Monster Roundup," 238). He then offers a theory of monstrosity that includes real, unreal, and part-real monsters. As his work suggests, the critical debates about Carroll's study have broadened the scope of his discussion in ways that are more inclusive and more compatible with popular understandings of the genre.

Horror and the Idea of Everyday Life

On Skeptical Threats in *Psycho* and *The Birds*

Philip J. Nickel

Sometimes art provokes outrage, fear, and disgust. In the case of horror, that is the point. Those who enjoy horror might seek no justification or defense for it. But because of the strong feelings elicited by horror and the outrageous acts that are depicted in it, to those sensitive to offense it is hard not to feel that some justification or defense is needed. There are some obvious strategies for this, for example, raising the flag of "art for art's sake" (or "entertainment for entertainment's sake"); or, by contrast, explicating the *value* of horror (for example, its moral or educational value—see Nietzsche 1968, 92–93). There are also strategies appealing to other categories of value, along the lines of Nietzsche's explanation of the value of tragedy as a Dionysian rallying cry. In this essay I intend to explain the value of horror in terms that are neither aesthetic nor moral. My goal is to show that horror has an *epistemological* value.[1]

The Concept of Horror

In what follows I will use the term *horror* mostly to refer to a literary and film genre (or, more broadly, a motif) instantiated in artistic works. I will also occasionally refer to horror as a particular emotion or a kind of psychological experience. The defense I propose of horror in the first sense (as a genre or motif) requires us to take up two philosophical questions: What is horror? and What is good about it? My main interest here is not in defining what horror is but rather in exploring the defense of horror—the prospects of an "apology" in the classical sense. But we cannot say in general what is good about horror unless we understand what it is. Thus I propose the following working definition. Horror has two central elements: (1) an appearance of the evil supernatural or of the monstrous (this includes the psychopath who kills monstrously); and (2) the intentional elicitation of dread, visceral disgust, fear, or startlement in the spectator or reader.[2] On this understanding, some of the most popular and critically acclaimed works of art and entertainment contain elements of horror. It is instantiated not only in contemporary film but in the whole history of literary and representational art (Dante's *Inferno*, Shakespeare's tragedies, paintings by Caravaggio and Goya, to mention some obvious examples).

This definition builds upon others offered in the philosophical literature on horror. Noël Carroll defines horror as a genre representing unnatural, threatening monsters (1990, 15–16, 27–29). According to Carroll, the genre plays upon a viewer's characteristic emotional aversion to the idea of such monsters as they are represented in his or her thoughts. For Carroll, monsters are essentially fictional, not something to be worried about in real life. The viewer knows that they do not exist. My definition is broader than Carroll's in that it allows for horror with no specific monster and also allows for "realistic" monsters. I have attempted in this way to respond to the criticism that Carroll's definition is too narrow, excluding works like *Psycho* and *The Shining*.[3] In my view, unlike Carroll's, the threats that horror presents are not always fictional but can bleed into the actual world.

The Value of Horror

The question of horror's value has been clouded in a couple of ways. First of all, some horror films emphasize graphic depictions of sadistic violence to the exclusion of almost everything else, in something like the way pornographic films focus on graphic depictions of sex to the exclusion of almost everything else. This has led many people to question the value of the horror genre as a whole. For example, Gianluca Di Muzio (2006) takes *The Texas Chainsaw Massacre* as a model. (In fact there is much more to this film than graphic violence, but let us set our quibbles aside.) In this film a few youths wander into the clutches of psychopaths who torture, murder, and eat them. The film depicts their sadistic torture and murder. One character narrowly escapes. Di Muzio argues that to enjoy such a film is to enjoy a depiction of the torture of children. He claims that it could only have a corrupting influence on one's moral character since it involves "silencing one's compassionate attitudes" in the face of (depictions of) terrific and pointless violence (287). Di Muzio argues that the spectator of such a show risks "atrophying her capacity for appropriate compassionate reactions and her ability to appraise correctly situations that make moral demands on her" (285).

There is no doubt that the violence of *The Texas Chainsaw Massacre* is shocking and perverse. But the basic claim of Di Muzio's argument nonetheless does not hold, even as applied to "slasher" horror. For it seems plausible to say that the experience of horror essentially involves the *engagement* of one's compassionate attitudes. That is what makes horror horrifying. Suppose I cringe with dread while watching Pam (one of the characters in the film) being hung on a meat hook. Suppose I can hardly watch and I feel nauseated. Later I cannot get the image out of my head, particularly at night and during my visits to the butcher counter at the supermarket. Although these reactions may be unpleasant and it may be puzzling to some people why I should ever wish to experience them, they are not desensitized reactions. On the contrary, the reaction to terror appears on its face to be a morally *engaged* reaction. And although a sensitive viewer may be morally overwhelmed by the violence depicted in horror films, there is no obvious causal link between being overwhelmed in this way and the atrophy of moral sensitivity. If there is such a link, it requires proof not offered by Di Muzio.

In any case, we are concerned with the value of horror as a contribution to art and entertainment in general, not only with the most graphic instances of the horror genre. Di Muzio does not discuss whether, in principle, horror can contribute something to great art and entertainment. Elements of horror such as dread and the sense of the uncanny add something to the artistry and interest of *Macbeth,* for example. It is doubtful that Di Muzio would deny this. Thus the focus on the graphic character of violence in slasher films diverts attention from basic issues about horror's value.

There is also a second way that the question of the value of horror has been improperly handled. Critical discussion has focused more on why horror is pleasurable rather than on why it is aesthetically or morally valuable. The appeal of horror as a theme or a genre, it has been said, is paradoxical.[4] Why should it be enjoyable or attractive to witness horrific events as they are depicted in films, fiction, and art? When Marion Crane is stabbed in the shower scene in *Psycho,* and when Norman Bates then disposes of her dead body, why do we enjoy watching it? (It is beautifully filmed, but then why don't the other aspects of the scene override or outweigh its cinematic beauty?) These are indeed fascinating questions, and have been answered in various ways by theorists of film. The gamut of explanations runs from a theory of repressed drives that pleasurably return to the viewer in his or her identification with the monster and/or the victim of horror to a more scientifically austere explanation of the neurophysiology of startle reactions and the social phenomenon of collective film-viewing experiences.[5]

The problem is that these are psychological answers to a psychological question, not philosophical answers to a philosophical question. Although philosophy certainly has something to contribute to the resolution of psychological questions (for example, by clarifying psychological concepts and the nature of psychological evidence), it cannot resolve these questions completely on its own. "Why is horror pleasurable?" is at least partly an empirical or scientific question about people, requiring that we understand regular and general principles of human psychology and anthropology. This is why I take the paradox of horror in a different way. If there is any philosophical puzzle here, it concerns what is *good* about horror, not just what is pleasurable about it.

In this essay I will try to put the philosophical discussion of horror back on track. I will argue that there is something good about horror—I mean, aesthetically interesting and epistemologically good. I shall argue that by the threats it presents to the everyday life of the viewer, horror gives us a perspective on so-called common sense. It helps us to see that a notion of everyday life completely secure against threats cannot be possible, and that the security of common sense is a persistent illusion. In order to make this clear, I will compare horror and philosophical skepticism, arguing that the threats they pose are structurally similar.[6] As with our purported philosophical solutions to skepticism, the idea of security in the everyday is based on an intellectually dubious but pragmatically attractive construction. We can hardly resist relying on the world not to annihilate us, and we can hardly resist trusting others not to do so. This is not because such reliance is rationally compulsory, but because we choose it as the most easy and natural strategy. One of the best things about horror is that it allows us viscerally to experience this as an epistemological choice.

Horror and Philosophical Skepticism

Philosophical skepticism deploys the following sorts of statements as premises in arguments intended to undermine our ordinary claim to knowledge or justified belief: *Consistent with what I can verify in my experience, it could be the case that everything that appears to me is the creation of an evil demon and that the world as I know it does not exist.*[7] This statement is distinctive for its sweeping implications for the epistemic rationality of belief. This sweeping generality is characteristic of philosophical skepticism as contrasted with more mundane or local forms of skepticism. Philosophical skepticism holds that no human being can have any knowledge or justification in a given area, for example, on questions of religion, the future, morality, or the external world. Global skepticism is a powerful philosophical weapon against ordinary belief. For ordinary believers it has the striking consequence that they should abandon their belief that the world is at all the way it appears. Philosophers often try to refute skeptical arguments, and surely this is one of the reasons why—because it threatens ordinary belief.

General skeptical premises similar to the one above are occasionally dramatized, as in the film *The Matrix*. But it is more common in works of art to dramatize local skeptical premises, such as: *Consistent with what I can verify in my experience, it could be the case that I will wake up tomorrow as a giant insect* (as in Franz Kafka, *The Metamorphosis*). Horror often dramatizes the ordinary or everyday world gone berserk and the transmogrification of the commonplace. The horror film makes the case that such a transmogrification, so far as any one of us can tell, might happen at any moment, and this casts our reliance on the everyday world around us into shadow. The persuasiveness of the case that a given horror film makes depends on how vivid or real the film can make the premise seem and on our background susceptibility to doubt or anxiety about the thing that the premise concerns. For example, although from day to day we are not worried about the possibility of flesh-eating zombies, perhaps the premise *Consistent with what I can verify in my experience, anybody I know (including myself) could turn into a rabid, contagious zombie* (as in *28 Days Later*) gains some of its psychological force from the real-life plausibility of an outbreak of deadly influenza or plague. There is a distinctive way that horror fiction and film can bring this threat home to the reader or viewer. A documentary about the flu pandemic of 1918, or about avian flu, could raise fears about a deadly outbreak, but unlike horror it would not depict very specific evils associated with such a flu (the sudden violation of one's body, the fear of death) as happening *now*. Hence it would not elicit fear in the same way that horror does when it represents events—even historical events—as happening in the present tense of the viewer with an open outcome.

The fact is, though, that even if horror does draw on everyday anxieties for its effectiveness, the connection with them does not have to be particularly close. It does not seem to be generally true that horror must bear a relation of symbolism or similarity to any real-life threat in order to create its characteristic emotional response. Horror can present its threats in a "realistic" and genuinely terrifying way even when the members of its audience do not act as if these threats were real after they have left the theater. There seems to be a deep reservoir of anxieties capable of fueling horror:

about dying and those who have died, about technology gone amok, about the deterioration of the body, about the collapse and unknowability of the human mind. These are not just everyday worries. They are the worries of the horror realm, even when they are occasioned by real life.

This contrast between the horror realm and the realm of the everyday is much like the contrast between skepticism and "common sense" (ordinary life, everyday life). Consider David Hume's famous account of skeptical philosophical arguments and their relation to everyday life. After presenting his own highly distinctive account of the "manifold contradictions and imperfections in human reason," he claims that the authority and legitimacy of reason have been thoroughly undermined. He "can look upon no opinion even as more probable or likely than another." The skeptical arguments he has put forward show that he is "in the most deplorable condition imaginable, environed with the deepest darkness, and utterly deprived of the use of every member and faculty." Reason itself cannot save him from this condition, for it is an examination of reason that originally led him into this state. But there is a silver lining: "Since reason is incapable of dispelling these clouds, Nature herself suffices to that purpose, and cures me of this philosophical melancholy and delirium. . . . I dine, I play a game of backgammon, I converse, and am merry with my friends; and when, after three or four hours' amusement, I would return to these speculations, they appear so cold, and strained, and ridiculous, that I cannot find in my heart to enter into them any further" (1969, 316). The return to everyday life restores our equilibrium.[8]

Something like this same return to everyday life and common sense is experienced as one walks out of the theater after a horror film into the parking lot on a sunny afternoon. As moments pass the worry that a monster or psychopath is about to drain one's blood into a tub is shaken off like the fears from a dream. Everyday fears and worries well up in the place of the "melancholy and delirium" induced by the horror.

Horror films often induce or suggest a particular state of uncertainty, experienced as epistemic anxiety, melancholia, or paranoia. My claim here is that this can be articulated as a kind of skeptical statement and forms the basis of a problematic argument that has no easy solution. Instead of trying to provide a general recipe for such a skeptical argument, I will take as examples two films by Alfred Hitchcock that are commonly said, individually or together, to be important milestones or turning points in the history of horror: *Psycho* and *The Birds*. These films initiate a new era of the horror genre in contemporary film, and each epitomizes different strands of that genre. The films are landmark horror films in part because, unlike some of their predecessors, they offer no moral reassurance that humans can dispel or effectively fight against the threats they present. These films merit extended analysis in their own right (and have received it). Of necessity, in this essay we can focus only on a few aspects of each and cannot take up the critical literature in detail. But I hope nevertheless to see how a kind of epistemic uncertainty emerges from these films—not just as a part of the plot but as a general and unresolved epistemic anxiety for the *viewer,* which he or she can resolve only by turning toward everyday life once again.

Each of these films dramatizes a paranoid scenario.[9] In *The Birds* the paranoid scenario is that, for all we can tell, a familiar and seemingly benign part of the background can suddenly change its basic nature and attempt to annihilate human life. In the case of *Psycho* the scenario is that for all we know a seemingly ordinary person (possibly including the viewer him- or herself) can turn out to be a homicidal "monster" without an integrated human mind. The way in which these films make an epistemological point is by making these scenarios vivid as terrifying alternatives to the everyday world. The situation at the beginning of each film is much like the everyday world. Their protagonists have ordinary kinds of motivations—love, sex, and money. But in each case their lives are thrown into a delirious rupture with expected patterns of nature and human interaction. These developments are presented as real in the films themselves. The crucial point is that the viewer is not in a position rationally to refuse the scenario of the film as impossible, and that the paranoid scenario thus threatens to annihilate the viewer. This is the similarity with philosophical skepticism, which threatens to annihilate our knowledge (including our knowledge of other minds and our own future existence). Viewers nonetheless return to their state of reliance on the world and on others as they go home after the film is over, because it is the only practical thing to do. One consequence of my account of these films and by extension of horror generally is that, as in Hume's account of skepticism, there is no resolution of our fears except to go on.

Epistemology and *The Birds*

In *The Birds* the paranoid scenario is: *Consistent with what I can verify in my experience, I could suddenly find that the birds of the world are now collectively trying to annihilate humans.* The genius of Hitchcock's film is partly that it makes this rather outlandish and unexpected specification of the skeptical premise seem so plausible. The plot is roughly as follows. Melanie Daniels arrives in Bodega Bay, a small coastal California town, to make a surprise delivery of two pet lovebirds to the young sister of a romantic interest, Mitch

Brenner. Just after she makes her delivery the seagulls begin to attack, pecking her forehead as she makes her way back from the Brenners' house to the town in a borrowed boat. Soon after birds kill a farmer by pecking his eyes out, and a schoolhouse is attacked by crows. After these attacks Melanie goes to a local diner to make some telephone calls. It is at the diner where the various reactions to this surprising and awful news are dramatized in a fourteen-minute "play within a play," including "a full-scale philosophical symposium" on the question of the birds (Paglia 1998, 69, 71). One might expect such a symposium to put a drag on the film, but the practical urgency of the questions raised gives it dramatic life. Moreover, in the middle of this episode the full avian attack on the town begins. Melanie retreats with Mitch's family to their house across the bay, where they board up the windows and doors and endure a harrowing battle with the birds. In the final scene of the film the birds are waiting outside in their millions as the humans try to creep away toward safety.

As Paglia suggests, the intellectual center of the film is the symposium at the diner concerning what to believe about the birds. In this episode Melanie has just experienced the birds' aggression firsthand and come to believe the paranoid scenario of the film. Some of the customers believe her. The dull-witted bartender, charmed by Melanie, gives her immediate and credulous support; the drunkard at the bar, citing scripture, hollers that it is the end of the world. But others at the diner react with caution or outright skepticism. The local cannery owner in the corner, Mr. Shoals, also has firsthand experience of the birds' aggression, but he doesn't believe they intend to start a war with humankind. There is also an amateur ornithologist present, the elderly Mrs. Bundy. After hearing Melanie's story she states her scientific opinion that "birds are not aggressive creatures," that different species do not flock together ("the very concept is unimaginable"), and that their " brainpans" are too small to coordinate an attack on the town. Mrs. Bundy, who has spent time observing the birds and even doing a yearly count of those in the area, exhibits confident expertise in her judgment that a coordinated bird attack of the kind Melanie has witnessed is impossible. Her wisdom is our wisdom. It is exactly the sort of rationale one would articulate, and rightly so, to refute a lurid tabloid story about UFOs or vampires. Here it is intended to refute the paranoid scenario.

The debate over what to believe goes on for some time, escalating into an exchange between Mitch, who thinks they're in "real trouble" and would be "crazy to ignore it," the dismissive Mrs. Bundy, and Mr. Shoals, who wants to stick to the facts and not draw any sweeping conclusions ("All I'm saying is that they attacked my boats"). Just a moment before a very worried mother dining with her two young children chided the others, "You're all sitting around debating. What do you want them to do next, crash into that window?" Now her worries become real and the horrific interruption occurs. The birds themselves impinge on the philosophical debate. Melanie, looking out the window, watches as a bird strategically knocks over a gas station attendant, causing a gasoline explosion, and shrieking birds terrorize everybody outside.

The scene at the diner particularly emphasizes the epistemological issues at stake. The characters have their initial doubts about what is happening, at least before they witness the full-scale bird attack. But the film ventures to show that even reassuring common sense or scientific claims based on careful observation do not preclude the possibility of a sudden rupture of our everyday expectations. The paranoid scenario is presented to the viewer—to *us,* outside the picture frame—and concerns whether what is depicted in the film is possible for us. To the extent that we are drawn into the film, or find it realistic, we accept this scenario as at least a logical possibility and we experience it as plausible. One of the common reactions after seeing this particular film is to see birds in an ominous light. Paul Wells writes about one person's recollection: "It was the day after *The Birds* had been shown on television and I was walking through Holland Park in central London. I saw a group of children, who had just visited the Commonwealth Institute, dive to the floor as a flock of pigeons rose into the air" (2000, 77). If we, like the children in the park, actually become fearful about the possibility of such a scenario even for a moment, we may find ourselves returning to the considerations raised by Mrs. Bundy: "Scientific explanations of animal behavior do not allow for interspecies cooperation; Birds have no motive to attack humans; Why would the birds wait until now to launch an attack on humans (and why here)?" These are all cogent considerations, and in ordinary life we take them to be conclusive reasons eliminating the possibility that birds will collectively attack. But what I wish to say, along with Hume, is that we are not compelled to do so by epistemic rationality. For the characters in the film raise exactly these reassuring considerations, and only a moment later are fearing for their lives. Mrs. Bundy doesn't say another word; she is cowering in the hallway with the others.

Thus, when we turn off the film or walk out of the theater, it is not as if we switch off our fear, or even reason our way back to an ordinary trust of birds (or whatever other forces in our everyday surroundings might suddenly and hideously turn against us—other films in this lineage such as *Cujo,*

Tippi Hedren (as Melanie Daniels) in *The Birds* (1963). Directed by Alfred Hitchcock. (MCA/Universal Pictures/Photofest)

Christine, and *Child's Play* exhibit variations). The fears are still there. They simply fade into the background as we go about our business, returning to conversation and backgammon, as Hume said.

Under the right circumstances most people can occasionally find themselves in a place where the paranoid scenario of horror is suddenly a live possibility. In 1992, while working part-time at the auditorium at the University of Colorado, I heard a story about a janitor who had worked there long before. In July 1966 he raped and murdered a woman in one of the towers of the neo-Gothic auditorium (Doligosa 2006). Campus folklore holds that her ghost haunts the building. One week I found out that I had to work alone in the building at night on the very anniversary of this horrific event. That evening I brought the vacuum cleaner up to the second floor and was just outside the spiral staircase to the tower. A chill crept over me, and I was ready to experience something bizarre—perhaps the ghost of the murdered woman would take her revenge on another employee. Then I went on with my job, and when I was finished walked back to my apartment. The fears were in my mind all along—I did not need to be in the grip of a fiction to experience them. But then I was back to everyday life.

Psycho

Despite some thematic similarities to *The Birds, Psycho* raises a rather different set of worries for the viewer.[10] In brief, Marion Crane, the short-lived protagonist of *Psycho,* steals forty thousand dollars from her employer and absconds from Phoenix to California. She is palpably alone. She cannot return to Phoenix (the city name is symbolic); she and her lover are separated; the journey away from her previous life is drawn out and lonely. Thus it is with a sense of relief that we find Marion striking up a conversation with the young clerk at the Bates Motel, Norman Bates. She goes back to her room, and she is murdered in the shower, apparently by Norman's deranged mother. Then Norman cleans up, wrapping her dead body in a plastic shower curtain and sending it into a muddy pool in the trunk of her car. During the remainder of the film we gradually learn that Norman is the murderer. He keeps his mother's dead body in the house and dresses in her clothes and a wig to enact his split personality. By the end of the film, after another killing, Norman is caught by the police. In the last scene we see him wrapped in a blanket and hear the inner voice of his mother asserting her innocence. A vision of his mother's skull is superimposed on Norman's face. Whereas in *The Birds* the threatening scenario is purely external, here it is psychological, arising from Norman's mental disintegration.

　　Psycho's psychological, internal orientation raises some questions of genre. According to Noël Carroll's account of horror, it is not a horror movie because it doesn't have a monster in the true sense: psychopaths are human beings, not monsters (except metaphorically). Vampires, zombies, even berserk birds can count as monsters. The weird guy running the motel off the highway cannot, at least not according to Carroll, because monsters exist only in fiction, whereas he exists (or might have existed) in reality. For Carroll, the fictionality of monsters is central to the account of what makes horror pleasurable: "The pleasure and interest that many horror fictions sustain . . . derive from the disclosure of unknown and impossible beings" (1990, 184). He continues, "Their [monsters'] very impossibility vis a vis our conceptual categories is what makes them function so compellingly in dramas of discovery and confirmation" (185).

　　Thus we should distinguish between two problems that Carroll's account raises, a conceptual problem and a problem in explaining what is good about horror. The conceptual question is whether *Psycho* counts as horror at all. To most people the answer to this question is straightforwardly yes. Conceptually, public sentiment and critical opinion do not square with Carroll's definition of horror. If Carroll were right about what horror is, not just *Psycho* but even *The Texas Chainsaw Massacre,* based on the same "true story" as *Psycho* (serial killer Ed Gein), would not be horror.[11] This cannot be right. But setting this conceptual issue aside, Carroll's analysis also presents a challenge to my account of why horror is good. "Internal" horror films such as *Psycho* traffic in abnormal psychology, not paranormal or supernatural phenomena. Hence they cannot offer the same epistemological fodder that a supernatural being could. For Carroll, the pleasure of horror is epistemological: it comes from "dramas of discovery and confirmation" that are uniquely exemplified in terms of supernatural creatures. Although my account of what is good about horror is different from Carroll's account of what is pleasurable about it, there is nonetheless an objection to my account of a film like *Psycho* that one might lodge on Carroll's behalf. One might argue that since psychopaths really exist, horror films such as *Psycho* and *The Texas Chainsaw Massacre* do not present a skeptical alternative to belief in everyday reality. Instead, they dramatize a scenario of which we are already aware *within* everyday reality. Hence they do not run in parallel with skeptical arguments.

My response to this challenge is to deny that the subject matter of *Psycho* and *The Texas Chainsaw Massacre* is a part of everyday reality. This is not to say that these films do not present their subject matter as real, nor is it to deny that serial killers exist in the real world. It is just to say that the everyday reality of the viewer—that is, the viewer's idea of what is normal, expected, and commonsensical—is typically insulated from these sorts of scenarios, and therefore the viewer finds them threatening when they are presented in film. Thus the critical discussion of *Psycho* admits a striking contrast between the world into which Marion Crane stumbles and that of everyday reality. As Paul Wells writes, "*Psycho* locates shockingly transgressive events in an everyday context, subject to ordinary conditions" (2000, 75).[12] Robin Wood writes of the opening sequence in which the camera zeroes in on a single window in a cityscape, which happens to be the hotel room of Marion and her lover, "This could be any place, any date, any time, any room: it could be us. . . . *Psycho* begins with the normal and draws us steadily deeper and deeper into the abnormal" (2004, 75). Whereas Carroll interprets the name Norman as "*Nor-man:* neither man nor woman but both" (1990, 39), I am more inclined to think of his name's ironic suggestion of normalcy: a normal man, an everyman. Norman represents an everyday person whom we find, in the journey of the film, to have an abnormally dark side. The paranoid scenario of the film is about the dark side of seeming everymen.

As in *The Birds,* the first intellectual flash point of the film is a conversation that comes just before the full onslaught of horror. Norman had originally proposed that Marion have dinner in the house on the hill, but his mother loudly objected as Marion listened from her hotel room below. She ends up dining in the motel office and conversing with Norman. Norman seeks affable collusion in his resentment toward his mother. When Marion casually suggests that Norman might try putting her in an institution, Norman suddenly goes cold. The threat to his mother—who, as we learn later, exists only as a part of Norman—cracks the brittle edges of his goofy, boyish sociability. (One of the unanswered questions of the film is whether Marion Crane's threatening stance toward Mrs. Bates in this scene is what leads to her murder, or whether she was already poised to become a victim.) Unlike the diner scene from *The Birds,* the conversation between Norman and Marion does not concern the paranoid scenario of the film, because the horror has not yet even started at that point in *Psycho.* But the scene is nonetheless pivotal in the epistemological drama, which in this case revolves around Marion's vulnerability and dependence. Marion is in a condition of total social isolation from all stable institutions (the law, her employer, married life). Her question is therefore about whom she can trust. She leaves her familiar environment and her place in it, and she is immediately placed in a condition of flailing anxiety and vulnerability. For example, she is subject to unscrupulous dealings as she sells the car linked with her crime, and she finds herself alone on the highway except for a mysterious cop on a motorcycle who trails her for hours and then parts ways. Arriving in the dark and rain at a vacant motel, she is at the end of her rope, choosing to rely on a complete stranger. In the office scene, at first we have the reassuring sense that there is nothing wrong with this choice. After all, Norman is sensitive enough to offer her dinner and polite enough to keep her company. She is not so vulnerable as to lose her composure and affability during their conversation even when it becomes uncomfortable.

But then her vulnerability is exploited. Norman first violates her privacy by peeping at her through a hole in the wall, and then he (as Mother) kills her in the shower. The particulars of Norman's psychopathy, particularly as expounded in the psychoanalytic cant of the film, are of no importance to the film's terror. What is fundamental is Marion's vulnerability and aloneness (symbolized by her nakedness in the shower) and the shocking consequences of her mistaken reliance on Norman. This is why, for some viewers, it was "the first horror movie which they could not forget, and felt frightened about it even within the apparent safety of their own homes" (Wells 2000, 31). Thus the paranoid scenario of *Psycho* is: *Consistent with what I can verify in my experience, it could be the case that the seemingly ordinary person I now rely upon in a moment of human vulnerability will murder me.* There are many details that make a crucial contribution to the horror of the shower scene: the gigantic knife, the translucent plastic curtain, the revolting sound the knife makes as it plunges into Marion's body, the famous shrieking music, and so on. But Marion's aloneness and vulnerability are fundamental. Moreover, the ordinariness of the beginning of the film and the viewer's knowledge that the film is based on a true story amplify the personal interest we have in the paranoid scenario. It is the shocking transition from everyday life to a murder in one's most vulnerable moment that gives the scenario its edge, Carroll's objections notwithstanding.

Everyday Life and Its Alternatives

Everyday life is saturated with our apparently justified reliance on others and on the world around us—saturated with trust. As Annette Baier writes, trust is like the air we breathe in that we only notice it when it disappears or goes bad (1986, 234). It is by understanding trust better that we can understand how horror relates to everyday life. So far I have left the notion of "everyday life" mostly unanalyzed and intuitive. Now we are in a position to say more by relating it to trusting reliance. The "everyday" encompasses those tacit assumptions of reliability that allow us to negotiate the world from one moment to the next: this bird will not attack me (if I thought it would I would not be able to walk down the street without terror); this person will not murder me (if I thought he would I would not be able to stay the night at a hotel without terror).

In order to refine this point, suppose we distinguish between practical and cognitive trust. Practical trust is based on well-founded confidence in our ability to act and carry out our intentions, whereas cognitive trust is well-founded confidence in our beliefs. Although they are conceptually different, these two kinds of trust are usually woven together. Suppose I want to cross a dark parking lot safely. On the one hand there is an action to be performed, crossing the parking lot. On the other hand there are a number of related beliefs I might have: there are no persons—or birds, or zombies—about to attack me, the surface of the parking lot will not rupture as I cross it, I am not in a nightmare induced by a demon, and so on. In most ordinary actions I have these backing beliefs implicitly and they make me feel confident or justified that my action will succeed. The beliefs are generally implicit or latent rather than conscious or occurrent. It is common in philosophy to point out that I have many latent beliefs, such as the belief that my gas pedal is connected to the engine of my car, that I do not entertain consciously, even though they provide backing for my actions. The beliefs that express and justify our intellectual willingness to rely upon the world and on other people are generally like this. They are latent or implicit.

There are, however, some nonordinary cases in which I perform an action even though I do not have the usual backing beliefs (latent or otherwise). I can walk across the parking lot even if I *don't* believe I won't be attacked by birds, just as Mitch walks out to his car at the end of *The Birds* as countless birds watch him ominously. I can act without having the usual backing beliefs by acting *as if* the relevant background propositions were true and simply stepping forward. If I am lucky, this *as-if* movement alone will carry me across the parking lot. But if so, I will be depending on luck, not on anything certain. It will be with no confidence that I will succeed in my action; it will be without the usual intellectual backing for practical trust.

With this discussion in hand I am now in a position to restate the thesis about horror and epistemology. As I have portrayed it, horror's bite is explained as a sudden tearing-away of the intellectual trust that stands behind our actions. Specifically, it is a *malicious* ripping-away of this intellectual trust, exposing our vulnerabilities in relying on the world and on other people. *Psycho* and *The Birds* exhibit this ripping-away for two different domains characteristic of the horror genre, the one for reliance on other people and the other for reliance on the natural world. Not all skepticism is based on malicious threats—some arguments for skepticism are based on reflections about human limitations or the possibility of sheer bad luck in the formation of beliefs. But there is a long tradition in epistemology of worrying about malicious threats to the possibility of justified belief. Descartes hypothesized that in the absence of a proof of the existence of God, there might for all we know be an evil demon manipulating our thoughts and our environment in such a way as to make our beliefs about the world radically mistaken (1986). More recent variants of this idea include the thought that we might be the puppets of a computer simulation (Bostrom 2003) or a mad scientist (Putnam 1982). Similarly, horror puts forward scenarios that through their vivid depiction threaten our background cognitive reliance on others and the world around us (and we should add, thinking perhaps of the films of David Cronenberg, our reliance on our own bodies and minds).

But what, it might be asked, could be good about that? There are three main things. First, it is a matter of not being deceived about the foundations of our practical trust. Horror helps us to experience the fact that the intellectual backing for our practical trust, consisting in the various background beliefs we have that our environment (natural and social) will behave in regular ways, cannot be made perfectly certain. Our reliance cannot be given a perfect philosophical "vindication"; all that can be done is to go on relying in the usual way. Once we give up the aim of providing a fail-safe intellectual backing for our actions, we gain intellectual clarity about our actual situation of dependence and trust on birds, people, cars, and ourselves. Our reliance on these things is inherently insecure, much more like Mitch's walk to the car than we are at first inclined to think.

Just as important, horror makes us realize that we can still go on, even in the absence of perfect certainty. In the climactic final assault on the house in *The Birds,* Melanie goes up the stairs to the second floor despite (or because of?) the fact that the birds are making a great stir up there. As noted in Urbano (2004), for many people Melanie's behavior is frustrating: "Melanie . . . should be more than able to assume that the noises she hears are made by birds that have managed to invade the rooms upstairs. What does she think her searchlight is going to throw light on up there? Is she stupid or what?" Urbano himself rejects this question: "Unless one is willing to accept that Melanie's reason for going upstairs is irrational, one will never be able to fully enjoy *The Birds*"—or the horror genre more generally (23). Urbano may be right to say this, but one thing the scene does illustrate is that Melanie can act from her motive, whatever it may be (curiosity? investigation?), even when she herself knows that the backing for her actions is extremely insecure. Just as Sam and Lila do when they go to the Bates Motel at the end of *Psycho* to find out what happened to Marion, Melanie continues to walk up the stairs even though her trust cannot be secured. It demonstrates that similarly, we continue to act in the presence of fear.

Horror also brings a third epistemological insight, which is that the construction of the everyday is necessary. This insight arises from the first two: that the intellectual backing for our practical trust is not perfectly secure and that, regardless, we can continue to act as if it were. The third epistemological insight is that we cannot remain content with this situation. It is necessary that we construct an idea of the everyday in which the intellectual backing for our practical trust *feels* secure, even when we know it is not. We must fabricate for ourselves a sphere in which we will not be attacked in our kitchens or showers, in which our own bodies will not turn suddenly against us, and in which the birds perched on the jungle gym are benign. There are a number of psychological reasons why this construction of the everyday is necessary, but one is simply that we cannot focus on all the possible paranoid scenarios at once. There are too many ways the world can threaten our trust for us to keep them all in mind. We must concentrate on the most salient threats to trust. This forces us to keep some of the myriad other paranoid scenarios off the table, at least provisionally. Once they are outside of the focus of our attention they are no longer threatening, and the idea of a regular, everyday world emerges. But the idea of a secure, regular everyday world is, then, a construction. One valuable thing about horror literature and film is that they keep this fact in view.

Notes

1. Epistemology is that branch of philosophy concerning knowledge, justification, and belief.

2. This definition implies that some suspense dramas, like *Klute, Basic Instinct,* and *No Country for Old Men,* involve at least a *motif* of horror. And since this motif (as I define it) is very prominent in these films, it is a puzzle for my account that they are not acknowledged as being inside the margin of the horror genre. It may be that they are styled with too much dramatic realism to count as meeting element (1) of the definition.

3. A criticism raised by Hills (2003), who cites Russell 1998; Schneider 2000; Jancovich 1992; and Freeland 2000.

4. For this way of formulating the paradox of horror, see Levine 2004, 46; Gaut 1993; and Turvey 2004, 70–71.

5. On this topic see the essays in Schneider 2004.

6. Here I am borrowing a theme about tragedy and skepticism from the philosopher Stanley Cavell, as developed in Cavell (2003) and earlier books.

7. "I will suppose therefore that . . . some malicious demon of the utmost power and cunning has employed all his energies in order to deceive me. I shall think that the sky, the air, the earth, colours, shapes, sounds and all external things are merely the delusions of dreams which he has devised to ensnare my judgment" (Descartes 1986, 15).

8. Coincidentally, Hume's view of tragedy has been deployed by Carroll (1990) to explain the pleasure of horror films.

9. This is loosely connected with what Andrew Tudor (1989) calls the "paranoid" strand of horror. According to Tudor, horror films in which there is "an ultimately successful struggle against disorder" are "secure," whereas horror films in which human action is ineffective and the threat continues to loom are "paranoid" (215). These two Hitchcock films are surely among the transitional instances as the genre moved toward the paranoid strand.

10. The thematic similarities include some very broad ideas, such as Hitchcock's preoccupation with mother-son relationships (and women's agency, as embodied by Melanie and Marion), and also some very specific connections, like the stuffed birds and bird art in the Bates Motel that prefigure the monstrous birds of the later film.

11. See the references in note 3.

12. Wells, however, does not convey much of the sense of contrast between the beginning of the film and the end: "[The world of *Psycho*] is everyday America, represented as an utterly remote place in which any semblance of moral or ethical security has been destabilized and proved to be illusory" (2000, 75).

Works Cited

Baier, Annette. 1986. "Trust and Antitrust." *Ethics* 96 (January): 231–60.

Bostrom, Nick. 2003. "Are We Living in a Computer Simulation?" *Philosophical Quarterly* 53 (April): 243–55.

Carroll, Noël. 1990. *The Philosophy of Horror; or, Paradoxes of the Heart*. New York: Routledge.

Cavell, Stanley. 2003. *Disowning Knowledge in Seven Plays of Shakespeare*. New York: Cambridge University Press.

Descartes, René. 1986. *Meditations on First Philosophy, with Selections from the Objections and Replies*. Ed. John Cottingham. New York: Cambridge University Press. (Orig. pub. 1642.)

Di Muzio, Gianluca. 2006. "The Immorality of Horror Films." *International Journal of Applied Philosophy* 20 (Fall): 277–95.

Doligosa, Felix, Jr. 2006. "In Memory of Lauri: Forty Years after Murder in Macky, Plaque Will Honor CU student." *Rocky Mountain News*, October 14. www.rockymountain news.com/drmn/local/article/0,1299,DRMN_15_5066491,00.html.

Freeland, Cynthia. 2000. *The Naked and the Undead: Evil and the Appeal of Horror*. Boulder, CO: Westview.

Gaut, Berys. 1993. "The Paradox of Horror." *British Journal of Aesthetics* 33 (4): 333–45.

Hills, Matt. 2003. "An Event-Based Definition of Horror." In *Dark Thoughts: Philosophic Reflections on Cinematic Horror*, ed. Steven Jay Schneider and Daniel Shaw, 138–57. Lanham, MD: Scarecrow.

Hume, David. 1969. *A Treatise of Human Nature*. Ed. Ernest C. Mossner. London: Penguin. (Orig. pub. 1739/40.)

Jancovich, Mark. 1992. *Horror*. London: Batsford.

Levine, Michael. 2004. "A Fun Night Out: Horror and Other Pleasures of the Cinema." In *Horror Film and Psychoanalysis: Freud's Worst Nightmare*, ed. Steven Jay Schneider, 35–54. Cambridge: Cambridge University Press.

Nietzsche, Friedrich. 1968. *Twilight of the Idols/The Anti-Christ*. Trans. R. J. Hollingdale. London: Penguin. (Orig. pub. 1889.)

Paglia, Camille. 1998. *The Birds*. London: British Film Institute.

Putnam, Hilary. 1982. "Brains in a Vat." In *Reason, Truth and History*, 1–21. Cambridge: Cambridge University Press.

Russell, David J. 1998. "Monster Roundup: Reintegrating the Horror Genre." In *Refiguring American Film Genres: History and Theory*, ed. Nick Browne, 233–54. Berkeley: University of California Press.

Schneider, Steven Jay. 2000. "Monsters as (Uncanny) Metaphors: Freud, Lakoff, and the Representation of Monstrosity in Cinematic Horror." In *Horror Film Reader,* ed. Alain Silver and James Ursini, 167–91. New York: Limelight.

———, ed. 2004. *Horror Film and Psychoanalysis: Freud's Worst Nightmare.* Cambridge: Cambridge University Press.

Tudor, Andrew. 1989. *Monsters and Mad Scientists.* London: Blackwell.

Turvey, Malcolm. 2004. "Philosophical Problems concerning the Concept of Pleasure in Psychoanalytic Theories of (the Horror) Film." In *Horror Film and Psychoanalysis: Freud's Worst Nightmare,* ed. Steven Jay Schneider, 68–83. Cambridge: Cambridge University Press..

Urbano, Cosimo. 2004. "'What's the Matter with Melanie?' Reflections on the Merits of Psychoanalytic Approaches to Modern Horror Cinema." In *Horror Film and Psychoanalysis: Freud's Worst Nightmare,* ed. Steven Jay Schneider, 17–34. Cambridge: Cambridge University Press.

Wells, Paul. 2000. *The Horror Genre from Beelzebub to Blair Witch.* London: Wallflower.

Wood, Robin. 2004. "Psycho." In *Alfred Hitchcock's Psycho: A Casebook,* ed. Robert Kolker, 74–99. New York: Oxford University Press.

Through a Mirror, Darkly
Art-Horror as a Medium for Moral Reflection
Philip Tallon

> The tale of the irrational is the sanest way I know of expressing the world in which I live. These tales have served me as instruments of both metaphor and morality; they continue to offer the best window I know on the question of how we perceive things and the question of how we do or do not behave on the basis of our perceptions.
> —Stephen King, *Four Past Midnight*

The Poetics of Horror

Works of art provide a means by which humans express, intuitively and explicitly, their assumptions about the world. We have all been moved by a sad story, gladdened by a funny story, and frightened by a scary story. In each case, it is very likely that the emotion produced depended on the effectiveness of the work of art to elicit those emotions by presenting to us a set of circumstances that we perceived as unfortunate, amusingly unexpected, or frightening. In other words, stories tend to need specific characteristics to produce the desired effect on us. Though fiction often seems to be about falsehood, "making things up," it actually very often adheres to a set of internal rules, specific to its genre type. To paraphrase *The Big Lebowski*'s Walter Sobchak: Art is not 'Nam; there are rules here.

In his *Poetics* Aristotle laid out the "rules" for tragic drama, dictating what could and could not be truly tragic. For instance, in Aristotle's view we cannot be moved to pity by the downfall of a truly wicked man. Seeing the violent deposition of a cruel dictator on CNN or reading about the murder of a vicious drug lord, very few of us feel genuinely sad, and many of us may even take pleasure in the news. Our tears do not flow because our minds accept the violent death of an evil man as, if not perfectly just, at the very least a fitting end.

Aristotle's approach to art assumes that narratives affect us in powerful ways because they interact with our *intuitive* understanding of life, the universe, and everything. For Aristotle, only the fall of a *great* man will move us to pity. Even better for tragic effect is if the great man has some flaw (like the rest of us) that brings him down, not randomly, but because of some mistake he has made. Our objective understanding of the man's greatness activates pity—while our objective understanding of his fatal flaw increases our identification and adds the element of fear. This cocktail of pity and fear is, for Aristotle, the essential effect of properly constructed tragic drama, and all of it depends on a certain understanding of the world.

Though Aristotle's *Poetics* discusses tragedy, much can also be said for the newer genre of horror as a medium for reflection on the ways that art interacts with, and disturbs, the way we see the world. In viewing a tragedy we grow to identify with the hero, especially with his inherent virtue, which is ultimately undone. In horror, however, what sympathy exists between the viewer and the victim will likely be *visceral* more than *emotional*. Seeing a woman hung on a meat hook, as *The Texas Chainsaw Massacre* invites us to do, isn't "very sad"—it is terrifying and nauseating. Rather than experience a cathartic purge of the emotions, we are more likely to want to purge the contents of our stomachs. The connection between spectator and spectacle is further seen in the way that the emotions of characters within horror fictions mirror those of our own. As Carroll points out, this is not the case with every genre of fiction. He writes,

> Aristotle is right about catharsis, for example, the emotional state of the audience does not double that of King Oedipus at the end of the play of the same name. Nor are we jealous, when Othello is. Also, when a comic character takes a pratfall, he hardly feels joyous, though we do. And though we feel suspense when the hero rushes to save the heroine tied to the railroad tracks he cannot afford to indulge such an emotion. Nevertheless, with horror, the situation is different. For in horror the emotions of the characters and those of the audience are synchronized in certain pertinent respects, as one can easily observe at a Saturday matinee in one's local cinema.[1]

This mirroring effect is found frequently in horror fiction, as described by

Jack Finney in *Invasion of the Body Snatchers*. In the book, the hero, Miles Bennell, encounters two of the alien pods that eventually take the form of humans. Finney describes Bennell's reaction as he seeks to destroy them: "They were weightless as children's balloons, harsh and dry on my palms and fingers. At the feel of them on my skin, I lost my mind completely, and then I was trampling them, smashing and crushing them under my plunging feet and legs, not even knowing that I was uttering a sort of hoarse, meaningless cry—Unhh! Unhh! Unhh!—of fright and animal disgust."[2] Bennell's horrorified trampling of the soon-to-be-human pods is easy to identify with. Similar examples can be seen in nearly any horror story where the protagonist or secondary character must enter a forbidding basement, venture out into the dark, or confront the monster. Like the character in the story, we are intended to feel fright and revulsion.

As genres go, horror is also the least friendly of the storytelling patterns. If genres were houseguests, romantic comedies would always be cooking you dinner, while historical dramas regaled you with stories, and science fiction kept you thinking about big ideas. Perhaps the broad comedies *might* leave the toilet seat up or fart at the dinner table, but, generally speaking, all these genres would behave themselves compared to horror. If horror were a houseguest, it would smash the china, flood the bathroom, and while you were cleaning off the gum it stuck to the living room TV, it would be trying to burn the house down.

As a genre, horror doesn't like you. Horror doesn't care if it causes you to lose sleep. Horror doesn't mind if it frightens you so much it makes you swear off something you love, like camping or swimming in the ocean. In essence, horror is a jerk. As an artistic category, horror trades in the random and meaningless: hence this description of *The Texas Chainsaw Massacre*, a movie whose story of innocent tourists caught in a house of horror clearly portrays cruelty and violence as meaningless, and thus defies positive description: "The film's archetypal structure is borrowed from fairy tales: this isn't far from Hansel and Gretel, with its children lost in the woods who find an attractive house inhabited by a fiend who kidnaps and wants to eat them. But while fairy tales tend to serve the function of preparing children for the rigors of adult life, and thus present a positive face for all their often considerable violence, *Texas* inverts their traditional values and presents an apocalyptic vision of unremitting negativity."[3] This unremitting negativity further calls into question the value of horror as an art form for consumption.

So what, then, can be learned from this most unpleasant of artistic genres? What of value could be uncovered about the way that we see the world by looking at horror's internal logic? In this essay I will look at the contribution horror makes to our thinking, arguing that horror can "illuminate" the way we see ourselves by showing us a much darker picture than we are used to seeing. Despite its frequent kinship with dark humor and its tendency toward vulgarity and schlock, I will suggest here that horror as a genre is worth taking seriously (at least for a while) because of how well it can inform and enlighten our vision of the world by reminding us of our inner moral frailty and by forcing us to take seriously the moral reality of evil.

John Ruskin, the famous artist and art critic, writes, "Great nations write their autobiographies in three manuscripts;—the book of their deeds, the book of their words, and the book of their art. Not one of these books can be understood unless we read the two others; but of the three the only quite trustworthy one is the last."[4] Art, then, following Ruskin, may be a better guide to understanding ourselves than even our words or deeds. I want to show that this is especially true of horror, as it clashes with and critiques (both explicitly and implicitly) two broad cultural movements (modern hubris and postmodern skepticism) by puncturing their philosophical posturing.

The Monsters Within: Horror and Enlightenment Hubris

There may be no more famous work of horror than the nineteenth-century masterpiece *Frankenstein*. It was a work both of its time and against its time. Created at the cusp of the modern scientific age, Shelley's work captures something of the spirit of the time, especially with regard to the sense that science would soon unlock the very secrets of life. In the preface to her book Mary Shelley wrote, "The event on which this fiction is founded has been supposed, by Dr. Darwin, and some of the physiological writers of Germany, as not of impossible occurrence."[5] By this Shelley meant to indicate that there was nothing, as far as she saw it, inherently supernatural about the tale she was about to tell. Though the stitching together and reanimation of corpses was not then (or now) possible, Shelley did not believe *Frankenstein* to be a story of "supernatural" terror. As such, Shelley's work of horror functions not so much as an external critique of the prevailing notions of the time—a strong affirmation of scientific investigation and a powerful faith in progress (compare Denis Diderot's statement "Free yourself from the yoke of religion ... [and] submit to nature, to humanity, to yourself again, and you will find flowers strewn all along the pathway of your life"[6])—but rather can function as an internal critique of the mood of the time.

Yet despite the fact that Shelley thought the events in the book were technically possible, she did recognize that they were also extraordinary, and extraordinarily disturbing. So she justified the tale in that it "affords a point of view to the imagination for the delineating of human passions more comprehensive and commanding than any which the ordinary relations of existing events can yield."[7] What passions, then, did Shelley think these extraordinary events could help us see and understand? What does *Frankenstein* show us?

First, it must be noted that when people say "Frankenstein" the first image that pops into our heads is the lumbering monster, with its flat forehead and the bolts emerging from the side of its neck. Yet in both the popular 1931 film version of *Frankenstein* and the novel on which it is based, "Frankenstein" properly refers to the creator, not the creature. This confusion is telling. In both the movie and the book, there is an essential humanity to the monster that, at moments, makes him a greater object of sympathy than his creator. Though we, like Dr. Victor Frankenstein, are horrified at the monster's destructive behavior (in the movie, most famously, the monster drowns a little girl; in the book the monster murders Frankenstein's new bride), in reality, it is the monster's abandonment by his creator that has allowed this to happen. Victor is unable to handle the work of his own hands; his attempt to play God turns into a nightmare as his scientific domination of "nature" overreaches his modest abilities to "nurture" what he has brought to life. Victor reaches beyond the normal limits of science, and manages to pluck the very secret of life from the heights of human knowledge. Yet here Victor destructively overreaches. The book's subtitle—"The Modern Prometheus"—echoes the theme of tragic overachievement, as it brings to mind another doomed attempt to bring divine "fire" down to the world of mortals. By painting a vivid picture of the horrific result of certain "human passions," Shelley seems to be showing the inherent dangers of scientific exploration, and more generally the weakness of Enlightenment hubris that Victor Frankenstein represents.

Now, of course, not all scientific exploration produces lumbering, fearsome monsters, but it is significant that the chaotic, regressive, and often supernatural genre of horror was born so closely together with the rise of Enlightenment values such as rationality, progress, and a generally naturalistic understanding of the world. Noël Carroll, writing about the genre of horror, therefore appropriately calls horror the "underside of the Enlightenment."[8]

The Enlightenment, of course, represented huge leaps forward in terms of human understanding of the world—the advance of scientific progress in the eighteenth and nineteenth centuries was astounding. But with every scientific advancement, new possibilities open up for abuse and corruption.

It is impossible to list every horror movie or work of fiction that raises a similar doubt to *Frankenstein,* but it is helpful to mention just a few examples in which we see similar themes: *The Fly, Jurassic Park, 28 Days Later, The Invisible Man, The Brain That Wouldn't Die, The Host, Them, Godzilla,* and *The Stand.* All of these stories cast doubt, in some way, on the human assumption that progress in knowledge is always good. All of them tell about human inventiveness unleashing destruction on humanity itself.

Horror, in this way, shows us our inherent skepticism about absolute progress. As we gain more and more mastery of the world, it can be easy to forget that, deep down, we still lack mastery of ourselves. Likewise, other works, such as *Dracula, The Call of Cthulu,* or *The Island of Dr. Moreau,* present a dark, regressive shadow image of the bright and progressive veneer of eighteenth- and nineteenth-century optimism. The origins of modern horror provide a vivid presentation of the inherent moral weakness and often-present darkness in the human condition. The presence of horror in the popular imagination suggests our cultural need to be reminded of our fallen state. Monsters like Mr. Hyde or the Wolfman make visible our inner corruption. Godzilla and "the Fly" metaphorically embody the dangers of recklessness and pride. Like Dorian Gray looking in horror on his portrait, the revulsion we feel at horror can be, in a sense, a revulsion at ourselves.

The Monsters Without: Postmodernism and Horror

However, as culture has shifted from eighteenth- and nineteenth-century optimism to a deeper suspicion of traditional universal values, horror's function as a medium for reflection has (to some degree) changed. Where the Enlightenment placed great confidence in our ability to understand and organize the world according to overarching "meta-narratives" (big stories), postmodern thinkers like Jean-François Lyotard (1924–98) have described our current condition as defined by "incredulity towards meta-narratives."[9] For Lyotard, postmodernism represented the failure of all large-scale systems to adequately explain the world. Where once Christian theology or Enlightenment rationalism attempted to understand everything (reality, morality, and aesthetics), we now get by with smaller narratives specific to our own contexts.

Often this incredulity toward meta-narratives shows itself in our casual attitude toward moral objectivity. Moral relativism, the view that moral evaluations are not universally true, is often found in public discourse. "To each his own," we find ourselves saying, trying not to pass judgment on the behavior of others. Tolerance, always a virtue for humans, has now become one of our highest virtues as we try to live peacefully in a broadly pluralistic society. Relativism is also seen regarding aesthetics. As we divide sharply over musical interests or favorite movies, our cultural "To each his own" philosophy expresses itself in phrases like "There is no accounting for taste" or "Beauty is in the eye of the beholder."

Yet there seems to be, despite the widespread trend toward relativism in morality and aesthetics, a deep human desire for bedrock order. Moral and aesthetic judgments, if much more difficult to make about many matters involving beauty or goodness, are still much easier to make about evil or ugliness, especially as they are taken to their extreme in horror. Philosophers like Cynthia Freeland have pointed out that horror involves a severe violation of our sense of moral, natural, and social order. Think of just about any horror film and you will find that it works upon us by tearing down some boundary we had in place, but perhaps forgot was there. Freeland writes that "monsters [are] beings that raise the specter of evil by overturning the natural order, whether it be an order concerning death, the body, God's laws, natural laws, or ordinary human values."[10] The key element is a sense of *violation*. Thus horror is often rooted in what feels most safe and secure: the home (*The Haunting* or *The Sixth Sense*), the family (*The Exorcist* or *The Shining*), or innocent and mundane activities such as checking into a motel or babysitting (*Psycho* or *Halloween*). So recent works of horror, from *Halloween* and *Psycho* to *The Birds* on to *The Texas Chainsaw Massacre*, all depend for their effect on an intuitive sense of order to the world. This is a discomforting aspect to horror, but there is also a desirable quality to it. It terrifies us *and* gives us a sense of moral, social, and aesthetic stability. Recently, sitting in a movie theater watching a screening of Alfred Hitchcock's 1960 classic film *Psycho,* I was struck with how the audience all startled at the same moments of surprising violence. The experience was communal in a way that few other experiences are: we all jumped *together* at the sudden appearance of "Mother" wielding a butcher knife. As a nation, of course, we have never been closer in recent memory than after the horrors of 9-11. Despite the divisions and problems that have followed in its wake, 9-11 itself provided a strong sense of national identity and purpose. Part of having moral order in the world necessitates having a real understanding of evil.

This is nowhere clearer in fiction, perhaps, than in Stephen King's modern retelling of *Dracula, 'Salem's Lot.* Where Bram Stoker's 1897 classic assumed much more easily the idea that there could be evil forces at work in the world, Stephen King's comfortable, peaceful twentieth-century Americans struggle to grasp that the nice new man who moved to town, Mr. Straker, could actually be a monster. Even the town priest must struggle to come to grips with the reality of absolute evil as represented by the town's vampire visitor. Yet in an extended passage, we hear in the priest's effort to accept the idea of evil the need for some rock-bottom reality: "He was being forced to the conclusion that there was no EVIL in the world at all but only evil—or perhaps (evil). At moments like this he suspected that Hitler had been nothing but a harried bureaucrat and Satan himself a mental defective with a rudimentary sense of humor—the kind that finds feeding firecrackers wrapped in bread to seagulls unutterably funny."[11]

This view of the world, however, the priest finds unutterably dull. Instead, as King writes, "[The priest] wanted to see EVIL with its cerements of deception cast aside. . . . He wanted to slug it out toe to toe with EVIL, like Muhummad Ali and Joe Frazier."[12] Fortunately (or unfortunately, depending on how you look at it), the priest *does* get a chance to face this evil, as does the rest of the town of 'Salem's Lot, and it destroys most of them. These days we often find ourselves in the position of the priest in King's novel, desiring to find a deeper meaning to our lives. Horror attempts, in the crudest and cruelest way possible, to give our world a shared sense of order.

The Dark Mirror: Horror and Moral Reflection

It seems, then, that horror not only provides a critique of our optimism about the world, but also expresses our pessimism about any sense of order: horror helps to illuminate aspects of our commonly held, if explicitly denied, underlying objective view of morality. Stephen King, in his full-length treatment of horror, wittily describes the conservative moral core of horror as a "Republican in a three-piece suit" hiding underneath a rubber monster costume.[13] Horror makes us recognize evils that must, if we know anything about the world at all, be wrong. Horror in this way is constructive.

Yet there is also something skeptical, or perhaps anarchical, about horror's view of the world. In criticizing postmodern relativism, horror pushes us to take seriously our deepest moral convictions, but in criticizing lofty Enlightenment values, it also casts doubt on our highest moral *intentions*. Horror forces us to take seriously the darkness within our own nature, which cannot be overcome with technological wizardry. In fact, the opposite is often true, as the twentieth century (and its horror stories) bluntly attest.

Horror, therefore, provides a dark mirror in which we can examine ourselves by honestly facing the shadow side of the human condition as well as our deepest intuitive (and inviolate) sense of right and wrong. If horror does not reassure us with glad tidings, it does provide us with the comforting sense that, while all may not be right with the world, or even within ourselves, there is order and meaning to the world. Monsters, inside us and outside us, still exist.

Notes

My epigraph is taken from Stephen King, *Four Past Midnight* (London: Hodder & Stroughton, 1990), 736.

1. Noël Carroll, *The Philosophy of Horror; or, Paradoxes of the Heart* (New York: Routledge, 1990), 28, 18.

2. Jack Finney, *Invasion of the Body Snatchers* (New York: Scribner, 1998), 114.

3. James Marriott, *Horror Films* (London: Virgin, 2007), 183.

4. John Ruskin, preface to *St. Mark's Rest,* quoted in Richard Viladesau, *Theology and the Arts* (Mahwah, NJ: Paulist, 2000), 124–25.

5. Mary Shelley, preface to *Frankenstein* (London: Gibbings, 1897), xii.

6. Ernst Cassirer, Fritz C. A. Koelin, and James P. Pettegrove, *The Philosophy of the Enlightenment* (Princeton, NJ: Princeton University Press, 1968), 135.

7. Shelley, preface, xii.

8. Carroll, *Philosophy of Horror,* 55.

9. Jean-François Lyotard, *The Postmodern Condition* (Minneapolis: University of Minnesota Press, 1984), xxiv.

10. Cynthia Freeland, *The Naked and the Undead: Evil and the Appeal of Horror* (Boulder, CO: Westview, 2000), 8.

11. Stephen King, *'Salem's Lot* (New York: Doubleday, 2005), 167.

12. Ibid., 166.

13. Stephen King, *Danse Macabre* (New York: Berkley, 1983), 24.

The Justification of Torture-Horror

Retribution and Sadism in *Saw, Hostel,* and *The Devil's Rejects*

Jeremy Morris

> Among other vices, I cruelly hate cruelty, both by nature and by judgment, as the extreme of all vices. But this is to such a point of softness that I do not see a chicken's neck wrung without distress, and I cannot bear to hear the scream of a hare in the teeth of my dogs, although the chase is a violent pleasure.
> —Michel de Montaigne, "Of Cruelty"

> Some of these movies are so viciously nihilistic that the only point seems to be to force you to suspend moral judgments altogether.
> —David Edelstein, "Now Playing at Your Local Multiplex: Torture Porn"

When in a decisive 1988 presidential debate Bernard Shaw asked Michael Dukakis what he would do to someone who had raped and murdered his wife, the response was supposed to be obvious; but it was not so for Dukakis. He stated his opposition to the death penalty without a trace of vengeful passion.[1] *Last House on the Left* (1972), on the other hand, indulged in its answer to the same sort of question: the film ends with the parents torturing and slaying their child's murderers. *Last House on the Left* became a classic model for some of the most popular horror films. Dukakis's answer became a model in its own right—for what not to do. It is now widely accepted, even by Dukakis himself, that his loss was partly due to that answer. To avoid

Dukakis's fate, presidential candidates must express hatred and even violent intentions toward the criminal when asked that sort of question. For instance, in a 2004 debate John Kerry answered: "My instinct is to want to strangle that person with my own hands. . . . I understand the instincts, I really do."[2] Though such a response is immediately tempered with a statement of the politician's real position, cruel and vengeful feelings toward the criminal are a must and are taken as a sign of empathy with the victim.

Cruelty is about as vivid an expression of immorality as there is, and yet cruelty is a perennial source of entertainment in our culture. We should resist the temptation to ascribe the popularity of films such as *Saw* (2004), *Hostel* (2005), and *The Devil's Rejects* (2005) to some exceptional depravity of our own time. A sober appraisal must recognize that torture-horror is a manifestation of a recurring form of recreation whose milestones include gladiator battles, inquisitions, and public executions. To dismiss the current popularity of the torture subgenre as a passing cinematic fetish is to ignore the depth of the important, if disturbing, questions raised. Is torture ever morally permissible? Is the enjoyment of torture ever morally justified? In what follows, I will explain how these questions relate to torture-horror movies. Whether or not torture can ever be justified, rationales for it, such as retribution, are important elements of the genre. A careful analysis of such elements may shed light on some of the moral issues raised by torture-horror. At the very least such an analysis can provide a deeper critical appreciation of torture-horror itself.

Elements of Torture-Horror

In true torture-horror, torture is the source of horror and not merely an accident of plot or character. It must include depictions of noninterrogational tortures that are realistic, accusatory, and essential to the narrative. Not every film that includes explicit depictions of torture is an example of the torture-horror genre, for at least the reason that not all depictions of torture occur in horror films. For example, the fact that a central character is tortured in *Syriana* (2005) does not mean that it is a torture-horror film. Rather, the apparent intent of *Syriana* is to lead its audience through situations that include torture for the sake of a story about international politics. Horror is very different: generally speaking, the intent is to lead the audience through horrifying experiences for the sake of those experiences. The larger horror genre has other distinctive features, but it should suffice to say that whatever features are essential to horror are also features of the torture subgenre. If the general aim of a horror film is to develop a frightening scenario that is to be enjoyed for the fear it creates, then the general goal of a torture-horror film is to develop such a scenario with depictions of torture. For torture-horror, it is important that torture and the characters of the torturers and tortured drive the narrative as the primary source of fear.

The different ends to which torture might be a means correspond to distinguishable elements of torture-horror.[3] Each purpose lays the groundwork for its particular answer to the justification questions: Is the torture justified? Is the audience's enjoyment of torture justified? These purposes include interrogation, punishment, deterrence, terrorism, and sadism. Torture is interrogational when its purpose, misguided or not, is to glean information by means of torture. Torture can also be used as a means of either punishment or deterrence. The purpose of terroristic torture is to subdue or otherwise manipulate a larger group by means of random torture of some of its members. The purpose of sadistic torture is to provide enjoyment to the torturer or a third party. Although a given act of cruelty often has more than one of these purposes, each can be distinguished and evaluated on its own merits.

Interrogational torture is prominent in many films, but not in torture-horror. The television series *24* includes, and in an important sense features, interrogational torture, but it is not torture-horror. Nonetheless, the series presents an answer to the justification question: extremely high stakes in the form of terrorist attacks are purported to justify the torture performed in interrogations. The recent fury of political debates over this answer gives the false impression that such scenarios are newly discovered possibilities, when in fact such high-stakes scenarios have for a long time figured in philosophers' arguments. For instance, high stakes are the basis of many arguments against utilitarianism, a view that seems to allow for the justification of torture in some cases. Even Aristotle comments on torture as a form of interrogation, rejecting it as unreliable.[4] I will leave these issues aside, since interrogational torture is not a distinctive feature of torture-horror. However, it is worth emphasizing an analogy between *24* and torture-horror. Both attempt to address the justification question through the intentions of the torturer. Although torture-horror must include noninterrogational torture, the intention of the torturer must be on display to or an issue for the audience. In torture-horror, the vengeful or sadistic purposes of the torture are a source of horror beyond the depiction of the torture itself, and it is through the torturer's purpose that the justification questions are addressed.

Another theme of torture-horror is the transformations of torturers and victims. Victims or their survivors sometimes return for retribution (for example, the Collingwood parents in *Last House on the Left* and Paxton in *Hostel*) or acquire an appreciation of torture themselves (Amanda in *Saw*

II–III) or both (Sheriff Wydell in *The Devil's Rejects*). Also, as in all of these films, the original torturers become the victims. In most torture-horror, one or more of the victims acquires at some point the intentions of a torturer. Such role reversals are one technique that encourages the audience to "be on the side of" the torturer. In this way the justification question is foisted on the audience.

Finally, there is an important realist element to torture-horror. Unlike other types of horror, torture-horror is never supernatural, magical, or religious—at least not primarily. Although reference is sometimes made to such common horror ingredients, for example, the sarcastically religious sacrifice in *House of 1000 Corpses* (2003), they are not real in the world of torture-horror. When the supernatural becomes a real part of a story that might be otherwise torture-horror, the story is transformed into something else, for example, *From Dusk Till Dawn* (1996) and *Videodrome* (1983). That torture-horror is naturalistic is integral to its other elements. Appreciation of the intentions and emotions of the victim and the torturer as well as recognition of their role reversal is facilitated by a realistic narrative undistracted by the wildly unfamiliar. The realism in torture-horror is thus relevant to justification as well. The less real the depictions of torture, the less real and the less pressing are the questions, asked of the audience, of whether the torture and its enjoyment are justified.

The distinctive features of torture-horror, besides those that are distinctive of horror generally, relate to the justification questions. These include focusing on realistic depictions of torture as the primary vehicle of fear, providing the torturer with a rationale, and the transformation of victims into torturers. Each can be found separately outside of the genre. Torture is by no means the exclusive province of horror. Role reversals can be found in almost any genre, as can realism. It is the particular combination of these elements that makes for torture-horror.

Retribution

A theory of retributive justice is defined by the claim that punishment is morally justified and made morally obligatory by the actions of the guilty. Immanuel Kant is perhaps the best defender of this view: "Juridical punishment can never be administered merely as a means for promoting another good either with regard to the criminal himself or to civil society, but must in all cases be imposed only because the individual on whom it is inflicted has committed a crime."[5] In a retributivist theory, the type of punishment that should be employed is also settled by the nature of the crime committed. The most basic standard is the principle of equality, according to which "If you slander another, you slander yourself; if you steal from another, you steal from yourself; if you strike another, you strike yourself; if you kill another, you kill yourself."[6] Now, it is not difficult to see how this principle can lead to absurdities: a rape for a rape, a mutilation for a mutilation, and so on. A code that assigns particular punishments to particular crimes, *lex talionis,* is an attempt to mitigate such complications. The same absurdities and compromises are present in torture-horror, a great deal of which can be understood as an exploration of *lex talionis.*

Kant's classical defense of equal-punishment retributivism is couched in terms of individual autonomy and responsibility. In Kant's conception, my autonomy is disrespected when another reaps the rewards or penalties of my actions. For instance, if every time I place a losing bet you are there to pick up the debt, it is not my gambling but *our* gambling. Something of mine other than money has been lost. In order to be really free, I need the world to react to my action without someone else in between. The same is true of my immoral acts if they go unpunished. If I am treated as a patient rather than an agent in action, then my action is no longer fully my own. Without responsibility, my sense of ownership of my actions is undermined. In Kant's view, my responsibility is to live by the rules I expect others to live by. By acting in a certain way toward others, I am accepting that others can act in that way toward me. If I murder and I am autonomous in this sense, then I should be treated as a murderer. In murdering I have chosen murder as the rule, and so I may be justly killed. The justification of punishment that is equal to its crime is a consequence of an immoral and autonomous act. By killing a murderer, we are doing no more than respecting his autonomy. According to this argument, the retributivist view of equal punishment is the only view that respects autonomy.[7]

Such retributivism and its related conceptions of responsibility and autonomy are frequent themes of torture-horror. *Last House on the Left,* as I have already mentioned, is a classic example. When young Mari Collingwood and her friend go to a concert, they happen upon a band of criminals on the run and are tortured, raped, and murdered in the first part of the film. By coincidence, the criminals are invited into the home of Mari's parents under the pretence of their being traveling salesmen with a broken-down car. Upon discovering that their houseguests are responsible for their daughter's death, the parents seek retribution. The roles are reversed; Mari's parents become the torturers. We are led by our empathy with Mari to our hatred of those who torture her, and so we find ourselves on the side of the parents.

The crimes against Mari serve as a retributivist justification for the cruel acts of her parents.

The retributivist element is developed in more elaborate ways in *Seven* (1995) and *Saw*. In both films the story centers on a torturer who devises ingenious punishments for various crimes. In *Seven* detectives Sommerset and Mills investigate a series of grisly murder scenes that are arranged to correspond to each of the seven deadly sins. A gluttonous man is force-fed until he literally explodes, a slothful man is bound to a bed for so long that he slowly wastes away, and so on. After turning himself in, the designer of these crimes announces that his purpose is to teach the world a lesson about human responsibility. This is also the purpose of the "Jigsaw Killer," John Kramer, who, in the *Saw* series, devises numerous torture traps that usually drive their victims to kill others or themselves. Scratchy recordings of Jigsaw's instructions to his victims explain the trap, how it can be escaped, and the lesson he intends to teach them. "Hello, Mark. If you're so sick, then why do I have so many photos of you up and about? Let's put your so-called illness to the test. Right now, there's a slow-acting poison in your veins. The antidote is inside the safe, the combination to the safe is written on the wall. Hurry up and program it in but watch your step. By the way, that's a flammable substance smeared on your body, so I would be careful with that candle, if I were you, or all the people you've burned with your act just might have their revenge." It is hard to miss the retributivism in Jigsaw's message to Mark. Mark does not die of the poison but, in a desperate attempt to avoid that fate, catches himself on fire and is burned to death. Mark's demise is only a brief flashback, but it illustrates the essentials of the multiple Jigsaw traps that drive the plots of each film in the series. Unlike *Last House on the Left*, the crimes of the victims in the *Saw* films are complex and not always explicit. There is no clear equivalent to lying, as in the case of Mark, or voyeurism, as in the case of Adam. Jigsaw has to compose his own *lex talionis*. The complex traps reveal the flaws and strengths of the victims' characters in ways that are intended to support Jigsaw's purposes. It is for the audience to decide the extent to which Jigsaw's tortures "fit" their victims, and this is undoubtedly a large part of the appeal.

What is common to *Saw, Seven*, and *Last House on the Left* is a theme of torture-horror generally: a narrative seeking for an appropriate code of punishment. Note that in this regard, the appeal of torture-horror is not unlike that offered by the carnival atmosphere of public executions, common until the last century. Now, before going any further, let me state clearly that I am not claiming that retribution is justification of torture in any case. I claim only that torture-horror offers a modern presentation of the implications of retributivism and that alone may be sufficient to justify the enjoyment of torture-horror. Retributive justice in film is no more immoral than witnessing actual retributive actions: "When someone who delights in annoying and vexing peace loving folk receives at last a right good beating, it is certainly an ill, but everyone approves of it and considers it as good in itself even if nothing further results from it."[8]

The appeal of retributivist torture-horror consists in a comprehension and evaluation of the torturer's motives and methods.

Sadism

Role reversal is sometimes employed to illuminate retributive intentions: our empathy with the victims is transformed into a shared feeling of vengeance when they perform retributive acts of torture. As I argued above, the protagonists of *Last House on the Left* become the torturers, and the audience is led to share their feelings not only as victims but as torturers.

It is difficult to find an instance of torture-horror that is completely devoid of retributivism. Nonetheless, it would be both inaccurate and naive to claim that retributivism can explain the appeal of all torture-horror films, since many focus more intently on a different kind of torture: that which is purely sadistic. Moreover, even with torture that is depicted as retributive, there is often a suspicion that there is something else going on as well. It is relatively easy to see that the retributivist rationale does not apply to most of the torture depicted in *The Texas Chainsaw Massacre* (1974), *Hostel,* or *The Devil's Rejects.*

Sometimes the motivation for cruelty is purely the pleasure and profit that torture brings to its practitioners. Pleasure and profit are the predominant motivations in *Hostel:* while touring Europe, a group of thrill-seeking young Americans is captured and sold to an industry that caters to thrill-seeking millionaires who pay to torture. Given that the torture is driven entirely by consumerism, justification questions go unanswered on retributivist grounds. So at first glance it may appear that enjoying *Hostel* is tantamount to partaking in the sadism. As it turns out, there is a last-minute retributivist aspect to *Hostel:* having escaped the torture factory, Paxton, one of the young tourists, corners and murders the Dutch businessman who, in one of the most intense torture scenes of the film, dismembered his friend. In this sense, *Hostel* provides a retributivist back door so that in the final scenes the audience is not left with the moral weight of pure sadism.

Sid Haig (as Captain J. T. Spaulding) in *The Devil's Rejects* (2005). Directed by Rob Zombie. (Lions Gate Films/Photofest)

There is less room for retributivist justification in *The Devil's Rejects*. Although part of the story is driven by Sheriff Wydell's quest for revenge for his brother's murder, the most prominent torture scenes of the film have no such retributive purposes. The scenes just after the Firefly family's initial escape from Wydell fill the first half of the film with seemingly pointless torture. Otis and Baby spend their time waiting for a rendezvous with Captain Spaulding by tormenting a hapless troupe of traveling musicians. Devoid of retributivism, these torture scenes display perhaps a deterrent, terroristic purpose, insofar as Otis and Baby need to control and ultimately employ their victims in uncovering a cache of weapons. Yet there is an undeniable emphasis placed on the sadistic joy of Otis and Baby as they torment their victims. By the second half of the film Otis and Baby are the heroes, reminiscing about their shared experiences as they plummet to their deaths while being chased by the police. The audience is left to accept their acts of torture as a kind of quirkiness to be appreciated for its uniqueness. Even in those scenes where retribution is the initial motivation, such as Sheriff Wydell's murder of Mama Firefly and later his torturing of Spaulding and Otis, his pleasure, even sexual pleasure, is emphasized.

What is morally wrong with this type of sadistic torture can be explained by a number of different principles. It is interesting to note that Kant's explanation of the wrongness of sadism is powered by the same arguments regarding autonomy that are invoked to explain the rightness of retributive punishment. Purely sadistic torture is by definition a violation of the victims' autonomy since it is a use of people merely as a means to pleasure. Though there is something right about the Kantian explanation, it is a bit peculiar, insofar as one might think the more natural explanation is that sadistic torture is wrong due to the intense suffering that it causes its victim. The concept of autonomy would hardly seem to exhaust the wrongness. Another explanation can be given by the utilitarian principle that the rightness or wrongness of an act is determined by its consequences with respect to the happiness or interests of those affected. Sadistic torture is wrong because on balance there is more harm caused to the victim than there is pleasure generated for the torturer (or others). However, the problem with the utilitarian explanation is that it allows that sadistic torture could be justified if a sufficient amount of pleasure is generated, such as a case with one victim and a large number of sadists. An even better explanation involves a condemnation of the intentions of the torturer: sadistic torture is wrong both because it causes harm to its victim and because it is the expression of a misguided sensibility—one that delights in controlling others and making them suffer.[9]

Given these arguments against sadistic torture, how can enjoyment of purely sadistic scenes in torture-horror be justified? One answer is that enjoyment, even that which is sadistic, is infectious. As an example, consider a torture-horror film that is totally devoid of the usual retributivist elements: *The Texas Chainsaw Massacre*. Explicit sadistic torture scenes include those that lead up to the grandfather's feeble attempts to murder Sally. After seeing her brother murdered by Leatherface, Sally escapes, only to be recaptured by Cook. As they return in Cook's truck to the house where Sally's friends have already met their end, Cook strikes Sally with the end of a broomstick while she is bound and covered in the passenger seat. Though the physical assault is minor relative to those that occur in the rest of the film, this is one of the most horrifying scenes. The source of horror and enjoyment is the infectious glee expressed by Cook with each jab of the broom handle. He has successfully duped Sally into thinking he would help her and is now on his way home with his prize: his satisfaction is something that is meant to be shared or at least recognized by the audience. It is not as if the audience empathizes with Cook's suffering; he is not suffering at all. It is Sally who is being tortured, but she is hidden in this scene and we hear only the faintest whimpers of pain. Rather, it is Cook's delight that is on display and it is an independent source of fear. That Cook's acts of cruelty are so clearly wrong implicates those in the audience led to giggle along with him.

An analogous explication can be given for the sadistic scenes in *The Devil's Rejects*. The persistent lightheartedness of Otis and Baby is always on display while they are taunting their victims. Their good cheer is made all the more contagious through their banter and joking with their victims and each other. Also, the classic rock and roll that plays as a soundtrack to their torture adventures works to further induce the audience to share their experiences. Here is the genius of sadistic torture-horror: it transforms the source of fear from a distant other to something familiar in ourselves. The terror of the victim is supplanted by the delight of the torturer, which is being consciously shared by the audience: *that* is the source of horror.

The appeal of sadistic torture-horror consists in careful manipulations of our moral sensibilities. The ability to share the suffering and joy of others naturally varies from person to person. Those that lack the ability completely are morally deficient, incapable of living a full life. Some sensitivity to the emotions of others is an obligatory characteristic of a morally good person. Yet, and this amounts to a serious theoretical difficulty much discussed in philosophy, according to rationalist theories such as Kant's, such empathic sensibilities are irrelevant to moral evaluation. In contrast, sentimentalist theories hold that empathic abilities are crucial to morality: we should be emotionally repulsed at the suffering, as well as partake in the happiness, of others. Our moral status is at least partially based on our capacity to feel the pain or the joy of others.

There are really two opposites to empathy: not sharing the feelings of another and sharing the feelings with an opposite effect. The former is a lack of empathetic ability, and the latter is when that ability is misguided. As wrong as it is to have no empathic abilities, it is every bit as immoral to have misguided sensibilities, for example, feeling pleasure at the suffering of others. In this way, sentimentalism can explain why the sadistic characters are immoral: they have misguided sensibilities. Yet torture-horror does not require an immoral audience, even according to sentimentalism. Torture-horror requires an audience both capable of empathy with the victims and able to share something of the joy of the torturers, however unsavory. Someone without both of these emotional capabilities does not get torture-horror and is morally deficient for the same reason. In order to enjoy sadistic torture-horror, the audience must experience both of these conflicting sentiments. Being conflicted in that way is not the mark of immorality; on the contrary, it is a moral vindication of the audience.

Utilitarianism gives another, albeit weaker, answer to the question of whether enjoyment of sadistic torture-horror can be justified. Utilitarianism holds that every interest, including the audience's, should be considered impartially. Now, this allows that sadistic torture will be justified just in cases where the harm caused is less than the resulting good, all things considered. Although it is not clear what numbers and intensities are involved in actual cases of sadism, in torture-horror, there is apparently no actual harm caused.[10] Enjoyment of sadistic torture-horror is, then, clearly justifiable according to utilitarianism. However, as I have already mentioned, utilitarianism has the implausible consequence that *real* sadistic torture itself may be justified.

As important as it is to defend the enjoyment of torture-horror, it is at least as important to condemn actual acts of sadistic torture. So a sentimentalist answer to the justification question is more plausible. A fully empathetic person can share the suffering of the victim but can also share the joy of the torturer. Our ability to share the joy of others is not limited to their morally permissible actions. Although one believes that torture is wrong, that does not mean that one thereby ceases to be sensitive to the amusement of sadists. This sort of sentimentalist account does not require that the audience condone or otherwise justify the torture itself, but it does explain how a good person can justifiably enjoy torture-horror.

From retributivist elements of torture-horror to sadistic elements, it is significant how the genre entangles moral questions about torture with moral questions about its own audience. Retributivist elements play on our sense of justice and vengeance, whereas sadistic elements can implicate our empathetic sensibilities. Pure cruelty obviously has no rationalistic justification along the lines of interrogation or retribution, but it may trouble us nonetheless as something we would enjoy if we were in the torturer's shoes. The implication of the audience through the torturer's purposes and experiences is both essential to the genre and a primary source of its appeal.

Realism

The attention to realistic detail in torture-horror is at least one reason critics have pigeonholed the genre as possessing a preoccupation with the newest advances in special effects. So why is torture-horror so realistic? Part of the answer has to be that realism supports the other elements discussed so far. Fantastical turns reduce our ability to identify with the characters, and the more visceral the violence, the more vivid are the impressions of empathy and cruelty. Being told about cruelty creates less of an impression than witnessing it. One sure way to induce sentiment is to make depictions of suffering and joy as vivid as possible. The retributivist and sentimentalist elements in torture-horror are amplified by such realism.

Few torture-horrors have dealt recursively with the realist element, save one possible example: *Videodrome*. In an attempt to gratify his taste for greater realism in depictions of torture, an obscure network executive, Max Renn, is willing to exploit pirated snuff films, first with foreign victims, then with familiar ones, and eventually with himself. One of the themes of *Videodrome* is that by seeking more realistic depictions of torture, we identify more with the victims as well as the perpetrators of the torture.[11] This summarizes one of the points of realism in torture-horror. One way to induce feelings of empathy is via self-identification with those whose feelings we empathize with. Realism, by definition, facilitates this identification and thus aids the implication and ultimately the fear and enjoyment of the audience.

Deriding our amusements is nearly as common as experiencing them. Boxing, sportfishing, and pornography are just some of the targets of moral denunciation.[12] Among the arguments one finds against these forms of entertainment are those that would seem to apply to torture-horror. For instance, the enjoyment of pornography is wrong, according to Helen Longino, since pornography features and endorses actions that are degrading to women: "Pornography is not just the explicit representation or description of sexual behavior . . . it is material that explicitly represents or describes degrading and abusive sexual behavior so as to endorse and/or recommend the behavior as described." She argues that pornography so defined should be restricted since its availability encourages harm to women: "As much as the materials themselves, the social tolerance of these degrading and distorted images of women in such quantities is harmful to us, since it indicates a general willingness to see women in ways incompatible with our fundamental human dignity and thus to justify treating us in those ways." For this reason, "both the manufacture and distribution of pornography and the enjoyment of it are instances of sexist behavior" and should be controlled.[13]

Is this kind of condemnation supported by the moral theories discussed so far? Because pornography endorses the use of women merely as means to sexual pleasure, it is clearly wrong on Kantian grounds. Moreover, pornography causes harm to women by promoting a general acceptance of violence toward them. If Longino is right, its enjoyment encourages harmful behavior. So it is wrong according to utilitarianism as well. But if these theories support the condemnation of pornography, is it then consistent to justify torture-horror on those same theories? That depends both on whether torture-horror is pornography, as some have claimed, and on whether the arguments for torture-horror and against pornography are all sound.

If we merely substitute the words "human being" for "women," Longino's argument against pornography applies easily to torture-horror: "As much as the materials themselves, the social tolerance of these degrading and distorted images of human beings in such quantities is harmful to us, since it indicates a general willingness to see human beings in ways incompatible with our fundamental human dignity and thus to justify treating us in those ways." In fact, such comparisons have bestowed on torture horror the derisive nickname "torture-porn."[14] The anti–torture-horror/pornography arguments, in order to be sound, must assume the truth of the following type of entailments: Degradation of women is wrong. Therefore, enjoyment of such degradation (for example, pornography) is wrong. Cruelty is wrong. Therefore, enjoying cruelty (for example, torture-horror) is wrong. But these entailments are not generally sound. To avoid begging the question, consider a case of dishonesty enjoyed by all. Assuming that lying is wrong in a given case does not show that enjoying lying, whether on your part or someone else's, is wrong. Consider the number of lies that it might require to arrange a surprise birthday party or the proliferation of lies in a typical comedy. Also, though some practical jokes are immoral, some are clearly morally permissible though they involve some lying. Whatever distinguishes morally permissible enjoyments from those that are wrong, it is not the moral status of the act that is enjoyed itself. This shows that anti-amusement arguments of this type are invalid. Thus Longino's argument fails in a general way even if it is assumed that torture-horror is a form of pornography.

As for whether torture-horror is really pornography, it should not be assumed that torture-horror endorses torture in any sense other than as a source of horror. The attempt to implicate the audience through retributivist justifications or with identification with the torturer is not the same thing as endorsing the torture committed. I have conducted this discussion with the less tendentious term *torture-horror* rather than *torture-porn* because it is not clear that torture-horror meets the endorsement condition.

The question of whether it is morally permissible to enjoy pornography parallels the justification question for torture-horror. But as I hope to have made clear, there is as much a distinction between an act of torture and enjoying an act of torture as between other immoral acts and the enjoyment of such things. This is not to say that pornographers or the makers of torture-horror films do not also enjoy what they are doing, but that such enjoyment, also shared by others, can be separated from the act itself. Insofar as cruelty is endorsed by one's enjoyment of torture-horror, such enjoyment is wrong. However, being disturbed, and enjoying being disturbed, by depictions of torture, or even the enjoyment of being confounded by the justification question itself, is not to endorse the torture. That the question is open as to whether the torture might be justified may itself be a source of horror.

The enjoyment of torture-horror is not necessarily immoral. The prevailing theme of the torture-horror genre is the attempt to share the purposes, intentions, and feelings behind realistic torture. By putting the audience on the side of the torturer in some way or other, the audience is disturbed in a way that goes beyond the fear generated by bare depictions of torture.

Notes

My epigraphs are taken from Michel de Montaigne, "Of Cruelty," in *The Complete Works*, trans. D. Frame (New York: Knopf, 2003), 372; and David Edelstein, "Now Playing at Your Local Multiplex: Torture Porn," *New York Magazine*, January 28, 2006.

1. The actual question was "You have two minutes to respond. Governor, if Kitty Dukakis were raped and murdered, would you favor an irrevocable death penalty for the killer?" Quoted from the transcript of the 1988 presidential debate provided by the Commission on Presidential Debates.

2. Quoted from the CNN transcript of the 2004 primary debate hosted by CNN and the *Los Angeles Times*.

3. Here I mean types distinguished not by technique but by intent. A similar distinction can be found in C. Tindale, "The Logic of Torture," *Social Theory and Practice* 22, no. 3 (1996): 349–77. "While the nature of the torture may vary very little from one case to another, the justification used to defend it may differ. . . . We can identify three distinct types, each distinguished by the goals that motivate the torturer" (350).

4. "Examination by torture is one form of evidence, to which great weight is often attached because it is in a sense compulsory. Here again it is not hard to point out the available grounds for magnifying its value, if it happens to tell in our favor, and arguing that it is the only form of evidence that is infallible; or, on the other hand, for refuting it if it tells against us and for our opponent, when we may say what is true of torture of every kind alike, that people under its compulsion tell lies quite as often as they tell the truth, sometimes persistently refusing to tell the truth, sometimes recklessly making a false charge in order to be let off sooner. We ought to be able to quote cases, familiar to the judges, in which this sort of thing has actually happened. [We must say that evidence under torture is not trustworthy, the fact being that many men whether thick-witted, tough-skinned, or stout of heart endure their ordeal nobly, while cowards and timid men are full of boldness till they see the ordeal of these others: so that no trust can be placed in evidence under torture.]" Aristotle, *Rhetoric*, book 1, chapter 15, [1377a].

5. Immanuel Kant, *The Metaphysical Elements of Justice*, trans. J. Ladd (Indianapolis: Bobbs-Merrill, 1965), 99–107.

6. Ibid., 99.

7. Since it is not clearly horror, it is not clear whether Kubrick's *A Clockwork Or-*

ange (1971) is a torture-horror, but it is clear that the "rehabilitation" of Alex, a sadistic torturer, destroys his sense of self in a way that echoes the Kantian view of autonomy and responsibility.

8. Immanuel Kant, *Critique of Practical Reason,* trans. L. Beck (Chicago: University of Chicago Press, 1949), 170.

9. Montaigne's expression of his natural disgust at cruelty in the first epigraph is a reference to his occasional preference for this type of sentimentalist virtue. See his "Of Cruelty," 372–86.

10. It is far from uncontroversial to state that no actual harm is caused by violent films, for example, those in the torture-horror genre. H. Longino argues that even if no one is actually harmed in filming, depictions of violence may cause violent behavior in their audience and thus actual harm ("Pornography, Oppression, and Freedom: A Closer Look," in *Social Ethics,* ed. T. Mappes and J. Zembaty [New York: McGraw-Hill, 1980], 234–41). I discuss Longino's argument in more detail below.

11. Ironically, *Videodrome* is itself too unrealistic to be clearly in the genre of torture-horror. Before taking his own life, for instance, Max is transformed into a video machine.

12. D. De Leeuw argues against the permissibility of sportfishing as a form of entertainment since he regards sportfishing as torture ("Contemplating the Interests of Fish: The Angler's Challenge," *Environmental Ethics* 18 [1996]: 373–90). L. Olson's criticism of his argument against sportfishing helped to inspire my response to moral attacks on torture-horror. See "Contemplating the Intentions of Anglers: The Ethicist's Challenge," *Environmental Ethics,* 25, no. 3 (2003), 267–79.

13. Longino, "Pornography, Oppression, and Freedom," 238, 240, 241.

14. See Edelstein, "Now Playing at Your Local Multiplex."

Hobbes, Human Nature, and the Culture of American Violence in Truman Capote's *In Cold Blood*

Thomas Fahy

> The life of man [is] solitary, poor, nasty, brutish, and short.
> —Thomas Hobbes, *Leviathan*

> [Men are] creatures among whose instinctual endowments is to be reckoned a powerful share of aggressiveness. As a result, their neighbor is for them not only a potential helper or sexual object, but also someone who tempts them to satisfy their aggressiveness on him, to exploit his capacity for work without compensation, to use him sexually without his consent, to seize his possessions, to humiliate him, to cause him pain, to torture and to kill him.
> —Sigmund Freud, *Civilization and Its Discontents*

On November 15, 1959, Dick Hickock and Perry Smith drove several hundred miles to the small town of Holcomb, Kansas, and brutally murdered four members of the Clutter family. Armed with a hunting knife and a twelve-gauge shotgun, the two men entered the house through an unlocked door just after midnight. They had been hoping to find a safe with thousands of dollars, but when Herb Clutter denied having one, they tied him up and gagged him. They did the same to his wife, Bonnie, his fifteen-year-old son, Kenyon, and his sixteen-year-old daughter, Nancy. Afterward, they placed each of them in separate rooms and searched the house for themselves. When they found no more than forty dollars, Smith slit Herb Clutter's throat and shot him in the face. He then proceeded to execute the rest of the family. Each one died from a point-blank shotgun wound to the head.

One month later, Truman Capote, who had first read about these crimes in the *New York Times,* arrived in Holcomb with his longtime friend, the author Nelle Harper Lee.[1] Both the horrifying details of the murders and the strangeness of the place appealed to Capote. Everything about Kansas—the landscape, dialect, social milieu, and customs—was completely alien to him, and he was energized by the prospect of trying to capture this world in prose. He recognized that the case might never be solved, since the police had no clues about the identity of Hickock and Smith at the time, but that didn't concern him. He primarily wanted to write about the impact of these horrific killings on the town. As biographer Gerald Clarke explains, Capote was less interested in the murders than in their potential "effect on that small and isolated community."[2] Six years later, after the execution of Hickock and Smith, he completed his "nonfiction novel" *In Cold Blood: A True Account of a Multiple Murder and Its Consequences*—a work that offers a chilling portrait of violence and fear in American culture.

But why is this book so terrifying? Before reading the first page, we know the outcome. Even if we haven't heard of the Clutter family, the description on the back of the book tells us that there is no mystery here. Capote even announces as much at the end of the first short chapter: "four shotgun blasts that, all told, ended six human lives." We know the Clutters will die and that the killers will be caught and executed. So what makes Capote's narrative so frightening and unsettling? The author gives some clue in the next sentence: "But afterward the townspeople, theretofore sufficiently unfearful of each other to seldom trouble to lock their doors, found fantasy re-creating them over and again—those somber explosions that stimulated fires of mistrust in the glare of which many old neighbors viewed each other strangely, and as strangers."[3] In Capote's rendering of this event, we, too, re-create "those somber explosions" and share in the fearful mistrust of others. We try to grapple with what these killings suggest about human nature, and in the process our neighbors become strangers, too. They become potential threats, undermining our own sense of safety and security.

Capote's book raises several disturbing questions for the reader as well: How and why were Hickock and Smith capable of such brutality? Could you or I do such things? These questions resonate with Thomas Hobbes's philosophy about the innate aggression and brutality of human beings. His pessimistic outlook can provide some insight into the source of terror in Capote's work—that such violence, resentment, and anger are in all of us. Before discussing this connection, I will situate *In Cold Blood* in the horror genre by focusing on its use of a horrific event and the imagined encounter with the monstrous. I will then discuss Hobbes's notion of human nature and the sovereign—a figure that promises to provide moral justice and prevent mankind from being in a perpetual state of war. But what happens if this source of moral authority (the sovereign) is absent? If the veneer of civilization is removed? Capote's answer, like the one offered by Hobbes, is clear: we will all act in cold blood.

The Horror of *In Cold Blood*

The horror of *In Cold Blood* operates on several levels: its realism, the brutality of the crime, the random selection of victims (Smith and Hickock had never met the Clutters before the night of the killing), the incongruity between the primary motive (theft) and the ultimate outcome (multiple murders), the fear that swept through the state in its aftermath, and the callous indifference and lack of remorse on the part of Hickock and Smith. So can *In Cold Blood,* which promises a journalistic account of actual events, be understood in terms of the horror genre as well?

By making this connection I'm not trying to minimize the real tragedy of these crimes. I'm merely suggesting that Capote uses some of the conventions of horror, as well as the suspense/thriller genres, to craft his rendering of these events. Capote himself labeled the work a nonfiction novel, and this invites us to think about the literary devices shaping *In Cold Blood.* "Journalism," he said, "always moves along a horizontal plane, telling a story, while fiction—good fiction—moves vertically, taking you deeper and deeper into character and events. By treating a real event with fictional techniques . . . it's possible to make this kind of synthesis."[4] Capote's fusion of reporting and fiction here enabled him to present Hickock and Smith's crime and its subsequent investigation as a novelist. He could make choices to create a certain effect and to manipulate the reader's response.

As suggested above, part of the momentum of *In Cold Blood* comes from the details that resonate with suspense/thriller fiction. A crime has been committed that launches a nationwide manhunt. Lead detectives work around the clock, piecing together clues and interviewing suspects in hopes of a lucky break. At one point, the special agent in charge learns that the men are back in Kansas, and the chase intensifies. But the facts of the case undermine these familiar-sounding conventions at every turn. The crime has been "solved" for the reader before the first page. The identity of the criminals is discovered by accident when Hickock's former cellmate, who told him about the Clutters in the first place, hears a radio broadcast about the murders and reveals Hickock's identity to the authorities. Smith and Hickock are caught not because of Special Agent Dewey's hard work and ingenuity; they are apprehended because of their own incompetence and arrogance. The book also suggests that Smith's abuse as a child, his family's neglect, his inability to pursue an education, and his association with people like Hickock helped shape him into a killer. Such revelations often occur in the suspense/thriller genres as well, but Capote is using them here to create sympathy for the killer—a response that complicates our response to his execution. When the people of Holcomb first see Smith and Hickock after they have been apprehended, for example, Capote notes that they all respond with stunned silence. "But when the crowd caught sight of the murderers, with their escort of blue-coated highway patrolmen, it fell silent, as though amazed to find them humanly shaped" (248). When faced with such horrible crimes, we expect the monstrous, the inhuman. Yet Capote's sympathetic characterization of Smith, in particular, makes it difficult for the reader to view him as a monster.

This is where *In Cold Blood* intersects with the horror genre as well—an encounter with the monstrous. Noël Carroll, in his influential work *The Philosophy of Horror; or, Paradoxes of the Heart,* argues that monsters are the central feature of horror. Vampires, werewolves, and zombies, for example, are recognizable threats, and the danger they pose must be destroyed/defeated to restore harmony. Monsters also elicit the emotional effect that the genre seeks—horror—because they literally embody the abnormal. As Carroll explains, "The objects of art-horror are essentially threatening and impure."[5] They inspire revulsion, disgust, and nausea.

A number of scholars have criticized this narrow definition, arguing that serial killers and more realistic monsters must be accounted for as well. David Russell, for example, offers a broader taxonomy for the horror genre, arguing that "some types of monsters may be explained as '*real*' . . . [in that they] are not remarkable in any physical sense. Their threat to normality is manifested solely through abnormal behavior challenging the rules of social regulation through 'monstrous' and transgressive behavior."[6] He labels these monsters "deviant"—a category that includes stalkers, slashers, and psychokillers. Critic Matt Hills also responds to Carroll's limited framework by suggesting an event-based definition of the genre (as opposed to Carroll's entity-based definition) so that "we can take in the widest possible range of texts that have been discussed as 'horror' by audiences and labeled as such by filmmakers and marketers."[7] Both of these characteristics are evident in Capote's book. As a ruthless killer, Smith is certainly a realistic monster, and the Clutter murders qualify as horrific events.

But let's return to Carroll's emphasis on monsters for a moment. Even though *In Cold Blood* doesn't fit the supernatural requirements of his definition of horror, Capote does present Hickock and Smith as monstrous on physical and psychological levels. His descriptions of their anomalous, damaged bodies attempt to ascribe some physical difference to their aberrant behavior. Smith is first depicted as a man with "stunted legs that seemed grotesquely inadequate to the grown-up bulk they supported" (15), and Special Agent Dewey takes note of Smith's disproportionate body at his execution: "He remembered his first meeting with Perry in the interrogation room at Police Headquarters in Las Vegas—the dwarfish boy-man seated in the metal chair, his small booted feet not quite brushing the floor" (341). Likewise, Hickock has a tattooed body, serpentine eyes "with a venomous, sickly-blue squint," and a face "composed of mismatched parts . . . as though his head had been halved like an apple, then put together a fraction off center" (31). As a boy-man (dwarf/adult) and serpent-man (with a divided face), Smith and Hickock are hybrid figures like the monsters that typically appear in horror fiction. Their bodies, like their actions, violate social norms and categories (moral/immoral, good/evil, human/inhuman), and this element resonates with Carroll's argument about monsters as repelling and compelling "because they violate standing categories."[8]

At the same time, these physical aberrations are not so pronounced that the townspeople of Holcomb can comfortably "Other" Hickock and Smith. Their bodies do not live up to the monsters whom they imagined responsible for the killings. As noted above, they initially responded to these men with stunned silence, "as though amazed to find them humanly shaped," but in many horror stories unreal monsters come in human form. The horror, in other words, resides within. Just like a serial killer who seems like a nice guy to his neighbors, werewolves "hide" inside human beings until a full moon; vampires can "pass" as human until they reveal their fangs. The notion of a threat from within is integral to the terror of *In Cold Blood.*[9] Smith isn't a werewolf or a vampire. He is a person just like us, but a killer lurks inside. Like these supernatural counterparts, he can transform at any moment from charming loner to ruthless murderer, which is evident in his confession: "I thought [Herb Clutter] was a very nice gentleman. Soft-spoken. I thought so right up to the moment I cut his throat" (244). What makes Smith so terrifying is not simply the suddenness of his transformation here, but the fact that he doesn't physically turn into a monster. At some level, the town of Holcomb, as well as the reader, fears this lack of visual otherness because it implies that *anyone* can be like Smith.

This implication also fuels fears in the community that the killer lives among them. On hearing the news of the murders, one townsperson responds: "If it wasn't him, maybe it was you. Or somebody across the street" (69). Another remarks: "What a terrible thing when neighbors can't look at each other without a kind of wondering!" (70) And even when the killers are apprehended, their suspicions don't vanish. "For the majority of Holcomb's population, having lived for seven weeks amid unwholesome rumors, general mistrust, and suspicion, appeared to feel disappointed at being told that the murderer was not someone among themselves" (231). Once they admit that anyone has the potential to be a monster, they can't stop being afraid of one another.

State of Nature: Man and the Need for Society

Thomas Hobbes makes this kind of fear the basis for his analysis of human nature in *Leviathan,* which was first published in 1651. For Hobbes, the natural state of man, which exists outside the context of society, is one of war. In this condition we are constantly pursuing pleasure, vying for power over others, and doing everything possible to avoid death. This creates an environment in which every man is "against every man," and he feels entitled to "every thing, even to one another's body."[10] Not only do these impulses motivate human action, they also cause us to live in constant fear. We recognize that even the strongest individual can be killed by the weakest and that we are continually at risk of having everything taken from us at any moment (including life itself).

Not surprisingly, morality is relative in this context. There is no absolute "good" and "evil" in a state of nature, only desire and aversion. "*Good,* and *evil,* are names that signify our appetites, and aversions; which in different tempers, customs, and doctrines of men, are different."[11] Each individual, in other words, determines morality: we desire what is good and have an aversion to what is bad. But because these things differ for everyone, we often pursue them at the expense of others. As Helen Thornton explains in *State of Nature or Eden? Thomas Hobbes and His Contemporaries on the Natural Condition of Human Beings:* "In the state of nature, every man, by right of nature, could do whatever he liked to whomever he liked. He could possess, use and enjoy anything, even another's body. Nature made men desire what was good for them, and avoid what was evil. Death, and the pain that accompanied it, was the greatest enemy of nature, so it was not against reason for an individual to do everything he could to preserve himself."[12] This instinct for self-preservation applies even to murder. Since everyone is against everyone else and the struggle for survival is paramount, the act of killing is not evil. It is completely justified. And this leads Hobbes to conclude that "the life of man [is] solitary, poor, nasty, brutish, and short."[13]

As an early Enlightenment figure, Hobbes believed that reason ultimately led to the formation of society. People realized that living in constant fear of someone taking their property or attempting to kill them was no way to live. Therefore, they came together in a large group and made agreements with one another to remove fear. Of course, society can't get rid of fear entirely. If it could, Hobbes points out, we wouldn't feel the need to lock our doors at night. But a social contract does provide some measure of security, and it keeps most of us from reverting to a warlike state.

At the same time, Hobbes insists that society must be governed by an individual or group of individuals with absolute authority. His central analogy for this society (commonwealth) is the leviathan—a large, healthy body with various parts that cooperate. It functions much like the parts of a human body, which work together to perform tasks, such as walking down the street or typing a sentence. In the social body, the sovereign is both the soul, giving it moral purpose by determining right and wrong, and the law, handing out rewards and punishment. It is important to note that the people agree to the decisions of this figure. As Hobbes explains, men "have made an artificial man, which we call a commonwealth; so also they made artificial chains, called *civil laws,* which they themselves, by mutual covenants, have fastened at one end, to the lips of that man, or assembly, to whom they have given sovereign power; and at the other end to their own ears."[14] We choose to subject ourselves to this authority because it holds together the commonwealth and maintains peace and security. It keeps us from being at war with our neighbors.

In many ways, Hickock and Smith operate in a state of nature throughout *In Cold Blood,* wantonly pursuing their own pleasure and power at the expense of others. Describing his own motivations, for example, Hickock explains that "at the time I never give any thought to whether it's right or wrong. The same with stealing. It seems to be an impulse" (278). Dr. Jones, the psychiatrist who examines him before the trial, comes to a similar conclusion: "[Hickock] is a person who is impulsive in action, likely to do things without thought of consequences or future discomfort to himself or to others" (294–95). Like a man in Hobbes's state of nature, Hickock pursues immediate pleasure without the thought of social (or personal) consequence. His penchant for statutory rape offers one example of this. When his desire for young girls comes into conflict with social norms, he simply rationalizes his behavior. "Seducing pubescent girls, as he had done 'eight or nine' times in the last several years, did not disprove [his normalcy], for if the truth were known, most real men had the same desires he had" (201). For Hickock, these urges are natural in men and shouldn't be considered wrong. This assertion of his own normalcy also gives Hickock another way to distance himself from social mores and the judgment of others.

Hickock is also motivated by what Hobbes describes as a "perpetual and restless desire for power after power, that ceaseth only in death."[15] As the narrator of *In Cold Blood* explains, "Envy was constantly with him; the Enemy was anyone who was someone he wanted to be or who had anything he wanted to have" (200). Envy causes Hickock to remain in a warlike state. He sees everyone and everything as something to conquer, and he feels completely justified in doing whatever he likes to others—including theft, rape, and murder. Hickock achieves this power primarily through violence. "With a knife in his hand, he, Dick, had power" (201). As Smith explains about his partner, "the glory of having everybody at his mercy, that's what excited him" (239). It is Hickock's use of violence that gives him both power and immediate pleasure (it "excited him")—the two impulses that determine human behavior for Hobbes.

Smith is also motivated by pleasure and power. In Capote's account, there is an underlying homoerotic attraction between the killers (Hickock even refers to Smith as "Honey" throughout the text), and Smith derives real pleasure from this relationship. "Dick's literalness, his pragmatic approach to every subject, was the primary reason Perry had been attracted to him, for it made Dick seem, compared to himself, so authentically tough, invulnerable, 'totally masculine'" (16). In a sense, Smith is not only "charmed" (124) by Hickock, he also experiences a vicarious power through him—an authenticity he lacks otherwise. Even after their arrest, which was largely due to Hickock's insistence on returning to the United States after they had successfully escaped to Mexico, and his confession blaming Smith for the murders, Smith misses him intensely. *"Many thoughts of Dick,* he wrote one day in his makeshift diary. . . . What he most desired [was] to talk to Dick, be with him again" (259). His greatest desire isn't freedom or forgiveness. It's to be with Hickock again because this relationship arguably fulfills his Hobbesian need for pleasure and power.

The lack of remorse from Hickock and Smith also resonates with the moral relativism in Hobbes's state of nature. As mentioned above, Hickock never thought about right and wrong while breaking the law, and Smith was also viewed as having no moral compass. "The rights of other people mean nothing to Smith," his sister explained. "He has no respect for anyone" (181). Smith later admits this lack of feeling about the Clutter murders. "I don't feel anything about it. I wish I did. But nothing about it bothers me a bit" (291). Smith and Hickock define right and wrong in Hobbesian terms of appetite and aversion, not social responsibility. This explains Smith's anger toward his sister, who rejects this kind of callous self-interest: "You are a human being with a *free will*. Which puts you above the animal level. But if you live your life without feeling and compassion for your fellow man—you are as an animal—'an eye for an eye, a tooth for a tooth.' . . . All of us are responsible to the community we live in & its laws" (142). Smith's sister clearly believes in the commonwealth, in a society of laws and justice, crimes and punishment. But Hickock and Smith, acting in accord only with their desires, see themselves as outside of the social contract. They remain outcasts, wanderers, "brothers in the breed of Cain" (260),[16] whose only purpose, as Hobbes would argue, is "to come prepared with forces united, to dispossess and deprive [another], not only of the fruit of his labour, but also of his life, or liberty."[17] Furthermore, since each individual defines right and wrong differently in a state of nature, men invariably come into conflict with each other. Hickock and Smith are no exception, and the gradual erosion of their friendship stems from the ways in which their different desires begin to clash.

Sovereigns and Eden on Earth

In Cold Blood also presents the sovereign (in this case two sovereigns) as essential for peace and safety: Clutter and Truman Capote himself. According to Hobbes, the sovereign establishes security and order, enforcing our agreements with others, resolving disputes, and imposing punishment. He also determines the ideology of the state (what is right and wrong, just and unjust). Under his authority, therefore, good and evil are absolute. And this is the kind of worldview that Clutter imposes on those around him.

In the first part of *In Cold Blood*, Clutter functions as a sovereign figure both for the community and for his family. He has a privileged place in and around Holcomb. He was "the community's most widely known citizen . . . and his name was everywhere respectfully recognized" (6). The narrator even describes him in regal terms: "Like royalty, he was famous for never carrying cash" (46). As a man with a large farm and the need to hire numerous employees, he has a certain power over others, which for Clutter includes issues of morality:

> The truth was he opposed all stimulants, however gentle. He did not smoke, and of course he did not drink. . . . While he was careful to avoid making a nuisance of his view, to adopt outside his realm an

externally uncensoring manner, he enforced them within his family
and among the employees at River Valley Farm. . . . [Every appli-
cant had to] sign a work contract containing a clause that declared
an agreement instantly void if the employee should be discovered
"harboring alcohol." A friend . . . had once told him, "You've got no
mercy. I swear, Herb, if you caught a hired man drinking, out he'd
go. And you wouldn't care if his family was starving." (10)

Clutter determines what is acceptable behavior for his employees, and his
friend's response suggests that Clutter perceives his own moral authority
as absolute. He even enforces this ideology in legally binding contracts.
This moralistic quality is apparent to the rest of the community as well,
and it goes hand in hand with Clutter's privileged place. "There wasn't any
other family like them. . . . Mr. Clutter may have been more strict about
some things—religion, and so on—but he never tried to make you feel he
was right and you were wrong" (50). The verb "tried" suggests that this is
exactly what Clutter did, however. He may not have wanted to make others
feel "wrong," but the town was completely aware of his moral expectations
and judgment.

Clutter exercises similar authoritarian rule over his family. He not
only demands that his daughter stop seeing her boyfriend, Bobby (he was
Roman Catholic, while the Clutters were Methodist), but he also keeps his
children in the local high school, as opposed to sending them to a better
institution in Garden City. In short, he "considered such defections an af-
front to community spirit" (21). This decision reflects not only his belief in
the importance of society; it also demonstrates his essential place in it. He
recognizes his power to hold the community together, and he doesn't want
to erode Holcomb's sense of solidarity by abandoning its school system.

Like the role of the sovereign in Hobbes, Clutter's "reign" is associated
with social stability. He presides over a peaceful, Eden-like atmosphere,
and he "often remarked, 'an inch more of rain and this country would be
paradise—Eden on earth'" (12). He even plants an orchard—"a patch of
paradise, the green, apple-scented Eden" (13)—to reinforce this illusion.
Hobbes reminds us that man needed a sovereign only after the Fall. Once
Adam and Eve were banished from the Garden of Eden, human beings lived
in a fallen world in which pain, suffering, hardship, and death were possible.[18]
The sovereign can't restore Eden but, like Clutter in his influence on his estate
and the town surrounding it, he can help establish a safe, secure, and peaceful
community. Not surprisingly, Holcomb is described in these terms. The locals
talk about it as a place where one couldn't ask for "friendlier people or fresher

air or sweeter drinking water." Folks passing through often stay because of the community. "Good neighbors, people who care about each other, that's what counts" (33). And this caring includes social equality, too: "All equal, regardless of wealth, color, or creed" (34). The narrator acknowledges that some of this rhetoric might overstate the case, but the people living there clearly perceive this community as beneficial and safe. And it's a place that Clutter's larger-than-life reputation seems to preside over.

For Hobbes, who was a monarchist, the power of the sovereign figure has to be absolute. There is no case in which overthrowing a sovereign is acceptable because without a ruler we will "return therefore to the sword again."[19] Thus a bad sovereign is better than having no society, and the death of Clutter illustrates this danger—a shift that is evident in the landscape itself. After the murders, the place itself becomes unnerving. "Monsters *howl*ing the bloody night long. A horrid racket. . . . That *hate*ful prairie wind" (115). This description comes right before the town learns that two of its longtime residents are moving away—not just from Finney County but from the state. The Eden-like home of the Clutters also changes after the murders. Now, people can smell "the odor of windfall apples rotting under the apple trees" (121), and the home, which had been under the meticulous care of Clutter, shows "the first threads of decay's cobweb. . . . A gravel rake lay rusting in the driveway; the lawn was parched and shabby. . . . The Clutter place seemed shadowed, and hushed, and motionless" (206–7). Howling monsters, rotting food, and decay now characterize the landscape. The loss of the sovereign here suggests a kind of Fall—from a verdant, Eden-like landscape to a place marked by desolation and decay.

This transformation also parallels a psychological shift in the community from comfort to fear. People can no longer sleep after the murders. No one feels safe—even the wife of Special Agent Dewey changes the locks on the house. And everyone becomes suspicious of everyone else. In short, these changes in Holcomb reflect Hobbes's view of the state of nature as a post-Edenic condition. "All the neighbors are rattlesnakes. Varmints looking for a chance to slam the door in your face. It's the same the world over. You know that" (69), one resident states, and the narrator summarizes the overall condition: "Old friends had suddenly to endure the unique experience of distrusting each other; understandably, they believed that the murderer was among themselves" (88). This intense mistrust and fear comes, in part, from the loss of the sovereign. Most of Holcomb acknowledges that the crime was worse because it happened to the Clutters: "Of all the people in the world, the Clutters were the least likely to be murdered" (85). One resident explains: "Feeling wouldn't run half so high if this had happened to anyone *except* the Clutters. Anyone *less* admired. Prosperous. Secure. But that family represented everything people hereabouts really value and respect, and that such a thing could happen to them—well it's like being told there is no God" (88). Clutter symbolizes safety, and the reference to God, like his comparison to royalty, suggests his sovereignlike status in the community.

We can also see Capote himself acting as a kind of sovereign. He rules over the text, shaping our responses to the Clutters, to the town of Holcomb, and to Hickock and Smith. Critic Trenton Hickman suggests this kind of reading in "'The Last to See Them Alive': Panopticism, the Supervisory Gaze, and Catharsis in Capote's *In Cold Blood.*" Hickman argues that the structure of the book parallels Foucault's discussion of Bentham's panopticon, placing the characters under the constant scrutiny of the narrator. "This strategy offers not only an angle into the criminal mind but a catharsis for an audience that can vent its own destructive energies through interaction with this novel rather than through violent action in the community." Capote, in other words, viewed the book as providing a safe outlet for the violent impulses of the reader. He stands in as a sovereign, dictating our response to the events and ultimately providing catharsis. He claims to have included so many details about Hickock's intention to rape Nancy, for example, as a "healthy form of release" for the reader. This strategy would, as Hickman explains, "[alleviate] the sorts of pressures that might drive someone into a pathological state if not released."[20]

Perhaps Capote's view of this healthy release and his role as sovereign in the text is best illustrated by the fictionalized ending of *In Cold Blood.* One of the questions that preoccupy the characters (and by extension the readers) after the arrest of Smith and Hickock is: What will restore peace and a sense of security to the town? That the crime's perpetrators are in captivity doesn't make the townspeople feel better. They remain suspicious that the killer is still in their midst. After the men were caught, one person believed that "there's more to it than that. Wait. Some day they'll get to the bottom, and when they do they'll find the one behind it" (231). Hickock's and Smith's confessions don't provide a satisfactory explanation or rationale for the crimes: "But the confessions, though they answered questions of how and why, failed to satisfy his sense of meaningful design" (245). And the executions don't offer closure either. As the narrator explains, "Dewey had imagined that with the deaths of Smith and Hickock, he would experience a sense of climax, release, of a design justly completed" (341). But his own sympathy for Smith, who reminds him of a wounded, exiled animal, doesn't bring Dewey closure, and for him (as well as the reader), the violent potential of human nature lingers at this moment. Capital punishment is just another form of brutality. It, too, speaks to our innate tendency toward violence. Once again, this is the source of *In Cold Blood*'s terror: the nagging reminder that we all have the potential to be killers. Capote isn't suggesting that we're all one Orange Blossom away from being psychopathic killers. (Orange Blossoms were Hickock's favorite alcoholic beverage, and he downed several to muster up courage to break into the Clutter house.) But the fear we share with the residents of Holcomb comes from our understanding that human beings all have this potential under certain circumstances. Perhaps this message isn't entirely surprising since the author felt a disconcerting kinship with Smith, who represented what Capote could have become under different circumstances—"the embodiment of his own accumulated angers and hurts."[21]

Nevertheless, Capote didn't want this Hobbesian message to close the book. He wanted to provide some kind of catharsis, and he fictionalized the ending to achieve this. Aristotle's notion of catharsis in Greek tragedy is that the final effect of this drama is to release or purge pent-up emotions. It restores a kind of equilibrium to the viewer, who has built up disproportionate levels of pity and fear. Capote achieves this release by having Dewey recall an encounter with Nancy's best friend, Susan Kidwell, at the graves of the Clutter family. Susan is now a junior at the University of Kansas. She is beautiful and thriving. "Her smooth hair swinging, shining—just such a young woman as Nancy might have been," Dewey thinks. The fact that her life has continued, that she is happy, gives Dewey hope, and he is able to walk away from the cemetery, "leaving behind him the big sky, the whisper of wind voices in the wind-bent wheat" (343). The story of this crime (the voices of the Clutters, of Smith's and Hickock's confessions, of the townspeople's speculations) are now whispers, and the image of rich land with its big sky and wind-bent wheat replaces that of the noose.

Capote once remarked: "I was criticized a lot for [the ending]. People thought I should have ended with the hangings, that awful last scene. But I felt I had to return to the town, to bring everything back full circle, to end with peace."[22] He takes on the role of the sovereign here to allow *us* to walk away from the story of this crime, too. The book restores the kind of peace that Holcomb felt before the murders. Late in the story, we even get a glimpse of the Clutter estate that shows hints of this renewal: "Mr. Clutter's orchard of pear and apple trees, the elms shading the lane—were lightly veiled in a haze of virginal green. The fine lawn surrounding the Clutter house was also newly green" (270). Virginal grass has replaced the rotting fruit and decay, suggesting that life goes on, wounds heal. Ultimately, this fictionalized ending demonstrates that Capote doesn't want to share Hobbes's pessimism about human nature. He incorporated this Hobbesian outlook as part of his use of the horror genre, recognizing that we all fear these darker sides of humanity. But Capote couldn't end with such a vision. He is more optimistic about our future, about our innate characteristics than Hobbes. Yet as *In Cold Blood* moves from nonfiction to fiction in these final moments, it leaves us with a more hopeful sense about our own humanity—but ironically, Capote's role as sovereign also suggests that Hobbes was right all along.

Notes

My epigraphs are taken from Thomas Hobbes, *Leviathan,* ed. J. C. A. Gaskin (Oxford: Oxford University Press, 1998); and Sigmund Freud, *Civilization and Its Discontents,* trans. and ed. James Strachey (New York: Norton, 1961).

1. Harper Lee's novel, *To Kill a Mockingbird,* was finished at the time but not yet published.

2. Gerald Clarke, *Capote: A Biography* (New York: Carroll & Graff, 2005), 319.

3. Truman Capote, *In Cold Blood: A True Account of a Multiple Murder and Its Consequences* (1965; reprint, New York: Vintage, 1994), 5. Subsequent page references to this work will be given parenthetically in the text.

4. Quoted in Clarke, *Capote,* 357.

5. Noël Carroll, *The Philosophy of Horror; or, Paradoxes of the Heart* (New York: Routledge, 1990), 42.

6. David J. Russell, "Monster Roundup: Reintegrating the Horror Genre," in *Refiguring American Film Genres: History and Theory,* ed. Nick Browne (Berkeley: University of California Press, 1998), 241.

7. Matt Hills, "An Event-Based Definition of Art-Horror," in *Dark Thoughts: Philosophic Reflections on Cinematic Horror,* ed. Steven Jay Schneider and Daniel Shaw (Lanham, MD: Scarecrow, 2003), 138.

8. Carroll, *Philosophy of Horror,* 188.

9. I'm using the terms *horror* and *terror* somewhat interchangeably here. Carroll argues that the presence of a literal monster distinguishes horror from works of terror, such as Edgar Allan Poe's "The Pit and the Pendulum" and "The Telltale Heart," which explore a psychological state or phenomenon. But I prefer seeing the terms as interconnected, which is the way Stephen King discusses them in *Danse Macabre.* He argues that horror operates on three levels: (1) *terror,* which comes not from seeing something terrible but from imagining it; (2) *horror,* or "the emotion of fear that underlies terror" and that is connected to a visible manifestation which is frightening; and (3) *revulsion,* or what King calls the "gross-out" (*Danse Macabre* [New York: Everest House, 1981], 35). In this paradigm, terror, which pulses through *In Cold Blood* as the town continues to imagine the crime and fears for its own safety, is the highest achievement of the horror genre.

10. Hobbes, *Leviathan,* chapters 13.8, p. 84, and 14.4, p. 87.

11. Ibid., chapter 15.40, p. 105.

12. Helen Thornton, *State of Nature or Eden? Thomas Hobbes and His Contemporaries on the Natural Condition of Human Beings* (Rochester, NY: University of Rochester Press, 2005), 102.

13. Hobbes, *Leviathan,* chapter 13.9, p. 84.

14. Ibid., chapter 12.5, p. 141.

15. Ibid., chapter 11.2, p. 66.

16. In the Old Testament, Cain and Abel were the sons of Adam and Eve. Cain feels jilted when God finds his brother's sacrifice more acceptable than his own, so he turns to violence, killing Abel and committing the first murder. God then rebukes him: "Listen! Your brother's blood cries out to me from the soil. And so, cursed shall you be by the soil that gaped with its mouth to take your brother's blood from your hand. . . . A restless wanderer shall you be on the earth" (Genesis 4:10–13). But Cain protests, fearing that others will kill him once they learn of his crime, so "the Lord set a mark upon Cain so that whoever found him would not slay him" (4:15). Smith and Hickock are certainly restless wanders, but they lack a significant physical marker, which makes it difficult for the town to believe that they are the killers. Robert Alter, *Genesis: Translation and Commentary* (New York: Norton & Norton, 1996), 18.

17. Hobbes, *Leviathan,* chapter 13.3, p. 83

18. Thornton examines the ways in which seventeenth-century readers interpreted Hobbes's view of human nature through the lens of the biblical account of Genesis and the Fall. There was a tension between the Hobbesian view and the religious view of human nature at the time because Hobbes's description of human nature contradicted the assumptions made about man's perfection in Genesis.

19. Hobbes, *Leviathan,* chapter 18.4, p. 116.

20. Trenton Hickman, "'The Last to See Them Alive': Panopticism, the Supervisory Gaze, and Catharsis in Capote's *In Cold Blood*," *Studies in the Novel* 37 (Winter 2005): 465, 472.

21. Clarke, *Capote,* 326.

22. Ibid., 359.

Making Their Presence Known

TV's Ghost-Hunter Phenomenon in a "Post-" World

Jessica O'Hara

> There are more things in heaven and earth, Horatio,
> than are dreamt of in your philosophy.
> —*Hamlet,* act I, scene V

In this young millennium, the television landscape has been shaped by a groundswell of reality-based and scripted shows investigating the supernatural, such as *A Haunting, Paranormal State, Most Haunted, Ghost Hunters, Ghost Hunters International, Ghostly Encounters, Ghost Trackers, Ghost Adventures, Haunted History, Ghost Whisperer, Medium,* and a landslide of one-off shows featuring things like the top ten most haunted hotels. What has caused this conspicuous "presencing," aside from the obvious cost savings that reality-based shows offer over scripted shows? And why is it that so many of our restless channel-surfing spirits find release in these shows?

The quick answer might be that spooky ghost stories are a staple of the human imagination—indeed, many cultures devote a whole holiday to the horrific. Thus, while TV's otherworldly programming dips into a deep well of cultural tradition, perhaps these shows also fascinate us because they plumb the depths of timeless philosophical questions and problems. For this piece we will focus specifically on ghost-hunter shows with a reality-based format that routinely consider these classic puzzlers: How can we trust our senses or truly know what we are experiencing? Is there an afterlife? What is the soul? Does God exist? Does evil—or even the demonic—exist? How do we deal with the so-called problem of evil? These, the themes that have occupied philosophers through the ages, bring us back again and again to ghost-hunting programs. Yet while ghost-hunter shows take on some classic philosophical questions, as we shall see, they do so with a distinctly postmodern approach to knowledge, discourse, and narrative. Moreover, their appearance at this particular moment may have as much to do with our own troubled, post-9/11 present day as with the ghosts of the past.

Plumbers of the Paranormal

The philosophical problem of verifying happenings outside of or in addition to sensory experience seems to be an overarching preoccupation on most of these shows, but none more so than on *Ghost Hunters.* Jason Hawes and Grant Wilson, who work for Roto-Rooter by day, lead the paranormal investigation team TAPS (the Atlantic Paranormal Society). For the majority of episodes the primary aim of TAPS is to validate what its "clients" are experiencing by using a wide array of ghost-detecting technologies such as electromagnetic field scanners (EMFs), digital thermometers, enhanced voice recorders, and night-vision and infrared cameras. The team also seeks to gather anecdotal "human" evidence as corollaries to the primary evidence provided by the technology. Unlike the investigators on *Paranormal State,* who do not assume a skeptical stance, the members of the TAPS team actively try to debunk the claims and experiences of the clients and themselves by privileging scientific methodology, which provides a kind of escape from the thorny problem of our fallible senses and easily deceived selves. Thus, that which cannot be explained is deemed not necessarily paranormal, but not normal either. When presenting its findings to the client, TAPS again highlights technology-based evidence, sprinkling in the team's human encounters during the investigation. The clients are usually pleased with "The Reveal," as it is called, for they are happy to have their experiences in the back bedroom, down the hall, or in the shed captured by technology and confirmed by experienced others. Thus, despite its relative skepticism, *Ghost Hunters* often validates our intuition and senses, as the client "knew there was something on the stairs" all along. When the evidence is inconclusive, it always disappoints.

Ghost Hunters, in particular, showcases some of the problems Descartes pondered centuries ago in *Meditations on First Philosophy.* In his First Meditation, Descartes names his foremost philosophical enterprise: "to demolish everything completely and start again right from the foundations if I wish to establish anything at all in the sciences that was stable and likely to last." He considers, "Whatever I have up until now accepted as most true I have acquired either from the senses or through the senses. But from time to time I have found that the senses deceive, and it is prudent never to trust completely those who have deceived us just once" (1990, 12). Descartes' endeavor to treat the epistemological problem of the fallible senses in order to discover objective reality and to establish the existence of God is not unlike the project of the ghost hunters: they, too, are pursuing proof of the supernatural and need a way to isolate and examine their evidence. In Descartes' time, a scientist was one who engaged philosophy and all the phenomena of the universe—even the mysteries of heaven and earth, as it were. Thus, the ghost-hunter teams (and their TV audiences) are aspiring "Renaissance" men and women, seeking to reintegrate the metaphysical domains of inquiry, which contemporary science has relegated to religion or quackery, with scientific methodology. Indeed, the TAPS investigators claim to apply such rigor and skepticism to their findings precisely because they would like to attract more "real" scientists, as it were, to investigate such phenomena ("The Converted Church" 2004).

Philosophers since Descartes have hardly given up on the question of how we experience the world. Rather, many of the great twentieth-century philosophers, such as Edmund Husserl, Martin Heidegger, Jean-Paul Sartre, and Maurice Merleau-Ponty, formalized and developed the field of phenomenology which, at its base, interrogates how we encounter phenomena, how consciousness operates in our encounters with the world, how things appear to us, and how we situate the meaning of our experiences. Ghost-hunter shows engage these questions because a haunting is inexorably a human perceptual experience. For instance, the investigators often implicitly deal with Edmund Husserl's concept of "intentionality." Husserl's idea of intentionality is described by Ronald McIntyre and David Woodruff Smith as

> a characteristic feature of our mental states and experiences, especially evident in what we commonly call being "conscious" or "aware." As conscious beings, or persons, we are not merely affected by the things in our environment: we are also *conscious of* these things—of physical objects and events, of our own selves and other persons, of abstract objects such as numbers and propositions, and of anything else we bring before our minds. Many, perhaps most, of the events that make up our mental life—our perceptions, thoughts, beliefs, hopes, fears, and so on—have this characteristic feature of being "of" and "about" something in our world. (1989, 148)

Thus intentionality, which Husserl deems "the fundamental property of consciousness," means that our experience is "directed toward—represents or 'intends'—things only *through* particular concepts, thoughts, ideas, images, etc. These make up the meaning or content of a given experience, and are distinct from the things they present or mean" (Smith 2008, sec. 1). The implications of Husserl's notion of intentionality loom large on ghost-hunter shows because if our individual consciousnesses do so much work to situate experience and even to order perception, then it seems like the investigators need to know the near impossible: the mostly unconscious inner workings of the clients' minds who have come to perceive that they might be haunted. More so, the investigators must somehow possess an incredibly heightened awareness of themselves *as* individuals *and* investigators. The shows often take refuge in the idea that if multiple people, all possessing varying frames of reference, attitudes, and knowledge about the space in question, report the same feelings and experiences, then there must be something going on outside of their individual minds. But truly, how different are their frames of reference? And how susceptible might they be to groupthink?

Paranormal State is perhaps more implicitly attuned to this issue of intentionality, at least with respect to the clients, than the other shows. As a prerequisite to be on the show, clients must submit to a psychiatric evaluation. Then, too, the investigators bring aboard a counselor to meet with the haunted, and the Paranormal Research Society (PRS) team probes the family situation, emotional state, and temperament of the clients. PRS is not necessarily questioning the sanity of the clients but rather exploring what aspects of their backgrounds or present situation might be causing them to interpret events in a certain way. For instance, in the episode "The Devil in Syracuse" (2007), which seemed to be a case of demonic haunting, investigation leader Ryan Buell perceives that the constant presence of a family friend might be "promoting fear and hysteria in the home." The house itself is shockingly cluttered and disorganized. The couple is unhappy in their marriage and on the verge of divorce. The PRS team cleans house, literally and figuratively. They perform a ritual religious cleansing, led by demonologist Keith Johnson, only after recommending that the living space be uncluttered and cleaned, the couple undergo marriage counseling, and the friend be removed as a constant presence. After the ritual the paranormal activity subsides, and the family feels that the oppressive presence has lifted. In the final interview the client Teena tells Ryan that "hope found [me]." She thanks Ryan for recommending the "baby steps" that have led to "a giant step" toward a brighter future for her and her family. Here the concept of intentionality inserts itself, as if a haunting is all in the attitude—a state of mind, as it were. Another *Paranormal State* episode, "The Fire" (2008), features estranged siblings being haunted by the spirits of their murdered parents. The sisters half suspect their estranged half brothers of committing the murder. In the end the murders remain unsolved, but PRS manages to reconcile the siblings, and once again the hauntings cease. Despite the seeming severity of the cases, we are left to wonder in these two episodes and many more if the family dysfunction *precipitates* the *perception* of "normal" phenomena as paranormal disturbance, as a metaphor for their "haunted" family dynamic. Or does their dysfunction actually invite in the supernatural, making their home "a playground for the demonic," as Episcopal priest Andrew Calder suggests in "The Devil in Syracuse?"

Ghost Hunters also worries about the role of intentionality in paranormal investigation. "The Converted Church" episode showcases a couple whose home is crowded with all things Gothic and macabre, and the incongruity of such items in the space of a former church creates a distinctly ghoulish vibe. During the investigation lead investigator Jason Hawes approaches demonologist Keith Johnson and starts up a conversation implicitly about intentionality:

> "So what do you think? You getting any feelings?"
> "Not so much impressions of the house, but after looking around, of course, and talking to Justin, I'm wondering if they so much wanted this house to be haunted that maybe they're seeing something they want to see. I mean, it's a possibility."
> "All the collections, and everything, ah, that's just—that breeds negativity."
> "Well, we know when someone has a preoccupation with the macabre, the fantastical, that that *can* produce phenomenon." (2004)

Hawes and Johnson's speculations move in two directions at once, much like the narrative arcs of the *Paranormal State* episodes in which the hauntings diminish as the family dysfunction is mitigated. Is it the case that the clients simply *think* they are experiencing a haunting because they *wish* it to be happening or because it is a projection of their dysfunction? In other words, can we apply Husserl's idea of intentionality to these situations? Or do these clients invite a *real* haunting because their "bad energy" or wishfulness brings it on? In other words, can you bring upon yourself a real haunting or only a fake one?

The implications of postmodern theorist Jean Baudrillard's work on simulation and the *hyperreal* certainly pose an enormous problem to those who wish to prove the *real* existence of ghosts. Baudrillard writes of simulation:

> To dissimulate is to feign not to have what one has. To simulate is to feign what one hasn't. One implies a presence, the other an

absence. But the matter is more complicated, since to simulate is not simply to feign: "Someone who feigns an illness can simply go to bed and pretend he is ill. Someone who simulates an illness produces in himself some of the symptoms" (Littre). Thus, feigning or dissimulating leaves the reality principle intact; whereas simulation threatens the difference between "true" and "false," between "real" and "imaginary." Since the simulator produces "true" symptoms, is he or she ill or not?" (1988, 168–69)

Something similar could be asked of a person simulating a haunting: is he or she haunted or not? Would not both a simulated and a real haunting produce the same terror? This is the big question that ghost hunters often leave to the viewers' imaginations, sidestepping the issue, for the investigators claim that their work is finished if they manage to stop the clients from *feeling* haunted.

Evil Happens

While ghost-hunter shows call forth a range of phenomenological questions, they wrestle with metaphysical ones as well. The concepts implicitly advanced by ghost-hunter shows about relationships between good and evil, heaven and hell, and the living and the dead draw upon millennia of theological and philosophical argument and speculation. For instance, let us reexamine Jason and Keith's conversation, which presents the troubling idea that "negative energy" can call forth the demonic or "bad spirits" of sorts. How are they conceptualizing the nature of ghosts? How do they frame our relationship to the diabolic? If the diabolic exists, is this evidence that God exists as well? *Paranormal State* and, to a lesser extent, *Ghost Hunters* sometimes will posit that this "negative energy," which can be a demonic entity or a disturbed spirit who was once touched by evil in life, either as victim or perpetrator, has manifested itself because of an absence of "positive energy," a Neoplatonic notion that conceives of evil as a privation of good.

Curiously, these shows put together this idea of privation with the biblical notion of Lucifer's fall and the "free will" hypothesis for the "problem of evil." On these shows the demons are really out there, functioning as a force opposed to good, which can be connected to the Manichean dualistic conception of darkness and light. Demons (who were never human) show up from time to time, especially on *Paranormal State*. Evil entities also seem capable of tethering spirits to the earth, preventing them from "going to the light," as it were. This seems like traditional biblical stuff, in which God and Satan battle over souls. However, Satan and his minions usually lose once again when some religion is applied to the situation, either as an expressly Catholic ritual or some other kind of cleansing that is associated with holiness.

But how does this evil make its way into our world to harass the living and the dead? Is God not paying attention? Did we do something wrong? These questions relate—at least obliquely—to the "problem of evil," a massive and incredibly intricate debate in the philosophy of religion which, at its heart, attempts to reconcile contradictory premises: How could God—who is all good, omniscient, and omnipotent—allow evil to happen? One answer to this problem is the free will defense, or greater good defense, which has been taken up by countless philosophers throughout the centuries. As Alvin Plantinga, a contemporary defender of the free will defense, argues, evil in the world exists because God gave us free will; as such:

> A world containing creatures who are sometimes significantly free (and freely perform more good than evil actions) is more valuable, all else being equal, than a world containing no free creatures at all. Now God can create free creatures, but he cannot *cause* or *determine* them to do only what is right. For if he does so, then they are not significantly free after all; they do not do what is right *freely*. To create creatures capable of *moral good,* therefore, he must create creatures capable of moral evil; and he cannot leave these creatures *free* to perform evil and at the same time prevent them from doing so. God did in fact create significantly free creatures; but some of them went wrong in the exercise of their freedom: this is the source of moral evil. The fact that these free creatures sometimes go wrong, however, counts neither against God's omnipotence nor against his goodness; for he could have forestalled the occurrence of moral evil only by excising the possibility of moral good. (1974, 30)

The possibility for evil, then, allows for creating more "good" because it provides the opportunity for us to *pursue* what is a moral good.

Paranormal State tacitly subscribes to these notions of free will and evil, since the show often suggests that humans, though their bad choices, dysfunction, and ungodly ways of living, often create a space for evil to enter. Then, too, the haunted bear witness to the poor deployment of free will from the past, as evil seems to collect around sites of trauma—places where evil rather than good was chosen or experienced. Usually, the haunted and the spirits can be set back on the path to moral good by choosing reconciliation, love, care for others, or, in the case of the spirit, "going to the light," and evil is vanquished by good with relatively little trouble.

However, *A Haunting* presents a more terrifying conception of the demonic and hell itself. By far the scariest of the ghost-themed shows, *A Haunting* deals almost exclusively with cases of demonic possession or harassment. Presenting itself as a documentary on past events, *A Haunting* mingles hair-raising reenactments, testimony from those involved with the case, and a narrative voice-over. The bad news in *A Haunting* is that we do not have to use our free will poorly to attract the demonic. Rather, evil preys upon the innocent and vulnerable, as it does in episodes in which a child is possessed ("The Demon Child" and "Spirits of the Dead"), another in which a mentally disabled young girl is the target of a demonic entity ("The Diabolical"), and yet another in which a pregnant woman is physically harassed and terrorized ("Gateway to Hell"). And the worse news? This evil is much more pesky to shake. The story arc will often feature the victims acquiring a talisman of sorts or procuring a quick blessing that might result in some temporary abeyance of the haunting but will ultimately prove to be inadequate protection. Then, even after a *lengthy* ritual cleansing or exorcism, an uneasy peace ensues, though the victims sometimes experience a recurrence of the haunting or a feeling of foreboding that the evil entity is plotting its return. Some episodes end with the victims simply abandoning their homes. On *A Haunting* you can never really beat the devil.

A Haunting and *Ghost Adventures* also present the idea that certain portals to hell exist. The voice-over introduction of every episode of *A Haunting* affirms this conception of our relation to all things hellish: "In this world, there is real evil in the darkest shadows and in the most ordinary places. These are the true stories of the innocent and the unimaginable. . . . Between the world we see and the things we fear, there are doors. When they are opened, nightmares become reality." As we know, these doors are not necessarily opened by our bad use of free will: we are more or less "innocent." In a sense, though, humans *are* culpable on *A Haunting* when they naively get in over their heads, inviting in the demonic by messing around with Satanic ritual, playing with a Ouija board, or uttering a curse. While humans can create these portals, these doors can also exist "naturally," an idea that *Ghost Adventures* floats by claiming that a particularly haunted site, Goldfield Hotel, is said to be built on certain "lay lines" to the seventh portal of hell (*Ghost Adventures: A Raw Documentary into the Paranormal* 2006). And on these two shows doors to hell are tough to close—or, at best, let in quite a draft.

Postmodern Ghost Stories

Despite their search for Truth, ghost-hunter shows resist offering consistent, definitive accounts of what they observe. Most of the shows conclude with no conclusion at all, thereby beginning and ending with uncertainty. Nor do the shows advance a consistent vision of the supernatural. In these senses, ghost-hunter shows take a distinctively postmodern approach to discourse and narrative in their preference for micro-narratives over grand narratives and their practice of bricolage.

In *The Postmodern Condition: A Report on Knowledge,* François Lyotard defines the postmodern broadly as "incredulity toward meta-narratives" (1989, xxiv). Lyotard identifies meta-narratives, otherwise known as grand narratives, as the sweeping stories that order our understanding of history and knowledge itself. Meta-narratives offer a narrative for all narratives, so to speak, by developing a totalizing explanation for *all* stories, thus providing some kind of universal truth. Examples of meta-narratives are the theologies of the world's major religions and the Enlightenment belief in human progress. Lyotard and others point out that meta-narratives have lost their power because they fail to account for that which is incompatible with their schema. As postmodern subjects, we have become aware of—and have embraced—difference and heterogeneity and have recognized that no narrative can be totalizing or representative; as such, we prefer localized "micro-narratives." Lyotard writes, "The postmodern would be that which, in the modern, puts forward the unpresentable in presentation itself; that which denies itself the solace of good forms, the consensus of a taste which would make it possible to share collectively the nostalgia for the unattainable; that which searches for new presentations, not in order to enjoy them but in order to impart a stronger sense of the unpresentable" (81). Lyotard advocates that we "wage a war on totality; let us be witness to the unpresentable; let us activate the differences and save the honor of the name " (82).

Ghost-hunter shows offer micro-narratives, since each ghost story stands on its own, and each haunting is specific and localized. While some common themes do emerge, the shows resist situating those themes and the episodes themselves into recognizable schema. Likewise, though scientific discourse is privileged in ghost-hunter narratives, these shows depend upon a variety of discourses, none of which are complete or authoritative and some of which would be traditionally considered mutually exclusive. This interplay of discourse allows for the convention of the "investigative team," which could include a medium, a priest, a building contractor, an occult expert, a pet trainer, a tech specialist, and a historian. This paradigm creates—without irony—a sense of incredible possibility and play yet also a measure of indeterminacy. Indeed, the shows practice "bricolage," which postmodern theorist Michel de Certeau describes as a "poetic 'making do'" (1988, xv). In "Structure, Sign, and Play," Jacques Derrida speaks of the *bricoleur* as one who forages among discourses without regard for disciplinarity: "The *bricoleur*, says Levi-Strauss, is someone who uses the 'means at hand,' that is, the instruments he finds at his disposition around him, those which are already there, which had not been especially conceived with an eye to the operation for which they are to be used and to which one tries by trial and error to adapt them, not hesitating to change them whenever it appears necessary, or to try several of them at once, even if their form and origin are heterogeneous" (quoted in Bruns 1998, 96). Thus, the ghost-hunting shows are more interested in efficacy than consistency and are not concerned if their experiences or practices do not hook up to a larger system of knowledge or belief. If it cannot hurt to say a Native American prayer while burning sage *in addition to* putting up crosses and sealing the entrances with a consecrated host, then why not do it? While the shows keep their distance from totalizing narratives, the relics, talismans, and tactics that come out of those systems *are embraced,* thus demonstrating Lyotard's assertion that micro-narratives and bricolage are preferred over meta-narratives in the postmodern age.

Specters of 9/11

We have established how ghost-hunter shows engage some of the great philosophical questions of the ages, and we have examined how they reflect both the dispositions and dominant narrative style of postmodernity. Thus ghost-hunter shows are both timeless and very *now* in their forms, but we may ask *why now:* why have they made their presence known at this *particular* cultural moment?

Perhaps it has something to do with September 11, an event that created seismic shifts in American thinking. That day of horror and tragedy, during which the scenes of sublime terror in a blockbuster disaster film became all too real, has prompted a collective interest in the nature of evil, haunted spaces (such as the destroyed World Trade Center towers), enduring trauma and mourning, and the debt the living owe the dead in seeking justice and reparation. Indeed, "We will never forget" is the motto that emerged in the aftermath of September 11; yet "not forgetting" is hardly an action in itself, and it remains unclear how we might go about remembering. In this post-

9/11 climate, it is thus not surprising that we have become so interested in ghosts, for they might provide just the metaphor we need to conceptualize the nature of history, trauma, and our relationship with the dead. Indeed, this is not the first time America has become interested in ghosts after national trauma: the Spiritualism movement became quite popular in the aftermath of the Civil War.

Jacques Derrida's work on ghosts has particular resonance when considering their meaning in the post-9/11 era. In his 1994 work *Spectres of Marx* Derrida develops a "hauntology" in which he theorizes the "spectre" and argues that mourning is work—the work of seeking justice. To animate his analysis Derrida examines the opening act of *Hamlet,* during which the ghost of King Hamlet appears. Derrida notes that the ghost demands that, above all, we *listen* as he issues an injunction for justice that we, as the living, must obey. The ghost also disorders time. "The time is out of joint," as Hamlet observes in the play and, as Derrida argues, the ghost calls upon his son "to put time on the right path, to do right, to render justice, and to redress history, the *wrong* [*tort*] of history" (21). The living then must work to reorder time through mourning, which is "in fact and by right interminable, without possible normality" and "responds to the injunction of a justice which, beyond right or law, rises up in the very respect owed to whoever is *not*, no longer or not yet, living, presently living." Thus the work of mourning, "which always follows a trauma," is without end, but has *as its end* acknowledging those not living and seeking justice and reparation on their behalf (97).

Since 9/11 history has presented itself as trauma, which invites us to imagine history's task as uncovering and authenticating sites of disturbance and tragedy, the haunts of restless spirits. This is certainly the work of ghost-hunter shows, which seek to recognize, acknowledge, and mourn the dead, thereby putting time in order again. Indeed, participants of the shows often "speak back" to the ghosts by acknowledging the spirits' presence and the injustice they suffered or caused. For instance, on *Ghost Adventures,* the team reassures the spirit of Elizabeth, a woman who was brutalized in Room 109 of Nevada's Goldfield Hotel, that they know what happened to her (*Ghost Adventures: A Raw Documentary into the Paranormal* 2006). More so, they call the spirit of her murderer a "coward," as if to work for justice on her behalf. The rhetoric of mourning and acknowledgement abounds on these shows, perhaps reaching its apex on an episode of *Paranormal State* in which the PRS team decides to hold a ceremony to bury an urn of cremated remains. Ryan, the director of PRS, approaches team member Eilfie, a pagan, to discuss the matter of the burial:

"I've never had to do this before . . . I never had to do a crash funeral. So what I was thinking is having a Christian burial; if you want to be there, you can be there, you know, just to pay respects or whatever."

"I think that's one of the main things. We don't know who the person was, but at least whoever is in there, we can give them respect." ("The Cemetery" 2008)

After we witness the funeral Ryan says into his director's log, "It's true charity, doing something for someone you don't know at all, with nothing to gain." The task of ghost hunting is thus the task of mourning and charity and, as those living in a post-9/11 world, we all must seek out the ghosts, as it were, so that we may "never forget."

September 11 casts its shadow in other ways as well. It has perhaps intensified a trend toward "nesting" and perfecting the home space, a trend that, oddly enough, can help to account for the popularity of ghost-hunting shows. On September 11 public space showed itself to be dangerous indeed. Thus the idea of retreating from the public into the private sphere became all the more appealing. The rhetoric of the home as "sanctuary" has certainly dominated the television airwaves over the last decade or so, perhaps because of this post-9/11 turn "inward." Another possibility for the HGTV orgy of late could be the secularization of our culture and our postmodern skepticism toward meta-narratives. If more and more of us do not regard churches as "sanctuaries" and have trouble believing in the meta-narratives of official religion, why not find spiritual solace and sanctuary—quite literally—in the comfort of our own homes? (And, of course, corporations promote such an ideology of the home, for it is a great engine for our consumer-based economy.) In any case, the home-improvement show trend is massive, and ghost-hunter programming can certainly be seen as an extension of the genre. Consider the home-improvement and ghost-hunter shows' common elements: clients call in experts to solve a problem with their home; the said problem compromises the clients' ability to enjoy the home as a sanctuary; the team applies its expertise and solves the problem. The only difference is that instead of moving a cooking island, adding granite countertops, and replacing tacky linoleum with earth-toned tile, ghost-hunting shows work on getting rid of the spirit hanging out by the refrigerator. Indeed, *Ghost Hunters* directly imitates the conventions of the home-improvement genre, including the up-tempo music, the infighting among team members, and the dramatic "reveal" to the clients, whose reaction of being pleased or not pleased draws upon the narrative structure of shows like *Trading Spaces* or *While You Were Out*. More so, in both kinds of shows, the home is fetishized and its space is made "holy."

Ghost-hunting and the Sublime

While it is easy to take a snarky stance toward ghost-hunting shows, in truth, they offer their viewers a bit more than most television programming, and that is the experience of the sublime. In *A Philosophical Inquiry into the Origin of Our Ideas of the Sublime and Beautiful,* eighteenth-century philosopher Edmund Burke understands the sublime to be an aesthetic experience: "Whatever is fitted in any sort to excite the ideas of pain, and danger, that is to say, whatever is in any sort terrible, or is conversant about terrible objects, or operates in a manner analogous to terror, is a source of the *sublime;* that is, it is productive of the strongest emotion which the mind is capable of feeling" (1844, 51). We thus experience the ideas of terror, yet as Burke, Kant, and others assert, we are not in any physical danger. Burke also develops the idea that ugliness has its own aesthetic, as does beauty, which is helpful for us to understand the pleasures of the Gothic. Lyotard, through Kant, configures the sublime as that which disturbs us and tests the limits of our reason: "Sublime feeling is analyzed as double defiance. Imagination at the limits of what it can present does violence to itself in order to present that which it can no longer present. Reason, for its part, seeks, unreasonably, to violate the interdict it imposes on itself and which is strictly critical, the interdict that prohibits it from finding objects corresponding to its concepts in sensible intuition. In these two aspects, thinking defies its own finitude, as if fascinated by its own excessiveness" (1994, 17).

Ghost-hunting shows, both by the nature of their content and through their style, offer us this aesthetic experience of the sublime. We witness that which tests the boundaries of our imagination and reason and that which creates a frisson of fear as we lounge on our couches. The hair on our necks stands on end as we glimpse the terrified faces of those in the presence of *something,* made more terrible by the chaotic movements of a night-vision handheld camera. As we get up to go to the bathroom, our chests tighten and our eyes widen as we take in the montage of fear-inducing images that often precede a commercial break. It is this Kantian mixture of terror and pleasure, as much as anything else, that makes our remote control stop at a ghost-themed show as abruptly as a Ouija board planchette during a séance. While these shows satisfy our desire to traffic in the great questions of heaven and earth, to feel as though we are closing in on a mystery, a part of us always remains unconvinced—and that doubt fuels both our pleasure and our addiction.

Note

My epigraph is taken from William Shakespeare, *Hamlet,* rev. ed., ed. T. J. B. Spencer (New York: Penguin, 1981), act I, scene V.

Works Cited

Baudrillard, Jean. 1988. "Simulacra and Simulations." In *Jean Baudrillard: Selected Writings,* ed. Marc Poster, 166–84. Stanford, CA: Stanford University Press.

Bruns, John. 1998. "Refiguring Pleasure: Itami and Postmodern Japanese Film." In *Postmodernism in the Cinema,* ed. Cristina Degli-Esposti, 93–112. New York: Berghahn.

Burke, Edmund. 1844. *A Philosophical Inquiry into the Origin of Our Ideas of the Sublime and Beautiful.* New York: Harper & Brothers. (Orig. pub. 1757.)

"The Cemetery." 2008. *Paranormal State.* Arts and Entertainment Network, January 7.

"The Converted Church." 2004. *Ghost Hunters.* Sci-Fi Channel, November 10.

De Certeau, Michel. 1988. *The Practice of Everyday Life.* Trans. Steven Randall. Berkeley: University of California Press.

Derrida, Jacques. 1994. *Spectres of Marx: The State of Debt, the Work of Mourning, and the New International.* Trans. Peggy Kamuf. New York: Routledge.

Descartes, René. 1990. *Meditations on First Philosophy.* Trans. John Cottingham. Cambridge: Cambridge University Press. (Orig. pub. 1641.)

"The Devil in Syracuse." 2007. *Paranormal State.* Arts and Entertainment Network, December 17.

"The Fire." 2008. *Paranormal State.* Arts and Entertainment Network, September 15.

Ghost Adventures: A Raw Documentary on the Paranormal. 2006. Perf. Zak Bagans and Nick Groff. Travel Channel. October 17, 2008.

A Haunting. 2005–8. Narr. Anthony Hall. Discovery Channel.

Lyotard, François. 1989. *The Postmodern Condition: A Report on Knowledge.* Trans. Geoff Bennington and Brian Massumi. Minneapolis: University of Minnesota Press. (Orig. pub. 1979.)

———. 1994. *Lessons on the Analytic of the Sublime.* Trans. Elizabeth Rottenberg. Stanford, CA: Stanford University Press.

McIntyre, Ronald, and David Woodruff Smith. 1989. "Theory of Intentionality." In *Husserl's Phenomenology: A Textbook,* ed. J. N. Mohanty and William R. McKenna, 147–79. Washington, DC: Center for Advanced Research in Phenomenology and University Press of America.

Plantinga, Alvin. 1974. *God, Freedom, and Evil.* New York: Harper & Row.

Smith, David Woodruff. 2008. "Phenomenology." In *Stanford Encyclopedia of Philosophy,* July 28. Metaphysics Research Lab, Stanford University. http://plato.stanford.edu/entries/phenomenology/.

The Vampire with a Soul
Angel and the Quest for Identity

Amy Kind

> To hell with you and your souls! . . . Why do you plague me about
> souls? Haven't I got enough to worry, and pain, and distract me
> already without thinking of souls?
> —R. M. Renfield to Dr. John Seward, *Dracula*

Perhaps no creature is more commonplace in horror fiction—both on
the page and on the screen—than the vampire. As typically depicted, the
vampire rises from the grave to a potentially immortal undead existence,
sustaining himself by drinking the blood of the innocent. With the kind of
charisma and cunning that is born only of evil, the garden-variety vampire
takes special pleasure in his actions, delighting in his wanton destruction
of human life.

Recently, however, the ingenious imagination of writer Joss Whedon has
given the classic vampire tale a new spin. What if a vampire had a conscience?
What if he could feel remorse? How could he live with what he has done?
Answers to these intriguing questions are explored through the character
Angel (David Boreanaz), initially introduced in the television series *Buffy
the Vampire Slayer* and then given an eponymous spin-off series.[1] The vampire Angelus had prided himself on the creativity he brought to the sadistic
seduction—and destruction—of his victims. But after a gypsy curse restores
his soul, everything changes. Tormented by his past evil deeds, he enters a
hell of his own making. Ultimately, renouncing his past identity, he renames
himself "Angel." Like an unhappy addict who wishes he could put an end to
his insatiable compulsion, Angel is repelled by his own unquenchable thirst
for blood. Neither comfortable nor welcome in either human or vampire
society, he struggles to find meaning in his continued existence and to make
his way in the world.

In addition to making for compelling television, the depiction of Angel/
Angelus presents an interesting test case for philosophical theories of

identity and moral responsibility. The people with whom he interacts are conflicted about what to make of his dual identity. His friends who reassure him that he's not Angelus nonetheless remind themselves not to forget who he really is. While some hold Angel accountable for the actions of Angelus, others convince themselves that they should think of those horrors as perpetrated by *someone else*. In this essay I explore how we should think about the identity of a vampire with a soul and what this means about the identity of us all.

Metaphysical Misfits

Buffy Summers (Sarah Michelle Gellar) may look like a typical teenage girl, but she's not. She's really a vampire slayer. The opening narration of *Buffy the Vampire Slayer* provides some background: "In every generation, there is a Chosen One. She alone will stand against the vampires, the demons, and the forces of darkness. She is the Slayer." Among other superhuman powers, a slayer has extraordinary strength and agility, heightened perceptual awareness, and the ability to heal far more quickly than a normal human. Each Slayer is also assigned a Watcher—a sort of mentor/adviser/coach on all matters relating to her special mission. Buffy's Watcher, Rupert Giles (Anthony Head), works by day as a librarian at Buffy's high school. Along with Giles and a group of friends referred to as the "Scooby Gang," Buffy saves the world, again and again, from the forces of evil. (Because her hometown of Sunnydale, California, is built on a hellmouth, it is a particular magnet for such forces.)

The show, which ran for seven seasons, featured Angel as Buffy's love interest during the first three seasons. When it becomes clear that a relationship between a vampire slayer and a vampire—even a vampire with a soul—is hopeless, Angel leaves Sunnydale for Los Angeles and gets a television series of his own. In *Angel,* which ran for five seasons (the first four concurrent with the final four seasons of *Buffy*), Angel opens a supernatural detective agency and continues the fight for good along with a motley assortment of supporting characters, including Cordelia Chase (Charisma Carpenter), formerly an occasional member of the Scooby Gang. The fight morphs into a personal crusade for Angel once he learns that he may have a special destiny. Contained in the ancient Scrolls of Aberjian, the Shanshu Prophecy predicts that the vampire with a soul, after enduring numerous trials and playing a key role in the apocalypse, will be rewarded with the gift of human life. Much of the series is thus framed by Angel's quest for redemption.

The Buffyverse—the world depicted in *Buffy* and *Angel*—is a lot like our world, only its evil is a lot more tangible. Importantly, the everyday folk in the Buffyverse don't easily accept the fact that there are vampires among them. When confronted with evidence of vampiric violence, they assume it must be the product of psychosis or pharmaceuticals. And even when they encounter vampires face-to-face, they're almost always unwilling to believe what they see with their own eyes. In this way the vampires and demons that populate the Buffyverse fit the standard horror prototype. As described by Noël Carroll in his influential work *The Philosophy of Horror,* what's distinctive about monsters of horror is that they disturb the natural order. Monsters appear in fairy tales as well as in works of horror, but in the latter, "it would appear that the monster is an extraordinary character in an ordinary world, whereas in fairy tales and the like the monster is an ordinary creature in an extraordinary world" (1990, 16).

Monsters of horror are thus "metaphysical misfits" (Carroll 1990, 54). Like zombies and ghosts, vampires are neither living nor dead—or perhaps they are both. In one of his many studies of occult phenomena, Montague Summers (no relation to Buffy) offers a similar assessment: "The vampire has a body, and it is his own body. He is neither dead nor alive; but living in death. He is an abnormality; the androgyne in the phantom world; a pariah among the fiends" (1960, 6).[2] Vampires thus fall between the cracks of our usual categories; in Carroll's terms, they are categorically interstitial or categorically contradictory (1990, 32).[3] In fact, their transgression of standard categorical and ontological boundaries is part of what makes the monsters of horror so horrific. We are both physically and cognitively threatened by their unnaturalness, their impurity, and we thus react to them with both fear and repugnance.

While all vampires defy easy classification, Angel presents a particular puzzle. Born as Liam in Galway, Ireland, in 1727, he is reborn as Angelus when sired by the vampire Darla (Julie Benz) in 1753. After discovering the pleasure of his first kill, he unhesitatingly murders his entire family—the first steps in a sociopathic rampage that lasts almost a century and a half. As Angel later describes that time: "I offered an ugly death to everyone I met. And I did it with a song in my heart." Even other vampires are awestruck by his capacity for evil; the legendary vampire known as the Master considers Angelus "the most vicious creature" he has ever encountered.[4] But with his murder of a gypsy girl in 1898, everything changes for Angelus. The gypsy elders conjure a perfect punishment to avenge their loss by restoring the soul that had departed from his body when he became a vampire. Regaining one's soul means regaining one's conscience. Instantly, he becomes tormented by his past. Able to remember in agonizing detail every life that he took, he now empathically experiences the incredible anguish of his victims. The crushing waves of guilt, shame, and remorse drive him to the brink of insanity.[5] He spends the next century trying to come to grips with his predicament. As Angel puts it, "You have no idea what it's like to have done the things I've done . . . and to care" (*Buffy*: "Angel").

When Buffy wonders whether it's possible for a vampire to be a good person, Giles responds negatively: "A vampire isn't a person at all. It may have the movements, the memories, even the personality of the person that it took over, but it's still a demon at the core. There is no halfway." But the case of Angel threatens to prove him wrong. Angel is not quite a vampire, but he's not quite human either:

> DARLA: Guess what precious? You're not one of them, are you?
> ANGEL: No. But I'm not exactly one of you, either. (*Buffy*: "Angel")

Angel thus perfectly epitomizes the kind of categorical contradiction described by Carroll. He's dead, but he's still living. He's a demon, but he has a soul. And he's in love with Buffy, a vampire slayer whose mission is to kill creatures like him. In fact, the mutual affection between Buffy and Angel leads to one of the most intriguing elements of his plight. When their romantic relationship is consummated, they discover an additional twist to the punishment inflicted by the gypsies: "Angel was meant to suffer. Not to live as human. One moment of true happiness, of contentment, one moment where the soul that we restored no longer plagues his thoughts, and that soul is taken from him" (*Buffy*: "Becoming," part 1). The upshot is that sex with Buffy might be said to literally make Angel a new man. His soul leaves his body and he once again becomes Angelus.[6]

A New Man?

During the eight years of events depicted on *Buffy the Vampire Slayer* and *Angel*, Angel twice makes the transition to Angelus and back again. After several months wreaking havoc as Angelus in *Buffy*, season 2, Angel returns in the closing moments of the season finale when Scooby Gang member Willow (Alyson Hannigan) is able to replicate the long-lost magic of the gypsies and restore his soul. Five years later, during *Angel*, season 4, Angel and his friends come up against a terrible demon, the Beast, who has turned Los Angeles into a land of permanent midnight as a first step toward the destruction of the world. When the gang discovers that Angelus might have information that Angel cannot access about how to stop the coming apocalypse, they engage a shaman to bring forth Angelus by extracting the vampire's soul. Later, after the Beast is defeated, Willow makes a guest appearance on *Angel* to once again perform the restoration spell and change Angelus back to Angel.

The Angel/Angelus duality suggests yet another categorical contradiction. We are encouraged to think of Angel and Angelus as being the same, and yet we are also encouraged to view them as different. During the time that the vampire's soul is restored, does Angelus cease to exist, or is he merely suppressed underneath Angel's humanity? Likewise, when the soul again departs his body, is Angel still somewhere deep inside? Do we have two different vampires here, or just one—albeit a fractured one? These questions are not easily answered.

Often Angel is presented as just the yin to Angelus's yang—two very different personalities, to be sure, but nonetheless personalities of *the same vampire*. The vampire himself—whether appearing as Angel or Angelus—at times describes the situation as a sort of multiple personality disorder, with one personality temporarily suppressed or cloaked by the other. Angelus claims that "I'm always here, deep in. I'm deep in . . . soul or no soul" (*Angel:* "Orpheus"), and he describes his time as Angel as having been just a phase he was going through:

> JENNY CALENDAR: He's not Angel anymore.
> ANGELUS: Wrong. I am Angel . . . at last. (*Buffy:* "Innocence")

This way of looking at the relationship between Angel and Angelus gains further support from the ongoing debate among other characters about which personality represents the vampire's true nature. Connor (Vincent Kartheiser), the son of Angel and Darla, gives Angelus primacy, referring to Angel as merely something that Angelus is "forced to wear" (*Angel:* "Soulless"). Darla takes a similar view. Trying to encourage Angel to return to the dark side, she warns him that he will not be able to suppress his "true nature" forever (*Buffy:* "Angel"). Angel's human friends disagree, trying to convince Angelus after he loses his soul that somewhere deep inside he must remember *who he really is* (*Buffy:* "Innocence"). Whatever the correct hierarchy of the personalities, this disagreement is framed by the shared presupposition that there's really only one vampire.

But this conclusion should not be too hastily accepted. Further reflection on individuals with multiple personality disorder muddies the picture, because it is not clear that they should be unequivocally seen as a single person. Consider Christine Beauchamp, whose consciousness fractured into three distinct personalities (called B1, B4, and Sally by her doctor) at the age of eighteen. Philosopher Kathleen Wilkes, in an interesting discussion of this case, notes that B1 was a refined and reticent saint, Sally was devilish, and B4 was an independent and aggressive woman. Sally and B4 loved to smoke and drink; B1 attended church and knitted. B4 and B1 were fluent in both English and French and well educated; Sally had poor command of English grammar and vocabulary, and spoke no French at all. According to Wilkes, each of the three personalities is best described as an independent character—"internally consistent and coherent"—and each differed dramatically from the others in terms of her "preferences, prejudices, outlooks, moods, ambitions, skills, tastes, and habits" (1988, 123). Ultimately, Wilkes concludes that we have good reason to maintain that three distinct persons occupied Beauchamp's body (128).[7]

The relationship between Angel and Angelus is often presented in a way that's similar to the relationships among the personalities of Beauchamp. One of the first things Angelus does when he returns is to light up a cigarette, whereas Angel doesn't smoke. Angelus mocks the clothes that Angel chooses to wear and hates his taste in music, particularly his fondness for Barry Manilow. Moreover, Angel and Angelus are generally taken to be mutually exclusive of one another. Despite Angelus's comment that he's always "deep in," the characters in the Buffyverse usually assume that Angel's presence means that Angelus has at least temporarily gone out of existence, and vice versa. In this way of looking at things, Angel and Angelus are best seen as two distinct vampires who alternately inhabit the same physical body.

Sorting out the relationship between Angel and Angelus is thus not easy, but it is an issue that matters deeply to the characters who interact with him—or with them. For example, when Angelus first returns after his century-long absence, he kidnaps, tortures, and brutally kills Jenny Calendar (Robia LaMorte), a teacher at Buffy's school who happens to be descended directly from the gypsies who originally cursed him with his soul. She also happens to be Giles's lover. Angelus then kidnaps and brutally tortures Giles as well, though he is ultimately thwarted from killing him. When Angel's soul is restored, should he be held accountable for these acts? Is he to blame for what Angelus did?

Here we need to be careful; as stated, these questions are ambiguous between *legal* accountability/blame and *moral* accountability/blame. While the two often go hand in hand, there are many cases in which they diverge. When your friend breaks a promise to pick you up at the airport, she may deserve your moral condemnation, but there are no legal consequences to what she's done. Conversely, when a motorcyclist fails to wear a helmet, her action is illegal—and imprudent—but not immoral.

Let us here restrict our focus to moral, not legal, responsibility. Criminal laws, after all, were not written with vampires in mind. So the issue before us is whether to hold Angel morally responsible for the actions of Angelus, whether Angel is morally blameworthy for what Angelus has done. To answer these questions it looks like we would first have to settle the issue of whether Angel should be identified with Angelus. If they're different individuals, then punishing Angel for what Angelus does is as arbitrary as punishing one identical twin for what the other does. We don't usually find it appropriate to hold one person accountable for what another person does; generally speaking, a person is morally responsible only for actions that are his own.[8] There are some obvious exceptions to this general rule: parents, for example, are often held responsible for the actions of their children, particularly their young children; military officers may be held responsible for the actions of troops under their command; and criminal accomplices may be held responsible for actions that they aid and abet but do not themselves commit. Moreover, in all of these alleged counterexamples, the moral responsibility in question seems merely derived or inherited from the individual's moral responsibility for actions of her own.[9] We hold the parent responsible for what the child does only because of the parent's prior actions in raising the child; we hold the officer responsible for the actions of someone under her command only because of the prior orders that she's issued. But the relationship between Angel/Angelus is not plausibly like parent/child or officer/subordinate; if Angel and Angelus are distinct individuals, there would be no reason that Angel should inherit responsibility for what Angelus has done. Thus, when it comes to all the horrible atrocities committed by Angelus, Angel should be held morally responsible only if those actions can be said to be his own. How can we make this determination?

Identity Revamped

Although philosophers have not been much concerned with issues relating to vampire identity, there has been considerable philosophical discussion about the problem of personal identity—the question of what makes an individual the same individual over time. This is often referred to as the problem of *reidentification:* what conditions must be met so that an individual in one context, under one name or description, and at one particular time, can be reidentified as the same individual in a different context, under a different name or description, or at a different time? As an example, consider author Anne Rice. Born Howard Allen O'Brien in 1941, she adopted the name Anne as a young girl. She started her adult life as an insurance claims agent but soon switched to writing. In the 1970s she authored numerous vampire tales including *Interview with a Vampire*. Then, in 1998, she rediscovered Catholicism. Since 2002 she has decided to write directly for Jesus Christ, consecrating her work to him.[10] So what makes it the case that, throughout all these changes, the same person has remained?

Philosophically, issues concerning personal identity date back at least to the British philosopher John Locke (1632–1704). In his *Essay Concerning Human Understanding,* Locke claims that personal identity consists in consciousness: "As far as this consciousness can be extended backwards to any past action or thought, so far reaches the identity of that person; it is the same self now it was then; and it is by the same self with this present one that now reflects on it, that that action was done" (1975, 39–40). Locke's notion of consciousness is usually understood in terms of *memory*. What it means for someone's consciousness to extend backward to one of her past actions is for her to *remember* it, experientially, from the inside. In contemporary discussion Lockean-inspired views typically broaden their focus from continuity of memory to continuity of psychology more generally. Derek Parfit, whose work on personal identity has been extremely influential, explicitly includes continuity of character, intention, belief, and desire along with continuity of memory (1984, 204–9). Parfit's view has become known as the *psychological theory* of personal identity: an individual at one time is identical to an individual at another time if and only if there are chains of psychological continuity between them.

Although the psychological theory is by far the dominant view in contemporary philosophy, some philosophers argue that the focus on psychological continuity is mistaken. Proponents of the bodily theory argue that an individual's personal identity consists in the continuity of his body, not the continuity of his psychology. Eric Olson, for example, notes that embryos and anencephalic babies "are human animals that manage to survive without having any psychological features at all," a point that casts doubt on the psychological theory (1997, 18). Olson describes his own view in terms of *biological* continuity: a person's survival through time consists in the continuity of his "purely animal functions—metabolism, the capacity to breathe and circulate one's blood, and the like" (16).

Although there is much to say about the relative merits of these two views, the events depicted in the Buffyverse generally support the psychological theory of personal identity. In season 4 of *Buffy*, the rogue vampire slayer Faith (Eliza Dushku) uses a mystical ring to "swap bodies" with Buffy ("This Year's Girl"). While Faith is wearing the ring, she and Buffy clasp hands. A glowing light flows through them, and then their "energies" switch. Although it takes everyone else a while to catch on, the magic of the ring has transported Buffy into Faith's body and Faith into Buffy's. Likewise, in season 3 of *Angel*, an elderly man who longs for his youth performs a spell in order to swap bodies with Angel and thereby escape the assisted living facility in which he's confined (*Angel:* "Carpe Noctem"). And in an odd turn of events in *Angel*, season 5, Angel is temporarily turned into a felt puppet ("Smile Time"). Though he no longer has a human body, he retains all of his psychological states. All of these body swap scenarios presuppose that personal identity consists in psychological continuity. We identify Buffy by where her psychology is, even if it is temporarily housed in Faith's body, and we identify Angel by wherever his psychology is, whether in his own body, the frail body of an elderly man, or the felt body of a puppet.

In fact, psychological theorists have long used thought experiments involving body swaps to motivate their views. Locke himself notes that "should the soul of a prince, carrying with it the consciousness of the prince's past life, enter and inform the body of a cobbler, as soon as deserted by his own soul, every one sees he would be the same person with the prince, accountable only for the prince's actions" (1975, 44). Here Locke also introduces the notion of accountability, and we can see how naturally one is led to a psychological theory of personal identity when thinking about moral responsibility. In fact, it may even seem that giving an adequate account of moral responsibility *requires* us to adopt a psychological theory of personal identity.[11] For example, assuming we knew about the body swap, we would be strongly disinclined to hold Buffy responsible should Faith commit a murder while inhabiting Buffy's body. Fingerprints and DNA would confirm that Buffy's *body* committed the crime, but can they show that Buffy *herself* was responsible for the action? In this case, though the murder would have been committed by Buffy's body, it seems implausible to suppose that it was something that Buffy herself did. For the action to be her own she must be psychologically connected to it in some way.[12]

The psychological theory, however, suggests that Angel and Angelus are one and the same vampire. Although many psychological connections are broken when Angel becomes Angelus or vice versa, there is still psychological continuity between them because they share memories. "I remember everything Angelus did," says Angel. "Every family butchered, every child slaughtered, every throat ripped out. I remember every detail" (*Angel*: "Awakening"). And this in turn seems to suggest that Angel is responsible for Angelus's actions. If the psychological theory of identity is correct, and if that theory suggests that Angel is identical to Angelus, then it would seem that any action undertaken by Angelus must be an action attributable to Angel. When it comes to all those butchered families, all those slaughtered children, all those mangled throats, Angel must be held responsible.

Crime and Punishment

But perhaps this reasoning is too quick. Earlier we said that an individual can be responsible *only* for actions that are her own. That does not mean, however, that an individual must be responsible for *all* of the actions that are her own. Identity may be necessary for moral responsibility, but that doesn't mean that it is sufficient for it. To some extent this is an obvious point. When an individual is brainwashed or coerced, the actions she performs are still her own, but that does not mean she is morally responsible for them. Granted, the situation involving Angel and Angelus is not similar to coercion or brainwashing, but the relation between them offers us a different kind of case in which identity comes apart from moral responsibility.

To see this it will be helpful to invoke a distinction made by Parfit between *psychological continuity* and *psychological connectedness*. Psychological continuity is all or nothing. There either is or is not a psychological chain from the present to the past, but there can be significant variation in the strength and number of the psychological connections that constitute the chain. As Parfit says, "Connectedness can hold to any degree. Between X today and Y yesterday there might be several thousand direct psychological connections, or only a single connection." Though a single weak psychological connection is not enough for psychological continuity, it is hard to specify exactly how much would be required. Parfit himself notes, "Since connectedness is a matter of degree, we cannot plausibly define precisely what counts as enough" (1984, 206).

Just as we cannot pinpoint exactly how much connectedness is needed to support psychological continuity, we also cannot pinpoint exactly how much psychological connectedness is needed to support moral responsibility. Certainly, when there is an unusual psychological disconnect between an individual's present self and the past self that committed some awful act, we are often conflicted about whether, and to what extent, we should hold the present self accountable. To her friends and neighbors in St. Paul, Minnesota, Sara Jane Olson appeared to be a typical suburban mom of three teenage girls. Married to an emergency room physician, she attended the local Methodist church, where she sang in the choir and cooked meals for the homeless. But it was discovered in 1999 that she was really Kathleen Soliah, a former member of the Symbionese Liberation Army who in the mid-1970s had allegedly planted pipe bombs under two Los Angeles police cars and participated in a bank robbery that left one person dead. At the time of her arrest there was considerable public hand-wringing about the extent to which Olson should bear responsibility for the crimes. According to one local newspaper story:

> For nearly 25 years, the question was "Where is Kathy Soliah?" If that question has been answered—if St. Paul model citizen Sara Jane Olson is Kathleen Soliah, the fugitive and alleged 1970s terrorist—two more questions take center stage. Can she be tried for crimes committed a quarter-century ago? Should she be tried for crimes committed a quarter-century ago? The first question is legal, procedural, practical. . . . The second question is moral, political, philosophical, but it is at the heart of the debate raging now over breakfast tables and on radio talk shows and in Internet chat rooms. (Haga 1999)

A similar situation had unfolded a few years earlier when Alice Metzinger, a chef and restaurant owner in Lebanon, Oregon, surrendered to police and revealed herself to be Katherine Ann Power, a former Vietnam War protester who had driven the getaway car during an armed bank robbery in 1970 that led to the killing of a police officer. A fugitive for twenty-three years, Power pled guilty to manslaughter and was sentenced to a prison term of eight to twelve years; she ultimately served six years before her parole. Writing about the case in the *New York Times,* columnist Anna Quindlen captures well our tangled intuitions about cases like these. While arguing that we must not forget that Power's actions left a woman widowed and a young girl to grow up without her father, Quindlen perceptively notes the difficult questions raised by Power's "odyssey" from radical activist to middle-aged mom: "Oh, do I recognize Katherine Power. She is the embodiment of the chasm between the 60's and the 90's, like someone with a multiple personality disorder. It is almost as though a different Kathy drove three ex-cons and her roommate to the scene of the crime. The other personalities, the cook, the mother, the middle-aged woman, perhaps feel as if they scarcely know her, as we scarcely know our younger selves" (1993). Should we take Quindlen literally here, that is, was it really a different woman who committed the crime? Had Katherine Power become a different person in 1993 from the one she was in 1970, and had Kathleen Soliah become a different person in 1999 from the one she was in 1974?

The conclusion that is beginning to emerge from this discussion is that these are the wrong questions to ask. Emotions run high about these real-life cases, in which real lives were lost, so it may be helpful to imagine a hypothetical scenario in which we just stipulate that the fugitive has changed so dramatically and so genuinely that the psychological connectedness between her present self and her former self is significantly diminished. Though she still remembers her past actions, she is now horrified by what she's done. She has completely repented, and having undergone a thoroughgoing transformation of character, she now lives an upstanding life. In this kind of situation, when psychological connectedness has significantly diminished, it seems reasonable to adjust our assignment of moral responsibility accordingly. But what's important to see is that we can do this without settling the question of identity, and in fact, the question of identity becomes essentially irrelevant. There may be enough psychological connectedness for us to find that the model citizen of the present is strictly identical to the criminal of the past, or there may not be. But making a judgment about identity does not itself settle the question of moral responsibility. Even if there is enough psychological connectedness for identity, that alone does not mean that there is enough psychological connectedness for us to hold someone morally responsible.

Lawrence Locke has helpfully presented these considerations in an essay on moral responsibility and personal identity: "Even if persons, in fact, last a lifetime, what is reprehensible or blameworthy about them does not, or might not" (1990, 62). In cases like the one we're imagining: "The facts about the persons before their character changes are especially galling, yet the end result is that we have little or no psychological connectivity and we are left with persons to whom the reasons we had for moral condemnation no longer apply. If we punish, we punish someone whose character is so far removed from that of the original person that *we might as well be punishing a different person.* In a sense, we would be punishing the son for the sins of the father" (63; my emphasis).

Above we suggested that we would need a theory of vampire identity in order to determine whether an action performed by Angelus could be justifiably counted as one of Angel's own. But it now seems that judgment was mistaken. In fact, the question of identity is orthogonal to the question of moral responsibility. We need to separate two questions, which might have different answers: (1) Who did the action? (2) Who should be held morally responsible for the action? Strictly speaking, Angel might be the same vampire as Angelus. The psychological continuity between them might be sufficient for the psychological theory of personal identity to reidentify them as one and the same person. But that is not enough to settle the question of moral responsibility. For moral responsibility we need not just bare identity, which arises from psychological continuity, but also significant psychological connectedness. Normally the two do not come apart. But when they do, as in the case of Angel/Angelus, we see that identity alone is not what matters for moral responsibility.[13] Even if Angel and Angelus *are* the same vampire, that does not mean Angel should be held responsible for the actions of Angelus. As Cordelia tells him, "You need to know that I can look back and see every horrible thing you've ever done as Angelus and it doesn't matter anymore because when I'm with you all I feel is the good you've done as Angel" (*Angel:* "Awakening").

Soul Justice

Given the unmitigated horror of Angelus's actions, we want clear-cut answers. And his victims understandably want justice. Unfortunately, however, this might be a case where there is no justice to be had, as Angel himself recognizes:

> HOLTZ: I will have justice.
> ANGEL: No, I don't think you will. There's no justice for the things
> I did to you. (*Angel:* "Lullaby")

In fact, there is something deeply ironic about the gypsy's curse that restores Angel's soul. By its very nature the curse is unable to achieve its intended purpose of causing Angelus torment. In one way of looking at things, Angelus's soul sends him out of existence and creates a new vampire. Angel, not Angelus, is thus the one who undergoes perpetual suffering. But even if Angel is identical to Angelus, by restoring the vampire's soul the curse itself has caused such psychological disconnect that the gypsies still seem to miss their target. Either way, the curse in and of itself ensures that its victim does not bear responsibility for the acts that motivated it in the first place.

Can we go so far as to say that the curse does Angel an injustice, that it is unjust for the gypsies to have caused him this perpetual suffering as revenge for acts for which he bears no responsibility? Here we might usefully recall the famous claim of John Stuart Mill: "It is better to be a human being dissatisfied than a pig satisfied; better to be Socrates dissatisfied than a fool satisfied" (2001, x). Surely, too, it is better to be Angel burdened by suffering than to be Angelus unburdened. As hard as it often is to have a soul, Angel is better off with one than without one—and so, too, are we all.

Notes

My epigraph is taken from Bram Stoker, *Dracula* (New York: Pocket, 2003), 324.

1. The television series *Buffy the Vampire Slayer* is loosely based on the 1992 movie of the same name, also written by Joss Whedon. Other than Buffy, who is played by Kristy Swanson in the movie, there is no character crossover between the movie and the television show.

2. Interestingly, Buffy herself—while not a monster—also fits the description of metaphysical misfit. She is human but superhuman. And she, too, is both living and dead, having been brought back from death . . . twice. She experiences clinical death in the season 1 finale before ultimately being revived. She is also killed (and buried) in the season 5 finale, though she is brought back from the dead through dark magic the following season.

3. In addition to the categorical transgressions already noted, Cynthia Freeland (among others) has argued that the vampire also "violates the norms of femininity and masculinity." According to Freeland, "Vampires are polymorphously perverse: In their search for blood, they can find physical intimacy with a person of almost any gender, age, race, or social class. . . . Transgressive and violent eroticism links the vampire's monstrousness to revolution against norms established by patriarchal institutions of religion, science, law, and the nuclear family" (2000, 124).

4. Having sired Darla, who in turns sires Angelus, the Master is essentially Angelus's vampiric grandfather.

5. The vampire Spike (James Marsters), who regains his soul at the end of *Buffy*, season 6, subsequently descends into madness as a result. As he describes the experience, "They put the spark back in and now all it does is burn" ("Beneath You"). The case of Spike raises several interesting issues of its own, but I do not have the space here to pursue them.

6. To simplify matters I will always refer to the soulless vampire as Angelus and the ensouled vampire as Angel.

7. Walter Glannon concludes something similar about individuals who suffer from disorders like schizophrenia or manic depression. These illnesses cause what he describes as "recurrent" or "successive" selves: "The self with normal mental states

develops into the self of schizophrenic delusion, which then once again returns to the self of normal mental states, and similarly for the self that moves back and forth between depressed and manic phases." In some cases these disorders may cause such severe breaks in psychological continuity between these selves that "affected individuals *effectively become different persons* from what they were at an earlier time" (1998, 240; my emphasis) And Schechtman argues that it is "at least uncontroversial to claim that in Multiple Personality Disorder we are not presented unproblematically with a single person. The fact that these cases seem to present, at least sometimes, genuinely independent streams of consciousness, which may have no awareness of one another, seems reason enough to say that there is some very important sense in which distinct persons co-occupy a body" (2005, 11).

   8. For discussion of this claim, see Schechtman 1996, 14, 157–59; Sider 2001, 203–8.

   9. Schechtman makes a similar point: in all of the alleged counterexamples, "we are holding the person responsible for actions that result from his prior actions, and so the assignment of responsibility for someone else's actions is always via a more primary ascription of another action to the person who is being held responsible" (1996, 14).

   10. See http://www.annerice.com/Chamber-Biography.html.

   11. In defending his own biological approach to personal identity, Olson vigorously rejects this claim (1997, 57–62).

   12. For further discussion of this point, see Shoemaker 2008, particularly section 5.

   13. This is directly in line with Parfit's (1984, 245–80) influential arguments that identity is not what matters for survival. According to Parfit, an individual may survive into the future even if no one exists who is strictly speaking identical to him.

Works Cited

"Angel." 1997. *Buffy the Vampire Slayer.* WB, April 14.
"Awakening." 2003. *Angel.* WB, January 29.
"Becoming," part 1. 1998. *Buffy the Vampire Slayer.* WB, May 12.
"Beneath You." 2002. *Buffy the Vampire Slayer.* UPN, October 1.
"Carpe Noctem." 2001. *Angel.* WB, October 15.
Carroll, Noël. 1990. *The Philosophy of Horror; or, Paradoxes of the Heart.* New York: Routledge.
Freeland, Cynthia. 2000. *The Naked and the Undead: Evil and the Appeal of Horror.* Boulder, CO: Westview.
Glannon, Walter. 1998. "Moral Responsibility and Personal Identity." *American Philosophical Quarterly* 35:231–49.
Haga, Chuck. 1999. "Soliah Case: Justice vs. What's Just; Sara Jane Olson's Arrest Evokes Passionate Debate." *Minneapolis Star Tribune,* June 20, 1A.
"Innocence." 1998. *Buffy the Vampire Slayer.* WB, January 20.
Locke, John. 1975. *Essay Concerning Human Understanding.* In *Personal Identity,* ed. John Perry, 33–52. Berkeley: University of California Press. (Orig. pub. 1694.)

Locke, Lawrence. 1990. "Personhood and Moral Responsibility." *Law and Philosophy* 9:39–66.

"Lullaby." 2001. *Angel.* WB, November 19.

Mill, John Stuart. 2001. *Utilitarianism.* Edited by George Sher. Indianapolis: Hackett. (Orig. pub. 1863.)

Olson, Eric T. 1997. *The Human Animal: Personal Identity without Psychology.* Oxford: Oxford University Press.

"Orpheus." 2003. *Angel.* WB, March 19.

Parfit, Derek. 1984. *Reasons and Persons.* Oxford: Clarendon.

Quindlen, Anna. 1993. "Public and Private: Our Radical, Ourselves." *New York Times,* October 10, sec. 4, p. 15.

Schechtman, Marya. 1996. *The Constitution of Selves.* Ithaca, NY: Cornell University Press.

———. 2005. "Personal Identity and the Past." *Philosophy, Psychiatry, and Psychology* 12:9–22.

Shoemaker, David. 2008. "Personal Identity and Ethics." In *Stanford Encyclopedia of Philosophy.* http://plato.stanford.edu/entries/identity-ethics/.

Sider, Theodore. 2001. *Four-Dimensionalism.* Oxford: Oxford University Press.

"Smile Time." 2004. *Angel.* WB, February 18.

"Soulless." 2003. *Angel.* WB, February 5.

Summers, Montague. 1960. *The Vampire: His Kith and Kin.* New Hyde Park, NY: University Books.

"This Year's Girl." 2000. *Buffy the Vampire Slayer.* WB, February 20.

Wilkes, Kathleen. 1988. *Real People: Personal Identity without Thought Experiments.* Oxford: Clarendon.

Ideological Formations of the Nuclear Family in *The Hills Have Eyes*

Lorena Russell

Horror and Ideology in *The Hills Have Eyes*

The Hills Have Eyes was originally filmed in 1977, directed and written by Wes Craven.[1] The 2006 remake (this time produced by Craven and directed by Alexandre Aja) revises the central concept of a family under siege to redirect the film's focus more pointedly toward a critique of the intensified discourse around "family values."[2] Both versions pit family against family, with violence marking the contact zone. But whereas Craven's 1977 film describes a mainstream American family under siege by an outlying "wild family" of hippies gone awry, in Aja's version the "wild family" are mutant miners living in the aftermath of the U.S. government's nuclear experimentations of the 1950s. In their explorations of the conflict between two families—one lawful, one outlawed—the films offer unique comment on the ideological force of this basic social unit. Both films mobilize the horror genre to discuss ideologies of family and the repercussions of state-sponsored violence, with the 2006 Aja film more clearly illustrating the links between family ideology and state power.

I want to begin my discussion of this dynamic by outlining my approach to film. In general, I understand film as a medium that holds the capacity to both reflect and challenge social values. In particular, horror, as a genre that appeals to its audience through multiple and contradictory modes of violence and disgust, complicates the way we view and understand the world. It is horror's close affinity with psychological processes that accounts in part for its uniqueness. As Rick Worland points out, "While we are likely to experience anxiety and fright in other violent genres—a war story, disaster movie, or crime drama, for instance—a horror film evokes deeper, more personal psychological fears in the starkest terms." It follows that horror has lent itself to critiques based on psychoanalytical criticism, largely based on the Freudian notion of repression, whereby the fear or terror that horror incites has a cathartic effect on our innermost traumas and anxieties. Catharsis may take place on a personal and individual level, but the anxieties and traumas themselves typically emerge out of a cultural context. As a result, we are ultimately dependent on a social framework for their psychological meanings. Worland describes how recent film critics extend their reading of psychoanalytical processes to include a sociopolitical critique, one that is based on an understanding of horror as "resonating with the return of any number of actions and desires repressed by the dominant social order." Horror functions in both the private and the public sphere: "A horror film may conjure private fantasies and dreads; its reception and interpretation remain a public and social phenomenon."[3] The divide between public and private is troubled by the psychological dynamics of horror, and that link between the social and psychological is strengthened.

Violence is another mechanism of horror that bridges the psychological and the ideological. In his analysis of the 1977 film, D. N. Rodowick maps out how "an 'ideology' of violence is an essential, if repressed, component in the figuration of the bourgeois family." He notes several narrative conventions regarding violence in horror films that help to maintain an opposition between the rationality of the bourgeois family and the manifestation of violence, and subsequently provide a "satisfying" conclusion that maintains the status quo of family. Violence in *The Hills Have Eyes*, however, repeatedly violates these conventions.[4] Thus *The Hills Have Eyes* may resonate with our own anxieties regarding sexuality or death, yet the very meanings of these seemingly primal elements are ultimately social in their expressions and effects. Social eras differ in their dominant issues. The ideology of family values has emerged as a particularly charged discourse in the late twentieth- and early twenty-first-century United States. The function of horror in *The Hills Have Eyes* is centrally linked to a critique of conservative American ideologies of family and family values. This analysis seeks to explore some of the nuances of cultural interpretation in its reading of the Craven and Aja versions of *The Hills Have Eyes*, and to do so through a reading of these films' complex relationship to the changing expressions of the ideology of family.

Cultural Criticism and Philosophy

In my reading of *The Hills Have Eyes*, I am drawing from post-structuralist theories, employing ideas from traditional Marxist as well as psychoanalyst thought. My claim that the films (both the 1977 and 2006 versions) are centrally concerned with family depends on an analysis that can account for how we understand family as an ideological construction. Recent articles outline a tension between scholars who approach film as philosophers and those who approach film as cultural critics. Members of the former group emerge out of an Anglo-American philosophical tradition and typically seek theoretical frameworks that help them to provide unified readings. Cultural critics tend to work from post-structural theories to understand the complex and sometimes contradictory ways meanings (and culture) are produced through textual forms like films. In their text *Film Theory and Philosophy,* Allen and Smith reject cultural film criticism largely because of its reliance on the "wholesale relativism" of post-structuralist theorists like Michel Foucault, Jacques Lacan, and Jacques Derrida.[5]

I believe that film holds the power to express the complexities of cultural attitudes around the political issues that mark a particular social period. As Henry A. Giroux puts it: "Films do more than entertain, they offer up subject positions, mobilize desires, influence us unconsciously, and help to construct the landscape of American culture. Deeply imbricated within material and symbolic relations of power, movies produce and incorporate ideologies that represent the outcome of struggles marked by the historical realities of power and the deep anxieties of the times; they also deploy power through the important role they play connecting the production of pleasure and meaning with the mechanisms and practices of powerful teaching machines."[6] Giroux's claims about films point to the underlying complexity of this process of cultural production and political intervention. Readings of films, and this essay is no exception, typically draw from a range of theoretical schools, including psychoanalysis (primarily apparent in discussions of repression) and Marxist or materialist critique (primarily apparent in discussions of social power arrangements and class struggle).

My reading of the film is in part a response to Noël Carroll's book on philosophy and horror; I want to counter Carroll's caricature of the political critic by noting how discourse and ideology function in multivalent and sometimes contradictory ways. In *The Philosophy of Horror; or, Paradoxes of the Heart,* Carroll dismisses the validity of ideological readings of horror, objecting that sociopolitical analysis inevitably explains the genre's appeal by virtue of its unilateral support of (or unilateral challenge to) the status quo. He objects to the reductive arguments of "[a] politically minded critic," one who argues that "horror exists because it is always in the service of the status quo; that is, horror is invariably an agent of the established order."[7]

For Carroll, any sociopolitical analysis will conclude that horror, insofar as it functions ideologically, works wholly at the service of the status quo or the state or, inversely, works wholly against the state. His concept of "ideological readings of horror" allows for little nuanced analysis, based as it is on a single, monolithic concept of power.

But Noël Carroll's imagined critic strikes me as unnecessarily rigid, and his extreme characterization ignores the more nuanced treatments of power and ideology that have evolved in post-structuralist thought. Carroll's oversimplified position is, predictably, quite easy for him to dismiss on the very basis of the rigidity he just described. I agree with him that such a reading practice would leave little space for nuance or for flexibility. What his position ignores, however, is the possibility of an ideological reading that would account for the complexity of ideological function, the gaps within the theory for partial resistance, and the allowance that a film might function as *both* resistant to and supportive of the dominant order.

Ideology and the State

For me, the ideological complications of *The Hills Have Eyes* (2006) can perhaps be best understood through the writings of Louis Althusser and Michel Foucault.[8] In my use of these ideas, I am most attracted to the nuanced ways the theorists account for how power operates through ideological formations. Althusser builds from Antonio Gramsci's concept of hegemony[9] to distinguish between "Repressive State Apparatus" (RSA) and "Ideological State Apparatus" (ISA), while Foucault develops Althusser to offer a multivalent concept of "technologies of power." Each of these theories seeks to accommodate the complexities of ideological formations such as "family" in ways that make sense given the plot, characters, and themes of *The Hills Have Eyes*.

Marxist theorist Louis Althusser (1919–90) explores how ideological formations (such as family, church, or education) might function to maintain, and in some cases resist, the status quo. In his 1970 essay "Ideology and Ideological State Apparatuses (Notes towards an Investigation)," Althusser distinguishes between the above-mentioned RSAs and ISAs, noting how both these categories of social and political formations help to reproduce the dominant state power: "the Repressive State Apparatus functions 'by violence,' whereas the Ideological State Apparatuses *function 'by ideology.'*" The RSAs include structures like the army and police force, those social institutions that play an active, often forceful role in maintaining state order and promoting state futurity. For Althusser, the state functions as "a force of repressive execution and intervention 'in the interests of the ruling classes' in the class struggle conducted by the bourgeoisie and its allies against the proletariat." The so-called ISAs complement the functioning of the repressive state structures through their ideological work. Institutions such as church, schools, and family make up the ISAs, and they play an equally powerful role in maintaining the state as do more forceful institutions like the army, but manage such intervention primarily through cultural and symbolic formulations. As Althusser describes it: "For their part the Ideological State Apparatuses function massively and predominantly by ideology, but they also function secondarily by repression, even if ultimately, but only ultimately, this is very attenuated and concealed, even symbolic."[10] The symbolic function of narrative, here expressed in film, thus can work to promote ideology. Later Althusser notes the potential of artistic forms, such as film, to resist the workings of the status quo, with sites of resistance located within the organizing structures of the ideology itself. Thus, as his student Michel Foucault will later develop, there is the possibility of power carrying the impulses of its own undermining.

My use of Althusser marks a point of tension between Anglo-American philosophical approaches to film and my position as a cultural critic. While my reading of *The Hills Have Eyes* largely depends on Althusser's accommodation of complexity, for philosophers Allen and Smith, it is this very complexity (and its violation of logical simplicity) that makes such approaches suspect. They argue that "the multiple confusions, ambiguities, and incoherencies that underlie the film theory derived from Althusser's all-encompassing and yet extremely sketchy theory of ideology have now been thoroughly exposed."[11] I object to this claim on several points. For one thing, Althusser's essay on ideology and the state is *intentionally* framed as tentative and preliminary. The essay's subtitle is "Notes towards an Investigation," and a footnote further invites the reader to consider the text as mere "introduction to a discussion."[12] This open-endedness is a large part of what makes the essay so useful and resists any claim of its status as "all-encompassing." But my primary difference is that where these critics see confusion, I see a level of complexity that brings us closer to understanding how art forms like film can at once further and challenge ideological struggles around complex political concepts like "family values."

One of Althusser's strengths is therefore that he complicates the explanation of how the state reproduces and maintains its hold on power. By distinguishing between various aspects of power, he paves the way for later theorists, most notably Foucault, to describe power as a multivalent and in some ways contradictory force. Althusser himself notes that a place for resistance may exist even within the ISAs, observing how "the Ideological State Apparatuses, may be not only the *stake,* but also the *site* of class struggle." Furthermore, his theory allows for intervention and resistance, so that even as cultural forms may function to replicate the dominant power, they also can reveal contradictions and breaks in the ideological formations: "the resistance of the exploited classes is able to find means and occasions to express itself . . . either by the utilization of their contradictions, or by conquering combat positions in them in struggle."[13] Althusser argues that art can find a way to highlight the gap between the ideological promise of the social forms and the lived reality, thus opening the way to resistance. *The Hills Have Eyes* operates in this gap between a conservative reiteration of family values (the standard plot of the family under siege) and, insofar as the films invite audience sympathy with the outlaw families, the radical possibility of how the social structure and ideological force of the family might assert itself against the state.

As Foucault describes it,

> Where there is power, there is resistance, and yet, or rather consequently, this resistance is never in a position of exteriority in relation to power. Should it be said that one is always inside power, there is no escaping it, there is no absolute outside where it is concerned, because one is subject to the law in any case? This would be to misunderstand the strictly relational character of power relationships. Their existence depends on a multiplicity of points of resistance: these play the role of adversary, target, support, or handle in power relations. These points of resistance are present everywhere in the power network. Hence there is no single locus of great Refusal, no soul of revolt, or pure law of the revolutionary.[14]

Foucault's characterization of ideological power takes it quite beyond a simplified notion whereby power can be understood as a monolithic, one-voiced entity. The ideological power carried in *The Hills Have Eyes* functions on multiple levels as well, with some elements working in favor of the status quo and others inviting points of radical opposition. Critical readings of the film, most notably by Robin Wood, Tony Williams, and Carol Clover, further the sense of ideological complication as developed by Foucault.

The Nuclear Family

Both versions of *The Hills Have Eyes* basically tell the same story. The films follow the misadventures of the Carters, a typical midwestern, middle-class family, as they travel across the American desert on their way to California. In both films, an ill-advised detour puts the family at the mercy of a murderous outlaw tribe run by a patriarch called Jupiter, and after a grueling series of violent encounters— Big Bob is burned alive, one of the family's dogs is killed and eaten, someone is raped, an infant is kidnapped—a remnant of the Carter family emerges from the fray. Both films contrast the families in terms of their class status, humanity, relationships, and loyalties, not to mention their propensity for violence. And both further place the stories in the context of the U.S. nuclear tests sites of the 1950s and 1960s though, as I will argue, the 2006 version accentuates the ideological powers of the state through its extended references to the nuclear military context, and in doing so speaks more directly to the complex interrelations between state and ideological influences.

On one level the films could be read as straightforward confrontations between good and evil. The Carters are clearly victims who stray into the nightmarish and violent world of social outcasts. But both films subtly manipulate audience sympathies and ultimately question clear distinctions between the "civilized" and "savage." While Jupiter and his family clearly outpace the Carters' capacity for brutality and evil, the audience is nevertheless repeatedly reminded to understand their disabilities and rage in the context of the hardships they have endured and to measure their violence against the specter of nuclear destruction and government deception.

While the original version of the film begins with a focus on the familial relationship between Ruby, Jupiter, and the gas station attendant (a connection not featured in Aja's version), in the second film the opening sequence firmly identifies the link between the repressive state apparatus (as indicated in the history of nuclear warfare) and the ideological state apparatus of family values. The 2006 film begins with a history lesson. The opening screen offers white text against a black screen that reads: "Between 1945 and 1962 the United States conducted 331 atmospheric nuclear tests. Today, the government still denies the genetic effects caused by the radioactive fallout." This textual preface clearly provides the historical context and political position through which viewers are invited to consider the fantastic events that will follow. The introduction indicts the U.S. government for its destructive policies of warfare and denial.

From this static and textual historical context, the film shifts to the alien environment of the desert, with hazy smoke shifting across the landscape and scientists in white decontamination suits (who could be astronauts on an alien planet) testing radiation levels and catching fish from a stream. A bloodied man approaches one of the scientists, pleading for help, before a pickax descends from offscreen, piercing the scientist's helmet and skull. A harrowing scene follows wherein bodies are violently flung against boulders before being dragged in chains behind a pickup truck. All the while the perpetrators remain unidentified to the viewer. From this surreal and bloody scene, the film shifts once again, to a 1950s commercial showing an iconic American housewife cooking in her kitchen and bragging about her new oven. The song "More and More I'm Forgetting the Past" plays in the background as the innocent commercial is displaced by images of nuclear blasts destroying test towns in the American desert. Mushroom clouds are then interpolated with images of mutations: several fetal images are positioned against circa 1960s mannequins in poses recalling the idealization of the family. This opening sequence puts into play the film's central concerns, linking the criminal negligence of the U.S. government with murderous violence and implicating the viewer's amnesiac understanding of history with the ideology of family. The scene poses the question "Why are we 'forgetting the past?'" One possible answer: we have been lulled into complacency through the ideological promise of family.

Urbanoia

The environmental destruction that this opening sequence describes provides another shared source of cultural anxiety and shame, and is cited as a recurrent motif in Carol Clover's 1992 text, *Men, Women, and Chain Saws*. Here Clover analyzes *The Hills Have Eyes* (1977) as typifying one of the staple plots of the horror film, a rape-revenge narrative dependent on the "city/country split." As in *Deliverance,* the evil country types represent "patriarchy run amok," and part of the problem lies outside the action of the film. In *Deliverance* the rural "hillbillies" will be displaced by a dam, while the environmental disaster of nuclear testing in *The Hills Have Eyes* sets the conflict into motion. In both versions the urban-rural divide further highlights class difference as it reenacts "the confrontation between haves and have-nots, or even more directly, between exploiters and their victims." But even though Jupiter's tribe demonstrates a capacity for incest, cannibalism, and rape, the historical background of nuclear testing effectively muddles the category of victimhood. As in *Deliverance,* the beleaguered city folk come to understand the savage Other "as the rural victims of their own city comfort."[15]

As Clover notes, it is in the challenge of boundaries that the basic element of horror resides, and a large part of what is so scary about both versions of *The Hills Have Eyes* is this muddling of the categories of "self" and "other." The point that the feral family somehow derives from the state allows Clover to speculates how "if in fact the feral family . . . came into being as a result of radiation . . . then we have yet another way that country folk are the direct victims of urban interests (in this case the military-industrial complex)."[16] One of the more horrifying implications of the film is that the cannibal mutants have basically emerged as part of the same system that has produced the "normal" Carter family. The families are linked, with the privileges and comforts the Carters enjoy dependent on the deprivation and miseries of an abused underclass.

Clover's analysis of slasher films is largely focused on psychoanalytical processes of audience response. She describes a process of sympathies and antipathies that enables a cross-gendered identification of the male audience with the "last girl" who has survived the mayhem. But alongside her analysis of gender, she identifies the significance of class struggle as a backdrop for *The Hills Have Eyes:* "In what I have called the hybrid film—the rape-revenge film staged on the city/country axis—two sets of politics come into play and are played off against one another: the politics of gender and the politics of urban/rural social class." While gender remains a central concern in Clover's analysis, she also notes how class conflict is central to the psychological guilt that powers the horror of these films. Clover identifies how films like *The Hills Have Eyes* often begin by establishing the deprivations and disenfran-chisement of the rural folk, so that "we know they have been (or are about to be) driven off their land, have been (or are about to be) deprived of their traditional livelihood, and so on."[17] Thus the strains of power dynamics in the films depend largely on audience identification and guilt, and in the case of *The Hills Have Eyes,* the points of identification and mobilization of guilt lead us paradoxically both toward the status quo and against it.

For Clover the emphasis on class difference often relates to a retelling of the Indian exploitation story: "In telling a new story, essentially a class story, about real estate plunder, we fall back on the terms of the older, originary story that haunts our national consciousness." This reading works quite well in her analysis of the 1977 film, where Jupiter's "tribe" clearly mimics Indians. As Clover describes it, "The mountain family of the *Hills Have Eyes* films is blatantly based on movie Indians (a tattered band of last survivors, living a subsistence life in the hills, wearing moccasins and headbands, engaging in pagan rites, and so on)." The link with Indians is perhaps less explicit in the 2006 film, where the mutants are set apart less by their primitivism and more by their physical abnormalities, mutations that define them as victims of an unjust and unaccountable industrial-military complex/state.

But in either case the resonance between racial and class struggle feeds the psychology of guilt underlying the plots. For Clover "urbanoia" describes the collective guilt behind so many horror films' plots: "The story is a familiar one in American popular culture. The city approaches the country guilty in much the same way that the capitalist approaches the proletarian guilty (for plundering her labor) or the settler approaches the Indian guilty (for taking his land)."[18] Again, Clover's reading of the film depends on a recognition of the imbrications of ideology and psychology, a dynamic that creates a guilt response in the reader, but one ultimately linked to social inequalities.

Gender and Family Ideology

Gendered norms of masculinity and femininity provide a stable field of identification for the viewer, a stability that is often intentionally disrupted or exploited by the horror genre. The wild "Coyote family" in the first film in many ways invites viewer identification more directly than the inhuman mutants of the second. In the Craven film, the daughter, Ruby, appears in the opening scene looking a bit like a scrappy version of Little Red Riding Hood. With the exception of her rabbit-pelt choker, tooth decay, and dirty face, she appears quite normal. She carries a basket of items to trade for food and begs the decrepit gas station owner (who will be later identified as her paternal grandfather) to help her escape from her immediate family. He laughs at the thought of her "passing" in society, dismissing her because she "doesn't know a knife and fork from her five fingers." This breach of etiquette seems like a minor flaw when compared to the physical deformities that mark the mutants in the second film, most of whom don't even have five fingers, let alone the use of language to distinguish them as human. In Aja's version, Ruby lurks as a shadowy presence throughout the film, never speaking a word. In both versions Ruby ultimately functions as a sympathetic presence, intervening to save the son-in-law, Doug, and his baby, Katherine, at the films' conclusions.

As is often the case in films centered on family ideology, gender identity and expression function as markers of individual growth. Ruby's motherly instincts allow her to develop as a sympathetic individual. She seems to actually bond with the baby, saving it from its execution at great risk to herself. The largest shifts of gender expression happen with the Carter family survivors. The son-in-law, Doug, the character who becomes a central figure of action and heroism, must change in ways that ultimately involve an enhanced machismo. Doug's initial clumsiness and effeminacy are associated with his technological dependence, a dependence that fatefully intersects with a mechanical ineptitude. He makes his entrance doing figurative battle with the RV's air-conditioning unit, and the air conditioner wins. The younger son, Bobby, though flawed by an arrogant impulsiveness, shows himself to be a more "manly man." He easily fixes the air conditioner. And significantly, Bobby is not afraid to carry a gun, but Doug, identified as an emasculated Democratic liberal, shies away from doing so. Part of the transformation Doug undergoes is from pacifist to warrior. He learns to be ingenious and violent, and as he grows more aggressive and more deadly, he gains a certain elegance of motion and a remarkable level of self-control. In the film's opening he struggles with a screwdriver, but by the end he is handy with a pickax. He strikes the very image of a manly man, striding along the hillside with his German shepherd and weapon, exuding a macho strength and manly determination he decidedly lacked at the film's start.

It is worth noting that Doug is not the only character who must "butch it up" in order to survive. The daughter, Brenda, begins as a timid and mindlessly seductive girl. When the trailer is stranded, she sets up a lounge chair and suns herself; creating her own imaginary world through a narcissistic gesture, she is delusional and seductive, recalling at once Blanche DuBois and Lolita. As the film progresses she is transformed through the violence she must endure, ultimately finding her way into the role of "Final Girl," dressed in a gray T-shirt and exhibiting great physical strength and focus, not to mention an ability with a pickax that rivals Doug's.

The 1977 version concludes with a focus on Doug's devolution from civilized man to savage: as he brutally kills the "wild man," the screen goes red, and the audience is invited to consider the horror that lies within the human capacity for violence, and to recognize that none of us are so different from the Others that haunt us. In an interview with Marc Mancini, Craven notes his early interest in individual psychology. Specifically, in his early films Craven was interested in exploring how the myth of the hero's journey reveals the paradox that a person can contain an equal capacity for good and evil: "recurring patterns about heroes descending into hell to face themselves on a primal level, and that hero and villain are two sides of a single personality."[19] Certainly this focus is apparent in the 1977 version, which ends with a shot highlighting Doug's descent into barbarianism, inviting viewer consideration of individual psychology, as opposed to the broader social implications of family or the state.

For Rodowick, the 1977 conclusion, with its freeze-frame on Doug, marks a potentially radical intervention in conservative ideology, set as it is against the ruin and devastation of what was once the Carter family. For him, "In a very real sense, the freeze frame which suspends the film is also the signifier of an ideological stalemate which marks not the triumph and affirmation of a culture, but its internal disintegration." He asks, "What kind of conclusion does this violence serve?" and then notes, with some relief, that "the film does not end with Doug reunited with his child or his brother and sister-in-law."[20] For Rodowick, such a resolution would have merely reiterated the survival of the bourgeois family against all odds, and therefore served a function of upholding the status quo.

The 2006 version notably ends with exactly the reconstituted family Rodowick imagines, as Doug, baby Katherine, Brenda, and Bobby (and the Beast) emerge as survivors against the backdrop of the destroyed trailer and charred family photos. For me, however, the conclusion lacks the sense of triumph that Rodowick imagines and, rather than reiterate cultural conservatism, instead points to the wreck the family has become. Despite the family tableau, the emphasis in Aja still concludes on a note about the evil capacity within the normalized "family," and raises the possibility of a new family emerging from the wreckage of their conservative past. Not only has each of these figures had to resort to extreme violence to survive, the configuration of the remnants, with Brenda the lone female in a heterosexual unit, points toward further, incestuous devolution. The future that the Carters are left with is ambivalent at best, and the audience is left pondering less about individual human nature and more about the possibilities of family. The irony of a 1950s idealized family is further highlighted with the syrupy and dated country-and-western tune playing in the background, "In the Valley of the Sun."

Cultural Repression and the American Family

In *Hearths of Desire*, Tony Williams describes the family as a "material cause of horrific events." He develops his reading through a cultural materialism involving "a continuous interaction between ideology and the material forces of history." In an approach that anticipates Clover's attention to psychological guilt and repression, he describes *The Hills Have Eyes* (1977) as typifying a class of films with a plot centered on a family under siege and struggling against outside forces: "These forces represent distorted embodiments of repressed tensions." He quotes Wes Craven from a 1979 interview; Craven's comments not only support Williams's central concern with repression but further the reading of the "monster within": "In *The Hills Have Eyes*, nobody even tells anybody what they saw. Everybody's trying to protect everyone else, so nobody tells the truth, [which] costs us in time and unpreparedness because you're not psychically facing what really is happening. So within the family I feel there are all these things. It's not that there are violent people waiting out there to break into our own affluent circle. No. We are those people."[21]

Williams's reading also points to class differences within the film, noting how "Craven's dark family" stands as "an extreme example" of "losers in the affluent American Dream." The battle between the families on one level represents a class struggle, as "Jupiter's family . . . destroys Bob, the patriarchal beneficiary of an economic system that condemns them to starvation and historic erasure." But on a broader, historical level, the central mechanism of repression Williams describes in the 1977 film is America's denial of the Vietnam War, a specter recalled through the guerilla tactics of the "dark family." The culture is at risk because of a shared historical repression, a repression acted out by the seemingly banal Carter family, whose family dog, Beast, signifies the family's "repressed violent tendencies." Williams notes how the end of the 1977 version places both families on a level playing field of violence as they trade atrocities: "Civilized family values are nonexistent; both families are identical."[22]

Whereas the 1977 film drew inspiration from American repression regarding the Vietnam War, the 2006 version and follow-ups use the desert setting to reference American wars in Afghanistan and Iran. The nuclear backstory is certainly present in the 1977 version of *The Hills Have Eyes*. The wild family in both films clearly stands outside the status quo, working against the normalcy and values the Carters represent. In the film the wild family launches raids using guerillalike tactics, military jets zoom dangerously close overhead, and the daughters read "Nuclear Testing Site" on the road map just before their trailer crashes. The specter of the military-industrial complex is even more apparent in the 2006 version of the film. It is established by the opening sequence of the film, and then reinforced throughout as the miners' mutated bodies bear the marks of oppression and deprivation. The nostalgia of the 1950s family is disrupted by the reality of the cold war and its victims, and the mutants themselves exist as "visible traces of the past's presence in the present."[23]

Both films refer to the cold war context that sets the scene, but the 2006 remake comments more directly on the link between the material impact of nuclear testing and the role of the U.S. government in creating the outlaw family of mutant miners. The film thereby increases the role of Repressive State Apparatuses by emphasizing the role of the military. The elaborated historical context of the later film functions on several levels. The historical period of the cold war coincides with the era of what many today see as a "golden age" of family values. The implicit pun on the mutants as the ultimate "nuclear family" is never stated, but nevertheless apparent. The use of mannequins as coinhabitants of the model nuclear town furthers the sense of family as constructed, comprising exchangeable individuals occupying established social roles. Again, the audience is reminded of the easy slippage of categories between "civilized" and "savage." The concept of the "constructed family" of mannequins points to the brutal environment of nuclear devastation that has created such monsters.

The Hills Have Eyes demonstrates the complications and contradictions that are inherent in any treatment of family in the contemporary United States, where national identification and religious belief are integral elements of how the bourgeois family asserts itself. Upon first recognizing they are stranded and isolated in a potentially threatening environment, the Carter family, with American flags fluttering on their RV, responds with prayer (with the mother, Ethel, leading the family with an appeal to the ISA of religion) and guns (with the ex-cop father, Bob, leading the family with an appeal to the RSA of the police). The inadequacies of these defenses become clear upon the deaths of the mother and the father as they are besieged by the purely antisocial (and in some ways post-human) mutant family.

Patriarchal Displacement

A key component of the family dynamic in both films relates to the cycles of the deaths of both patriarchal and matriarchal figures in the film. The films' treatment of patriarchal demise marks a key point of ambivalence in their treatment of the ideology of family. In his analysis of the 1977 film, Rodo-wick notes that the death of Big Bob, a "literal representative of bourgeois authority in the text," marks a critical moment in a cycle of displacement that sets off the action of the film. The violence in the film is in some sense centrally dependent on this displacement of patriarchal authority. Bob's death follows the death of Fred (the gas station attendant and father of Jupiter) and opens a space for Doug to avenge the remaining family. For Rodowick, what is notable about how the revenge cycle operates as events unfold is how the violence becomes a part of the Carters, not the monsters. As he describes it, "The film moves towards a resolution, but this will not mean the restoration of order and ideological stability. It is, rather, a movement of equivalence in which the [Carters] will be identified with the ideology of 'violence' previously reserved for the monsters."[24] It is this critical point of blurred identification between Big Bob's conservative family and Jupiter's outlawed tribe that creates one significant space for radical intervention.

Horror films are notorious for their exercise of violence against women, and *The Hills Have Eyes* is no exception. Big Bob's immolation is part of a violent sequence of action in which Jupiter's sons invade the Carters' trailer and wreak havoc upon the women in the family. In this disturbing sequence, the mutants set off the explosion that engulfs Big Bob in flames, creating a diversion that effectively draws Bobby, Ethel, and Lynn away while Mars and Pluto ravage the trailer, bite the head off the pet parakeet, rape Brenda, and ultimately kill Lynn and Ethel before absconding with the baby. For many critics, including Rodowick, such moments would inevitably point to a re-assertion of patriarchal norms and the status quo. In her article "Breached Bodies and Home Invasions: Horrific Representations of the Feminized Body and Home," Marcia England explores the ambivalent dynamic of the violence of penetration in three films, *The Others, Evil Dead II,* and *I Walked with a Zombie,* concluding that while home invasions and rape might in some cases be read as a violent transgression of patriarchal spaces and a radical disruption of boundaries, the conclusions of these particular films serve to reinstate patriarchal order, thereby reinforcing "gendered codings of space."[25] In *The Hills Have Eyes,* both the horror and the theme of patriarchal displacement come together in this pivotal scene of penetrative violence.

England does not specifically reference *The Hills Have Eyes* in her discussion, but the dynamic whereby home invasion marks a radical intervention within the ideology of family certainly holds true in this film. As England comments, "The home becomes a conduit within these horror stories, one that is permeable to the outside. It is no longer isolated and segregated; it is invaded. It is from this fuzziness that we begin to see the fragility of the constructions of public and private space, of the home and of family, of society as a whole."[26] For England the level of extreme punishment that the perpetrators suffer serves to restore patriarchal norms, but for me the radical displacement of the normative family in *The Hills Have Eyes* contributes to the films' ultimate critique of the dominant ideology.

The cycle of displaced patriarchal authority and the exercise of violence against women might seem to gesture toward a conservative ending, but the Carter family's ability (in both films) to adapt to the same level of excessive violence as the monsters ultimately destabilizes the family's ideological co-herence. As Rodowick puts it in his description of the 1977 Craven film, "Instead of celebrating the triumph of the bourgeois family, the final moments of the film only serve to inscribe them in the place of their victimizers."[27] While in the Aja 2006 version, the final shot of the reconfigured family might be seen as the family prevailing in a heroic tableau, the narrative excesses of violence undermine any conservative sense of reassurance. The strict boundaries of gender roles have been disrupted, and the haunting presence of the sins of the past are ever present, effectively disrupting the ideological link between family, god, and country. The final shot of the Aja film, taken from the perspective of the mutants, signals that the threat is not over, and that the past is still very much present.

Conclusion

A key scene in the 2006 film exemplifies the concept of ISAs and also marks a departure from the 1977 original. As Doug develops as an action hero, he makes the critical decision to track the miners to their town and retrieve baby Katherine. As he emerges from the mineshaft with weapon and dog, he enters the ghost town that was once the village for nuclear testing, with tattered mannequins still in place. The mannequins, inanimate human replicates, are symbolic by their nature, and here their symbolism functions to mimic the everyday life of a bourgeois American family from the 1960s. A young boy and girl sit on the creaking swings in the yard of a house in a deserted middle-class neighborhood— a ghostly replication of normalcy in which mannequins "play" on swings and tumbleweeds blow through a bright desert day.

The mannequins' symbolic force gestures to ways that we humans inhabit social roles: more like puppets or dolls set in position than individual agents with free will, these figures have been placed into positions that mark them as inanimate leftovers, but they are still somehow are recognizable as "family." The mannequins manage to be representative and ironic at once, straddling the ground between innocence and danger. These figures were pawns in the nuclear testing, and are therefore (like the mutants themselves) representative of devastation. As inhabitants of this ghost town, they further signal danger insofar as they are "neighbors" of the mutant miners. Yet their iconic meaning as white, middle-class American children of the 1960s strongly signals a nostalgic pull of normalcy, stability, and comfort. It is in this ironic play between the immediate danger signaled by the plot of the film and the iconic comfort of the symbolism of family that we can understand the strength of the ISA.[28]

The nuclear ghost town is an eerie echo of the middle-class 1960s, with mannequins standing in for neighbors and family units. It also holds the iconic appeal of the American Western, situating the miners within the symbolic framework of "Americanness." Even the living rooms are set up as lifeless tableaux, with kids lounging on the floor before the television set. Yet all these signifiers of normalcy and family exist in a ghost town, an empty and evacuated scene of traces with no visible sign of life. Part of what makes this all so scary is the way that the world of the mutant miners mirrors the world of the bourgeois Carter family and their symbols of normalcy. This is more like a fun-house mirror, with odd distortions and horrific violence displacing the banal predictability of the iconic American family. This group looks the part in many ways. In one shocking scene, Doug enters a room and comes across a pair of live little children sitting on the floor watching TV. After so many mannequins, their presence is shocking, as is their clichéd request to him: "Come play with us, mister." Another shot of the mannequins shows them posed alternatively as family and then (in a quick shot almost beyond recognition) as a couple engaged in fellatio. A shadow of marginality, perhaps a technician's prank, it nevertheless contributes to the uncanny feel of the ghost village, a place at once familiar and strange, and alienating largely because of the strong appeal of family ideology.

Mannequins point to notions of the sterility and exchangeability of the working classes. When Doug wakes up in the meat freezer, he finds himself surrounded by body parts, and it is only the blood that helps us realize the limbs are not from dismembered mannequins but from human victims. Disassembled, the limbs imply that the parts are in some sense exchangeable, subject to production and reproduction. The bodies have been cheapened through their "use value" of cannibalism and also through their association to the mannequins. As Robin Wood notes, "Cannibalism represents the ultimate in possessiveness, hence the logical end of human relations under capitalism."[29]

While on the surface *The Hills Have Eyes* rehearses the time-worn theme of a family under siege, thus seemingly reiterating American family values, on another level the films radically revise assumptions about the legacy of the "nuclear family" and its uneasy place in American history. The mechanisms of horror and its relationship to family ideology demand a complex set of reading practices. My response to the films is in line with that of Rodowick, who concludes with a similar mixed response: "In the final analysis, I'm not sure whether I would consider *The Hills Have Eyes* to be a progressive text or not."[30] For me such ambivalence is in keeping with the complexities of the horror film, as well as the ambivalent and often mixed nature of ideological power. Sociopolitical readings of film must account for the paradoxical complexity of ideological discourses that achieve their power by appealing on multiple, sometimes conflicting, levels. Althusser and Foucault's theories of discourse, ideology, and subject formation allow a rich space for understanding the ideology of family values in America and the horror that such seemingly banal discourse carries in its wake.

Notes

1. Wes Craven, *The Hills Have Eyes* (Troy, MI: Anchor Bay Entertainment, 1977).

2. Alexandre Aja, *The Hills Have Eyes* (Beverly Hills: Fox Searchlight Pictures, 2006).

3. Rick Worland, *The Horror Film: An Introduction,* New Approaches to Film Genre (Malden, MA: Blackwell, 2007), 7, 15.

4. D. N. Rodowick, "The Enemy Within: The Economy of Violence in *The Hills Have Eyes,*" in *Planks of Reason: Essays on the Horror Film,* ed. Barry Keith Grant (Metuchen, NJ, and London: Scarecrow, 1984), 323.

5. Richard Allen and Murray Smith, eds., *Film Theory and Philosophy* (Oxford: Clarendon, 1997), 16.

6. Henry A. Giroux, *Breaking in to the Movies: Film and the Culture of Politics* (Malden, MA: Blackwell, 2002), 3.

7. Noël Carroll, *The Philosophy of Horror; or, Paradoxes of the Heart* (New York Routledge, 1990), 196.

8. Louis Althusser, *On Ideology,* Radical Thinkers 26 (London and New York: Verso, 2008); Michel Foucault, *The History of Sexuality* (New York: Vintage, 1990).

9. Antonio Gramsci (1891–1937) was an Italian Marxist whose theories account for the complexity of consent and resistance through the notion of hegemony. He argues that workers acquiesce to the dominant economic order because cultural forces legitimate the value system that makes up that order. Hegemony is that dynamic of manufactured consent via cultural forces that unifies a society despite the oppression and exploitation of certain classes. See Antonio Gramsci, *Selections from the Prison Notebooks of Antonio Gramsci,* trans. Quintin Hoare and Geoffrey Nowell-Smith (New York: International, 1971).

10. Althusser, *On Ideology,* 19, 11.

11. Allen and Smith, *Film Theory and Philosophy,* 241.

12. Althusser, *On Ideology,* 1.

13. Ibid., 21.

14. Foucault, *History of Sexuality,* 95.

15. Carol J. Clover, *Men, Women, and Chain Saws: Gender in the Modern Horror Film* (Princeton, NJ: Princeton University Press, 1992), 124, 125, 126, 129.

16. Ibid., 129.

17. Ibid., 160, 161.

18. Ibid., 163, 136, 134.

19. Marc Mancini, "Professor Gore," *Film Comment* 25 (1989): 8.

20. Rodowick, "The Enemy Within," 330, 329.

21. Tony Williams, *Hearths of Darkness: The Family in the American Horror Film* (Madison, NY: Farleigh Dickinson University Press, 1996), 13, 22, 129, 130.

22. Ibid., 143, 145, 147, 148.

23. Vivian Sobchack, "Bringing It All Back Home: Family Economy and Generic

Exchange," in *American Horrors: Essays on the Modern American Horror Film,* ed. Gregory A. Waller (Urbana: University of Illinois Press, 1987), 180.

24. Rodowick, "The Enemy Within," 327–28.

25. Marcia England, "Breached Bodies and Home Invasions: Horrific Representations of the Feminized Body and Home," *Gender, Place and Culture: A Journal of Feminist Geography* 13, no. 4 (2006): 359.

26. Ibid.

27. Rodowick, "The Enemy Within," 324.

28. In fact, the ideology of family has in many ways superseded the power of education (identified by Althusser as the premiere ISA) in its ability to fashion social responses.

29. Robin Wood, *Hollywood from Vietnam to Reagan* (New York: Columbia University Press, 1986), 91.

30. Rodowick, "The Enemy Within," 329.

Zombies of the World, Unite

Class Struggle and Alienation in *Land of the Dead*

John Lutz

> MIKE: It's like they're pretending to be alive.
> RILEY: Isn't that what we're doing, pretending to be alive?
> —*Land of the Dead*

In a 2005 review of George A. Romero's *Land of the Dead,* Roger Ebert notes the class structure of the society of surviving humans residing in Pittsburgh, pointing out the contrast between the luxurious (and apparently completely idle) lifestyle of the residents of Fiddler's Green, a luxury skyscraper at the center of the city, and the dehumanized condition of the poorer inhabitants surrounding it. Ebert goes on to note how the functioning of money is never explained in this economy, "where possessions are acquired by looting and retained by force."[1] This provocative description is not pursued any further in the review, but it provides a point of departure for examining the film's satiric treatment of American capitalism and, by extension, a global economic order predicated upon class exploitation. Indeed, the economic system depicted in *Land of the Dead* has a remarkable parallel with Marx's representation of capitalist society. According to Marx, capitalism is defined by an unremitting conflict between classes with antagonistic and irreconcilable interests. In the Marxian view, class struggle represents a central feature of human history. This is a struggle in which, from one economic system to its successor, oppressor and oppressed have "stood in constant opposition to one another, carried on an uninterrupted, now hidden, now open fight, a fight that each time ended, either in the revolutionary reconstitution of society at large, or in the common ruin of the contending classes."[2] One of the fundamental characteristics of Marx's description pertains to the sometimes "hidden" nature of class conflict. This insight suggests that members of classes with antagonistic interests may not always recognize themselves as representatives of a particular class, nor recognize the precise nature of their true interests. In the United States, a country where discussions of class rarely find their way directly into public discourse, representations of class conflict sometimes appear in unlikely places. Romero's film is one such place: an ostensible representation of what is known as a survival narrative, that is to say, "a story in which a group of characters undergoes a crisis that tests their individual and collective capacity to survive,"[3] that actually represents a complex, sustained allegorical treatment of class conflict in America and exploitation on a global scale. At the same time, the film represents an interesting variation on the genre of survival horror and, in particular, the zombie film, which, like its prototype *The Birds,* usually involves a relatively small group trapped in a house or mall. In *Land of the Dead,* this principle is applied on a grand scale. The besieged house is transformed into an entire city allegorically representing America and its relationship to the underdeveloped, exploited nations on the periphery of empire.

Furthermore, like Romero's earlier films in this genre, *Land of the Dead* seems preoccupied with making comparisons between the cannibalistic zombies and uninfected humans. The opening scene depicts members of a zombie brass band playing their instruments pathetically. A teenaged couple, the unlaced sneakers of the male very much like the style currently fashionable, parades past. And, when the gas station bell rings, the African American attendant, Big Daddy, who will later lead the zombie "revolution" against the businessman Kaufman, emerges to answer the bell and picks up the gas handle in imitation of his former life. The choice of an African American for this role contributes to the film's allegorical exploration of class and privilege on two levels. Even as it evokes the zombie figure's origin in the history of African slavery in the Caribbean, it comments upon the relationship between race and class in the United States by pointing to the disproportionate number of African Americans in impoverished conditions and the role of violence in enforcing these conditions. Indeed, in a discussion of George Romero's *Night of the Living Dead* cycle, Noël Carroll points out that these films are "explicitly anti-racist as well as critical of the consumerism and viciousness of American society."[4] Similarly, in a discussion of the original *Night of the Living Dead,* Tony Williams suggests that the film represents "a devastating critique upon the deformations of human personality operating within a ruthless capitalist society."[5] *Land of the Dead* carries on this tradition, emphasizing how racism and brutally competitive consumerism function on a global level by reinforcing the underdevelop-

Eugene Clark (as Big Daddy) in *Land of the Dead* (2005). Directed by George A. Romero. (Universal Studios/Photofest)

ment and exploitation of nations primarily populated by nonwhites. Big Daddy's response to the assault on his town is particularly suggestive here, since he clearly expresses rage over the killing of his fellow zombies. When provided with an opportunity, he grabs a gun from a soldier passing on a motorcycle and begins to teach himself how to use it. In arming himself, Big Daddy figuratively sets foot on the path of violent resistance and revolution. In this connection, it is worthwhile noting that "the original narrative of Caribbean cannibalism in Columbus's journals rested upon a distinction between those who would work docilely for European colonizers, and those 'cannibals' who staged resistance and could thus be enslaved or killed."[6] Like Columbus's cannibals, these zombies will not stand peacefully by and allow their town to be emptied of its resources. As the soldiers leave the town, Big Daddy puts the gun over his shoulder in military fashion, begins walking in the direction of the departing soldiers, and successfully exhorts his fellow zombies to follow him.

Although Roger Ebert's review mentioned earlier may seem to foreground class, in the final analysis it proves to be quite typical of American public discourse to the degree that it fails to pursue the full allegorical implications of the film. Early in the review, Ebert points out that the healthy humans surviving in Pittsburgh "have evolved a class system."[7] This is an interesting, if not symptomatic, phrase that directs attention away from the film's allegorical treatment of class and race by suggesting that before the zombie outbreak there were no classes. Ebert's use of the word *evolved* implies that the residents of Pittsburgh have constructed a class system in order to survive rather than merely reproduced the one that existed before. A full exploration of the film's allegorical (and sometimes bitingly satiric) depiction of American capitalism requires shifting from an exclusive focus upon the inhabitants of Pittsburgh and extending the analysis of class struggle to encompass the zombies as well. In many respects, the zombies prove to have more in common with the poorer inhabitants of the Pittsburgh fortress than these poorer inhabitants have with the wealthy residents of Fiddler's Green. Ruled over by the dictatorial businessman Paul Kaufman, who enforces the city's system of privilege with direct violence and allocates the resources pillaged from the surrounding countryside, Pittsburgh represents only an apparent oasis of partial stability in a world characterized by utter chaos and insecurity. Although initially Kaufman seems to exert absolute control over the city and the surrounding land of the dead, he can be viewed as a symbol of modern capitalist society with its exploitative class relations and inequitable distribution of property. Marx describes the modern capitalist with a provocative Gothic metaphor as one who has "conjured up . . . gigantic means of production and exchange" but "is like the sorcerer, who is no longer able to control the powers of the nether world whom he has called up by his spells."[8] The zombies surrounding the fortress of Pittsburgh are apt symbols of these "powers of the nether world" constantly threatening capitalist society with destruction. They signify not only the countless individuals impoverished by the system and the disruptive potential of their unrest, but also the commercial crises that periodically threaten the prosperity of the privileged classes.

In this respect, the film can also be seen as an explicit commentary upon America's place at the center of global economic imperialism. Bordered by two rivers and an electric barricade, the city of Pittsburgh in *Land of the Dead* serves as a figure for America's place (bordered by two oceans and a barricade between it and Mexico) in the global economic order. The militarism apparent in the city emphasizes the degree to which America's global hegemony is maintained by imperialistic violence while pointing out how the sharpening contradictions between capital and labor have created social instability and political chaos. Similarly divided between a class of wealthy survivors living in luxury in the city's center and the poor living on its outlying edges, Pittsburgh exists in a permanently antagonistic relationship with the surrounding territory, populated by the undead. This relationship signifies America's exploitative relationship to the underdeveloped nations of the world. Using its heavy firepower and accompanying assault team to gather commodities from the territory of the undead, the armored vehicle named *Dead Reckoning* represents the military enforcement of U.S. economic imperialism as it relies upon violent coercion to appropriate raw materials and perpetuates the exploitation of cheap labor.

Furthermore, the subhuman condition of the zombie masses, permanently afflicted with an insatiable hunger coupled with rudimentary intellectual skills, serves as a powerful allegory for the condition of alienation described by Marx. The title of the film, *Land of the Dead,* metaphorically represents the living death experienced by the brutalized and exploited worker. The worker's domination by the system of production has a dehumanizing effect upon his or her psyche, creating psychological forms of degradation and impoverishment to accompany the physical ones. As Marx describes this process of domination:

> They [conditions of labor] distort the worker into a fragment of a man, they degrade him to the level of an appendage of a machine, they destroy the actual content of his labor by turning it into a torment; they alienate [*entfremden*] from him the intellectual potentialities of the labor process in the same proportion as science is incorporated in it as an independent power; they deform the conditions under which he works, subject him during the labor process to a despotism the more hateful for its meanness; they transform his life-time into working-time, and drag his wife and child beneath the juggernaut of capital.[9]

More than the poor inhabitants of Pittsburgh, the zombies populating the surrounding land of the dead reflect this psychological condition. The horrifying facial expressions, distorted posture, and subhuman grunting of the zombies clearly suggest a condition of unrelenting torment and misery. Their frequent appearance in clothing suggesting working-class roles (more on this later) and their wielding of various tools and vestiges of material culture all point to their dehumanized, alienated condition.

Indeed, the metaphorical significance of the zombie as a representation of a victim of exploitation can be traced back to its origins in Caribbean folklore. In a book examining the consumption of the Caribbean from the initial stages of European conquest to the present, Mimi Sheller emphasizes its defining condition of enslavement and points out that the Haitian *zombi,* "a living-dead slave deprived of will and physically controlled by a sorcerer," functions as "the ultimate representation of the psychic state of one whose body/spirit is consumed."[10] Making a similar point, Joan Dayan views the zombie as a way of representing the twentieth-century history of forced labor and denigration during America's occupation of Haiti, in which "the phantasm of the zombie—a soulless husk deprived of freedom—is the ultimate sign of loss and dispossession."[11] Although there is no apparent sorcerer controlling the zombies in *Land of the Dead,* unless it be the capitalist sorcerer described by Marx, they are clearly driven by forces beyond their own rational control and exist in a state of constant hunger. This condition reflects the physical impoverishment of the exploited worker. In this respect, the title of the film represents an ironic commentary upon the alienated condition of the mass of humanity under global capitalism.

In an interesting exchange that underscores this commentary, Riley, the leader of the strike team assembled to raid supplies from the region surrounding Pittsburgh and the ostensible hero of the film, comments upon the similarity of the zombies to humans:

MIKE: They're trying to be us.
RILEY: No, they used to be us. Learning to be us again.
MIKE: No way. Some germ or some devil got those things up and walking . . . but there's a big difference between us and them. They're dead.
MIKE: It's like they're pretending to be alive.
RILEY: Isn't that what we're doing, pretending to be alive?

Riley alone seems to recognize the humanity of the zombies and later comments that they are learning to be useful. This theme will come up frequently in assessing the value of various characters. The usefulness of the zombies serves as an implicit condemnation of the comparatively "useless" wealthy residents of Fiddler's Green who spend all of their time in complete leisure. At the same time, Riley's recognition of the humanity of the zombies initially only goes so far, since he is leading a raid against the town in which they reside. In several respects this raid resembles the military enforcement of U.S. imperialism. As Riley and Mike observe the gas station, Riley notices that Big Daddy seems to be communicating with the other zombies and even thinking on a rudimentary level. Riley's perception of the zombies is quite similar to standard imperialist perceptions of colonized peoples during the height of European imperialism. The grunts and groans that have a meaning opaque to Riley and Mike present the standard stereotypical view of the savage cannibal, and indeed, as Mimi Sheller points out, there is a close association between zombies, cannibalism, and the exploitation of labor in which "the dialectics of eating and being eaten pertain as much to the hollowing out of human agency by degraded forms of labor (the zombie) as to the actual appropriation, objectification, fragmentation, and ingestion of the physical body itself (to be cannibalized)."[12]

Furthermore, the fireworks display that is used to mesmerize the zombies signifies the superior technological and military might of the United States, a "shock and awe" display of force that is intended to make the zombies submissive so that the strike team can gather the resources they need without interference. The raid itself, reminiscent of any number of Western imperialist military adventures in which civilians have been indiscriminately killed alongside soldiers, quickly degenerates into the random gunning down of zombies in the street. The whooping and yelling of the members of the assault team as they leave the town evokes lawless pillage and presents the zombies as victims of random violence. This leads one of the soldiers on Riley's team to comment, "I thought this was going to be a battle. It's a fucking massacre," an observation no doubt made by more than one soldier enforcing the imperatives of U.S. economic and political hegemony abroad.

Riley's attitude to all of this is clearly ambivalent, and we learn during the raid that this is his last night performing this kind of work. At one point Riley mentions that he doesn't want anything to go wrong and expresses his commitment to getting the job done. Riley's comment represents an interesting representation of the work ethic. Not unlike the character of Marlow in Conrad's *Heart of Darkness,* whose perception of Africans has some remarkable parallels with the film's representation of the cannibalistic zombies, Riley places a value on work for its own sake, independent of the kind of work in which he is engaged. Evocations of imperialism are also evident in the way the zombies react to the raid. As the zombies are mesmerized by the fireworks display, that is to say, the superior technological might of Western capitalism, the African American zombie Big Daddy alone seems immune to it and attempts to rouse his companions.

In addition to its allegorical exploration of global capitalism, the film explores class relations in America by focusing upon the contrasting living conditions of Pittsburgh's wealthy and poor residents. One focus of this exploration is the relationship between Kaufman and his henchman Cholo. Cholo has been procuring luxury items for Kaufman in the raids upon the countryside and disposing of the bodies of those whom Kaufman has had killed to preserve his power and position. In one of the more interesting segments of the film, a conversation between Riley and Cholo takes place underneath a television screen playing an advertisement for Fiddler's Green.

In his review of the film, Roger Ebert takes note of the commercial and expresses perplexity about its possible purpose in this world;[13] however, even though there are no consumers left who can aspire to live in Fiddler's Green, the entire segment represents a complex commentary upon the manner in which advertising works as a purveyor of what Marx referred to as ideology. Marx defined ideology as the "false consciousness" adopted by workers and capitalists alike that participates in the reproduction of the system by persuading the workers in particular that its institutions are arranged to support their interests. In his theoretical work, Marx frequently concerned himself with the role of ideology in capitalist society since he realized that it played a powerful part in preventing workers from developing a direct awareness of their exploitation. However, one of the most provocative descriptions of ideology in the Marxist tradition was arrived at by Louis Althusser, who defined ideology as "the imaginary relationship of individuals to their real conditions of existence."[14] This definition represents an ideal characterization of Cholo's initial perception of his place in the order of things. As the commercial announces, "Life goes on in Fiddler's Green in the heart of one of America's oldest and greatest cities," it advertises its six fine restaurants and endless shopping opportunities. When it goes on to point out that there is a difference between Fiddler's Green and other places, Cholo announces to Riley his intention to have his own home in Fiddler's Green. He then goes on to characterize the world as a place of ruthless competition where only those who act selfishly in their own interests can get ahead. Essentially, Cholo has fully internalized the competitive ethic of capitalism, subordinating all moral considerations to personal enrichment and drowning everything, like the capitalist whom he serves, "in the icy waters of egotistical calculation."[15]

Cholo's attitudes explain the continuing function of advertising even in this postapocalyptic world. Cholo announces his intention to gain entry to the Green as he is watching the advertisement. This detail participates in the film's critique of how advertising functions not only to literally sell products but also to inculcate the lower classes with an ethic of consumption and persuade them that they have the opportunity to join the ranks of the privileged. In his aspirations for a life of wealth and privilege, Cholo can be viewed as a direct representation of a worker whose investment in an "imaginary" relationship to the real conditions of his existence deludes him into believing that he can achieve the American dream. Later, when Kaufman rejects his bid to live in the Green and Cholo steals *Dead Reckoning*, he continues to hold onto this delusion, believing that the power that the assault vehicle gives him will enable him to extort 5 million dollars from Kaufman and still achieve his goal of reaching a privileged lifestyle.

In the course of a conversation in which Cholo has come to understand the world as a place where all advantages are gained by the ruthless application of violent force, he glances at the monitor of the assault vehicle to see a Latino zombie pushing a manual lawnmower in meaningless circles. Before shooting the zombie, Cholo, Latino himself, points out that the power that *Dead Reckoning* gives him represents the only thing that sets him apart from the "Mexican bastard" with the lawnmower. In addition to directing social criticism at the racist tendency to label all Latino workers as "Mexicans," the segment directly comments upon the widespread exploitation of undocumented workers in the United States as landscapers. Simultaneously, it provides a powerful image of how the extensive use of machinery reduces the worker to an "appendage of the machine" from whom "only the most simple, most monotonous, and most easily acquired knack" is required.[16] Although Cholo has developed a better understanding of his real place in the world, his individualistic focus compels him to see all human relations in terms of ruthless competition. The conversation between Riley and Cholo about Cholo's aspirations provides additional insight into the function of ideology. Riley recognizes the absurdity of Cholo's goals, assuring him that his desire to get a place in Fiddler's Green, that is, become a member of the capitalist class, will never come to pass because both of them are the "wrong kind." Cholo refuses to accept Riley's point of view and, as their conversation ends, the camera returns to the television screen and the voice-over saying, "Isn't it time? Isn't it your time for Fiddler's Green?" Taken as a whole, this segment of the film represents a caustic satire upon the vast discrepancy between the ideals of the American dream and the underlying brutal reality of American society.

Even though the world is in complete disorder and the Green is closed to any new members, the commercial still serves a crucial function as a source of ideology. It is intended to keep the poor surviving residents of Pittsburgh buying into the system in order to preserve the privileges of the ruling class. The final voice-over of the commercial comments upon the delusional nature of Cholo's aspirations, and allegorically exposes the imaginary nature of the American dream. It demonstrates how ideology functions as a means of getting people to reproduce the system without the state having to use direct repressive violence. After this exchange, it really comes as no surprise when Kaufman tells Cholo that there isn't enough space for him in the Green. At the same time, not only does the commercial serve as a vehicle for reinforcing the aspirations of the lower class, but it also comments allegorically upon the American obsession with commodity consumption. In addition to being a place of residence, Fiddler's Green is essentially a luxury shopping and dining center. In one of the few glimpses we have of the inside of the tower, the wealthy white residents, none of whom are shown working, spend all of their time shopping and dining. As Cholo walks through the Green to deliver the whiskey he has procured for Kaufman, the viewer is given a glimpse of an insulated world of privilege with virtually unlimited opportunities for consumption. This world of privilege stands in stark contrast to the conditions of scarcity and competition that exist in the rest of the city and the surrounding land of the dead.

However, the poor residents of the city and the zombies, despite their condition of deprivation, share with the wealthy residents of the tower an obsession with consumption. As in the second installment of Romero's earlier trilogy, *Dawn of the Dead,* "humans and zombies become equal partners in a goal of conspicuous consumption dominating personal behavior."[17] The opening shot of the film emphasizes this point by lingering upon an old sign with the word "Eats" with an arrow pointing in the direction of zombies wandering in an abandoned churchyard. This segment provides a satiric commentary upon America's origins in a Puritan ethic and its abandonment of Puritan religious ideals for the ideals of unlimited consumption. The sign itself is ambiguous and raises interesting questions about the nature and limits of human consumption. While the main activity of the zombies is the consumption of human flesh, an activity that serves as a figure for capitalist competition and the social and economic construction of scarcity through the exploitation of labor and the unequal distribution of wealth, Riley's team is also coming to the town to gather resources. If the zombies serve as a figure for the exploited workers of the underdeveloped world, then there is a clear sense in which they are being eaten as well. Marx's understanding of how commodities are produced makes this process more explicit. According to Marx, commodities are a form of "dead labor," that is to say, they represent living flesh transformed into a fetishized commodity available for consumption. Understood in this sense, those who consume commodities are consumers of bodies. Consequently, Riley's raid on the town for commodities allegorically represents the Northern Hemisphere's consumption of the "dead" labor of the underdeveloped South.

The link between consumption and human exploitation is made explicit in the segment of the film in which Riley and Charlie visit what is clearly the commercial hub of the city. This area serves as a marketplace, casino, strip club, and entertainment center. Interestingly, this mini Las Vegas is the only place where the wealthy are seen mingling with the poor. The one activity that apparently unites the residents of Pittsburgh is consumption. In this section of the city, zombies and humans alike are objects for exploitation.

Zombies are used as targets for paintball guns and as props for the wealthy to pose with for pictures. However, the most overt example of exploitation is depicted when the young heroine Slack, a former soldier and prostitute who has challenged Kaufman's authority, is placed in a cage with two zombies in order to induce them to fight. The cage occupies the center of a strip club, and the spectators are placing bets on which zombie will get the food (Slack) first. In this context, the zombie fight serves as a clear example of the way in which the film uses cannibalism to characterize Western consumer culture as "a culture of excessive consumption and insatiable hunger, feeding off human bodies for profit."[18] At the same time, this segment represents a commentary upon the sexual exploitation of women as objects of consumption. The literal threat of dismemberment that faces Slack is emblematic of the process of objectification of women's bodies and the fragmentation (in this case, literal morselization) of women for economic gain. Although Slack finds herself in the cage as a result of her resistance to Kaufman, her exploitation there is merely the extension of the sexual exploitation she experiences as a prostitute. With the exception of the forms of entertainment involving zombies, the remaining ones differ in no way from what can be found in any of the gambling centers of America or elsewhere. Later in the film, when Kaufman, like any good capitalist, takes credit for the privileges of the Green as the product of his ingenuity, he points out that it was his idea to set up the gambling and other vices to keep the poorer residents off the streets. The representation of Pittsburgh's mini Las Vegas, in tandem with Kaufman's explanation of its true purpose, offers a critique of the American entertainment industry and its role as a purveyor of an ethic of consumption designed to distract the poor and exploited from their oppression and keep them from unrest and revolt. When these measures fail, Kaufman relies upon both overt and covert acts of direct violence to suppress any resistance to his regime.

Indeed, when Riley and Charlie put an end to the zombie fight and save Slack from certain death, they all find themselves in prison as a result. While in prison, they see Mulligan, a resident of Pittsburgh who has been calling for the overthrow of Kaufman, being led past. Lurking behind the apparent tranquility of the life of privilege in the Green and the fevered pursuit of consumption in Pittsburgh's commercial hub and entertainment industry, one encounters the specter of a patriarchal and totalitarian political regime driven by the vicissitudes of profit. This regime is appropriately surrounded by a wasteland that, following the logic of competition, is presided over by the last capitalist left standing. Evoking the conflict between Harry and Ben in the isolated farmhouse in *Night of the Living Dead*, *Land of the*

Dead exhibits a similar awareness "that the competitive arena of patriarchal aggression is no solution for the besieged humans."[19] Through its representation of the antagonism and conflict between the survivors in Pittsburgh, the film explores not only the institutionalized forms of violence endemic to American society, but also the violent coercion that lies in wait for those who pose an actual threat to the system.

Furthermore, the existence of a repressive military apparatus in postapocalyptic Pittsburgh serves as a means of allegorically exploring the forms of militarism that emerged in the wake of the September 11 attacks on the World Trade Center and the Pentagon. When Riley and Charlie are about to enter Pittsburgh's entertainment center, they are stopped by two guards in front of a barricade. In a remarkable image, one of the soldiers stands in front of a mural of the Statue of Liberty. The arm of Liberty's torch is outstretched and the soldier stands directly beneath and next to it. The soldier appears seamlessly nestled beside her in an image intended to demonstrate the discrepancy between the ideology of American democracy, with its promise of freedom, and the violent coercion that the system relies upon to perpetuate the exploitation of one class by another. Directly invoking the environment of New York City after 9/11, the deeper aim of the image is to point out the sham character of American democracy, a system reinforced by imperialist violence abroad and more subtle repressive measures on the domestic front, where wealth and property are protected by the threat of violence should ideology fail. These repressive measures extend beyond the borders of the United States but are justified by pointing to real or imagined threats to those borders. Unlike the soldiers who stop Riley and Charlie, who are present to exert control over Pittsburgh's poor population, the soldiers who guard the only overland access to the city play a different role. They patrol the border in order to protect the survivors of the city from the zombies. However, viewed allegorically, the fences barricading the third side of Pittsburgh signify the border between the United States and Mexico and, by extension, the underdeveloped, exploited countries of the Southern Hemisphere. The soldiers who guard the overland access to the city refer to it as the "throat." This description provides yet another image of consumption that metaphorically registers America's consumption of a disproportionate quantity of the world's resources and its exploitative relationship to the underdeveloped world. At the same time, the rigorously patrolled border allegorically represents the attempt to limit the flow of undocumented workers across the U.S./Mexican border. The threat of invasion by the zombies provides a means of representing American xenophobic anxiety about immigration. As it turns out, the zombies will not invade the city by the overland route; they will cross the water by walking on the bottom of the riverbed and emerge (literally with wet backs) on the other side.

In addition to metaphorically representing the class character of American society and the global contradictions between capital and labor, *Land of the Dead* ultimately finds a way to figuratively present socialist revolution. Early in the film Riley encounters Mulligan in the poor section of the city exhorting his fellow citizens to overthrow Kaufman, who didn't "build" Fiddler's Green but merely took it over. He goes on to point out that if they all joined together they could transform the city into a fit place for all of them to live. When he speaks to Mulligan, Riley observes that although they may be locked out of the Green, they're also locked in the city. He goes on to say that he is "looking for a world where there are no fences." If the fences signify the differences between the American ruling class, the American working class, and the classes of the underdeveloped world, Riley's statement amounts to the search for a world without classes and, by implication, a world without exploitation.

At the same time that Mulligan is involved in generating a revolt among the citizens of Pittsburgh, the zombies are pursuing a parallel revolt of their own. The assault on the city led by Big Daddy is accompanied by a process whereby the zombies begin to regain social skills from their former lives. This development of intellectual capacities signifies the growth of class consciousness among the alienated "undead." In an interesting parallel to Marx's description of class consciousness as a product of revolutionary struggle, the zombies begin to regain their humanity only when they revolt against the wealthy denizens of Pittsburgh who have been appropriating and consuming the commodities taken from their territory. The long march from their town ends with Big Daddy learning how to cross the bottom of the river. This act is preceded by an image of the crowd of zombies lined up on the river's edge, looking longingly across at the lit-up tower of Fiddler's Green at the center of the city. Figuratively, this is a powerful image of deprivation and the longing for a decent life, an image of the masses of deprived humanity looking at America with desire but also with rage at those who have exploited them. The emergence of the zombies from the river after crossing is perhaps the most frightening scene in the film and was used in the advertising trailer. The camera pans over the seemingly endless crowd of zombies as they rise from the water to begin their assault on the city. This metaphorical rebirth signifies the awakening of the masses as they develop a revolutionary consciousness. As they draw closer to the tower, the zombies begin to learn how to use tools. They begin to recover their lost humanity in the process of revolt. At one point Big Daddy even teaches a female baseball player how to use a gun, taking away the bat she is carrying and demonstrating to her how to fire the weapon.

While all of this is going on, Riley and his team have regained control over *Dead Reckoning,* and Cholo, bitten by a zombie, decides not to kill himself, claiming that he always wanted to "see how the other half lives." This satiric comment adds emphasis to the film's treatment of class, as does Cholo's confrontation with Kaufman once he has transformed into a zombie. Kaufman refers to him as a "fucking spic bastard," echoing Cholo's earlier reference to the Mexican zombie as a bastard and reinforcing the ethnic and racial dimension of the privilege enjoyed by the white residents of Fiddler's Green. As Cholo and Kaufman struggle and the zombies eat the wealthy residents of the Green, Big Daddy returns to the scene. After having earlier pumped gasoline into Kaufman's Cadillac, Big Daddy rolls a burning can down the slope of the garage and kills both Kaufman and Cholo in a massive explosion.

The killing of Kaufman and the destruction of the Green effectively abolish the economic system as well as the classes it supports. In an echo of Marx's description of the revolutionary association of the proletariat in the *Manifesto,* those who have the least to lose and the most to gain by abolishing the system, the zombies, prove to be, in a wonderfully ironic twist, the "grave-diggers" of the ruling class.[20] The allegorical revolution undertaken by the zombies is given further emphasis when it turns out that many of the poor residents of the city have survived and are led by Mulligan. Mulligan has armed himself and his companions and encourages Riley to stay and "turn this place into what we always wanted it to be." Mulligan and his companions are an allegorical representation of socialist revolution, inspired with the goal of transforming America into a place more consistent with its democratic ideals. The destruction of the wealthy center of the city along with its privileged citizens, in tandem with the survival of the city's poor inhabitants, suggests a common set of economic interests between the zombies and the impoverished inhabitants of Pittsburgh. As in Romero's earlier zombie trilogy, "the real threat to survival [proves to be] the class-based verbal savagery different characters exhibit towards each other rather than the zombies outside."[21] The common ground discovered with the zombies points toward a resolution of the global contradictions between capital and labor as well as the universal economic exploitation endemic to capitalism. The destruction of the city effectively abolishes the class system dominating the city and, in a displaced form, offers a representation of socialist revolution. Still resolved in his intention to go north to Canada, Riley is concerned about what Mulligan and his comrades might turn into in the process of rebuilding the city, a possible reference to the failures of historical communism that Mulligan optimistically responds to with a noncommittal "We'll see, won't we?"

As Riley leaves for Canada, he spares the life of Big Daddy and the retreating zombies, claiming, "They're just looking for a place to go. Just like us." With the zombies as the primary agents of change, all of the fences have been destroyed. On an allegorical level, it turns out that the most wretched of the earth, that is to say, the exploited and impoverished masses of the underdeveloped world, serve as the primary agents of this transformation. The poor and working class of the developed world follow their lead. With the departure of the zombies, class distinctions and privilege have been abolished, but it remains to be seen what kind of world will replace the capitalist one. At the same time, Riley's perception of some common interests with the zombies humanizes them and metaphorically suggests a common set of needs and desires between America and the rest of humanity in the underdeveloped world that transcends the barriers of race, class, and ethnicity. Indeed, if we understand the figure of the cannibal as Elsbeth Probyn does in her work *Carnal Appetites* as "a historicized spectre of Western appetite" offering a critique of excessive consumption that points to an "an ethics and practice of restraint,"[22] and the cannibal/zombie as a metaphor for a society in which consumption has exceeded all moral limits, then the film can be viewed as a powerful condemnation of capitalist society and its economic imperatives that require human beings to consume one another in order to survive. The final moments of the film even hint at an ethical alternative to capitalism. As *Dead Reckoning* heads north, it fires off the rest of its fireworks in an evocation of freedom that deliberately echoes Fourth of July celebrations. However, in a significant departure from other installments in this genre, the zombies turn out to be among the survivors, and the enemy is not a monster but the monstrous exploitative institutions of global capitalism. After all, in this postapocalyptic land of the dead characterized by insecurity, scarcity, and profound deprivation, the zombies have nothing to lose but their chains.

Notes

My epigraph is taken from *Land of the Dead,* dir. George A. Romero (Universal Pictures, 2005).

   1. Roger Ebert, "*Land of the Dead*: This '*Land*' is Gore Land," June 24, 2005, http://rogeregbert.suntimes.com.

2. Karl Marx and Frederick Engels, *The Communist Manifesto* (New York: Verso, 1998), 35.

3. Kirsten Moana Thompson, *Apocalyptic Dread: American Film at the Turn of the Millennium* (New York: State University of New York Press, 2007), 127–28.

4. Noël Carroll, *The Philosophy of Horror; or, Paradoxes of the Heart* (New York: Routledge, 1990), 198.

5. Tony Williams, *The Cinema of George A. Romero: Knight of the Living Dead* (London: Wallflower, 2003), 21.

6. Mimi Sheller, *Consuming the Caribbean: From Arawaks to Zombies* (New York: Routledge, 2003), 148.

7. Ebert, "*Land of the Dead.*"

8. Marx and Engels, *Communist Manifesto,* 41.

9. Karl Marx, *Capital,* vol. 1, trans. Ben Fowkes (New York: Vintage, 1977), 799.

10. Sheller, *Consuming the Caribbean,* 145.

11. Joan Dayan, *Haiti, History, and the Gods* (Berkeley: University of California Press, 1998), 37–38.

12. Sheller, *Consuming the Caribbean,* 145.

13. Ebert, "*Land of the Dead.*"

14. Louis Althusser, "Ideology and Ideological State Apparatuses," in *Lenin and Philosophy* (New York: Monthly Review, 1971), 162.

15. Marx, and Engels, *Communist Manifesto,* 37.

16. Ibid., 43.

17. Williams, *Cinema of Romero,* 93.

18. Sheller, *Consuming the Caribbean,* 148.

19. Williams, *Cinema of Romero,* 28.

20. Marx, *Manifesto,* 50.

21. Williams, *Cinema of Romero,* 131.

22. Elsbeth Probyn, *Carnal Appetites: Foodsexidentities* (New York: Routledge, 2000), 99.

The Fall of the House of Ulmer
Europe vs. America in the Gothic Vision of *The Black Cat*

Paul A. Cantor

> The American public apparently does not want us to give screen-plays a natural ending, because movie fans really do not want motion pictures like the books from which they are adapted. . . . In Europe a realistic production is considered splendid entertainment by the masses, even though it is a stark tragedy. In America, however, every picture must end with the hero and heroine dying in each other's arms. They must live happily ever after, but life isn't like that.
> —Carl Laemmle Sr.

Importing Horror

The horror story is one of the many exotic goods that Americans have traditionally imported from Europe. This was already true in American Gothic fiction in the early nineteenth century, but the situation persisted even in the twentieth century and the new medium of cinema.[1] To be sure, the horror movie seems at first to be a quintessentially American phenomenon—a rite of passage for American teenagers and a genre in which America has come to dominate the world. It is due to American movies that the faces of Dracula and the Frankenstein monster are known all around the globe. Yet both these creatures were originally the creations of European authors (Bram Stoker for Dracula and Mary Shelley for the Frankenstein monster). Even as motion picture figures, they can be traced back to European precursors in German expressionist cinema—*Nosferatu* (1922) for *Dracula* (1931), and *The Golem* (1920) and *Metropolis* (1927) for *Frankenstein* (1931).

An excellent example of the equivocally American character of the horror movie is *The Black Cat* (1934), one of the highlights of the groundbreaking series of horror movies that the Hollywood studio Universal turned out in the 1930s.[2] Several commentators regard it as one of the all-time greatest achievements in the genre.[3] As its title indicates, *The Black Cat* was intended to evoke the spirit of America's most famous native exponent of the horror story, Edgar Allan Poe.[4] But at the same time, the movie was made to capitalize on the popularity of Universal's two most famous—and exotic—horror movie stars, an Englishman named William Henry Pratt, who had adopted the very European-sounding stage name of Boris Karloff, and a Hungarian actor with the equally European name of Bela Lugosi.[5] The director of the film, Edgar G. Ulmer, was an émigré from the defunct Austro-Hungarian Empire who had worked with several German expressionist film directors, including the great F. W. Murnau.[6] The film has a European feel in all its aspects, including the art direction and the casting of the minor roles (Ulmer drew upon fellow émigrés to fill several of the parts).[7] With its abstract, geometric sets, unusual camera angles and tracking shots, and artful use of light and shadow, *The Black Cat* at times looks like pure German expressionism on the screen.[8] The musical score is one of the most remarkable in Hollywood history for its unabashed use of European classical music, with passages from Bach, Beethoven, Brahms, Chopin, Liszt, Schubert, Schumann, and Tchaikovsky, often used as Wagnerian leitmotifs to highlight the action.[9]

Thus, one of the greatest of American horror movies appears, upon closer inspection, to be European through and through. Moreover, the film turns out to have Europe as a theme. It stages a confrontation between the Old World and the New and attempts to define the one way of life by comparison with the other. Ulmer draws upon the European Gothic tradition to create a ruined castle for the twentieth century, a haunted house shadowed by the new horrors of the modern world, specifically the nightmare of the Great War, 1914–18. Faced with the task of creating an American horror movie, Ulmer had a brilliant idea. He realized that if Americans wanted to see something horrific in 1934, all they had to do was to look across the Atlantic to a European landscape permanently scarred by World War I. But at the same time, as a sophisticated European himself, Ulmer could not avoid a certain condescension in the way he portrays his American protagonists in the film.[10] He sees something childish in his Americans, with their naïveté and lack of culture.

Ulmer thus joins a long line of Europeans who regard the United States as posing a philosophical problem, as offering an alternative to Europe as a way of life and thus a challenge to its assumptions. If Americans have been fascinated by Europe as the source of their culture, Europeans have been obsessed with America as "the child that got away," the offspring of Europe that rebelled against it and in many ways went on to surpass it, but only by taking culture in a democratic direction that Europeans, with their aristocratic traditions in the arts, looked down upon. Like many Europeans, Ulmer could not help treating Americans with a mixture of admiration and contempt. Yet in the end he seems to turn to them as the only hope of escaping, as he himself had just done, from a Europe morbidly fixated on its own conflicted past and becoming self-destructive in its obsessions. *The Black Cat* is a fascinating case study of how Europeans looked to Americans at one moment of cultural history and how Americans looked to Europeans—all in a film created by a man who, as an émigré filmmaker, was moving between the two worlds himself.[11]

The Haunted House of Edgar Ulmer

The Black Cat tells the story of Peter and Joan Alison, an American couple who have come to central Europe for their honeymoon. Boarding the Orient Express, they are thrown together in the same train compartment with a cultivated European gentleman, a Hungarian psychiatrist named Vitus Werdegast (played by Lugosi). Soon they transfer to a bus and set off with Werdegast to their hotel; he is headed for the home of an old friend, an architect named Hjalmar Poelzig (played by Karloff). In a rainstorm the bus overturns; the driver is killed and Mrs. Alison is injured; Werdegast takes the young couple to Poelzig's house. Due to this series of accidents, the Americans get caught up in a European power struggle, as Werdegast fights bitterly to revenge himself on Poelzig for wrongs done to him fifteen years earlier.

The backstory of the revenge plot emerges only gradually in the course of the movie, and it turns out to be rooted in the genuine horrors of World War I. The ill-fated bus driver sounds the keynote of the film when he narrates a grim travelogue for his passengers just before his own death: "All of this country was one of the greatest battlefields of the war. Tens of thousands of men died here. The ravine down there was piled twelve deep with dead and wounded men. The little river below was swollen, red, a raging torrent of blood."[12] The driver's catalogue of the carnage of the Great War culminates in his description of Fort Marmaros, "the greatest graveyard in the world." It turns out that Poelzig commanded Marmaros, and we later learn that he sold out the fort to the Russians, saving his own skin but sending thousands of men to their deaths and condemning the others to imprisonment in Siberia. Werdegast was one of those prisoners; after fifteen years he has returned to Hungary to get his revenge on the man who betrayed him and his country. He has tracked Poelzig down to his magnificent new home, a showcase of modernist architecture constructed on the ruins of Fort Marmaros.

Upon this very real foundation of the horrors of the war, Ulmer builds up one Gothic element upon another. Werdegast has come back not only to avenge his wrongs but also to regain his wife and daughter. After the war Poelzig told Werdegast's wife that he was dead and stole her from him, marrying her and running off with her and the daughter she had with Werdegast (both wife and daughter are named Karen). To his horror Werdegast now learns that his wife is dead; he suspects that Poelzig killed her; what he can see with his own eyes is that Poelzig has embalmed her corpse and keeps it in a display case in a room of the old fort that lies beneath his house. Earlier we have seen several other dead women mysteriously on view in the fort's nether regions. *The Black Cat* consists of a series of increasingly disturbing revelations. Eventually Werdegast learns that his daughter did not die, as Poelzig originally claimed. Instead the architect went on to marry his stepdaughter, and in the course of the film he kills her, too, intending to add her to the gruesome collection he keeps below his house.

To the Gothic motifs of necrophilia and incest, Ulmer adds Satanism to the morbid mix of Poelzig's perversions. He is the high priest of a Satanic cult, and with a Black Mass scheduled for the night of the full moon, he decides to take advantage of the accident that has brought Joan Alison within his grasp and to use her as a sacrifice in the ceremony. Much of the movie is devoted to a battle between Poelzig and Werdegast over the fate of the young and innocent Americans, played out literally and figuratively as a chess match. At the last minute Werdegast manages to rescue Joan from Poelzig's evil clutches. In the ensuing combat between them Werdegast overpowers his mortal foe with the help of his faithful servant. Together they stretch the architect out on his own embalming rack, and the crazed doctor proceeds to flay him alive, to tear the skin from his body, "slowly, bit by bit," while Poelzig can only howl like an animal. Werdegast shows the Alisons the way out of what has come to seem like a madhouse to them. He then pulls the "red switch," initiating a self-destruction sequence in the old fort, which is still thoroughly undermined with dynamite. The Americans barely escape in time to watch Werdegast achieve his revenge (though at the cost of his own life)—he blows Poelzig and his "rotten cult" sky-high.

Even in a bare summary, the plot of *The Black Cat* seems extraordinarily daring, especially for the 1930s, and one wonders how Ulmer managed to get some of the film's elements past studio censorship.[13] Such a story of father-daughter incest would still be shocking today.[14] The Black Mass is vividly realized on the screen, centering on a crooked, modernistic cross, with Ulmer making full use of every cinematic trick he had learned from German expressionist cinema. The scene would have done Murnau himself proud. But *The Black Cat* has more to offer than just its shock value. The horror of the film does not depend on monsters or special effects. It is genuinely psychological, growing largely out of Poelzig's fiendish obsessions.[15] Moreover, the horror is ultimately rooted, as we have seen, in something very real—the horror of the Great War.[16] In an interview with Peter Bogdanovich, Ulmer traced the genesis of *The Black Cat* back to a conversation he had in the 1920s with the novelist Gustav Meyrinck (best known for having written *The Golem*): "Meyrinck at that time was contemplating a play based upon Doumont, which was a French fortress the Germans had shelled to pieces during World War I; there were some survivors who didn't come out for years. And the commander was a strange Euripides figure who went crazy three years later, when he was brought back to Paris, because he had walked on that mountain of bodies. I thought it was an important subject, and that feeling was in the air in the twenties." Ulmer went on to explain that he made *The Black Cat* in order to counter falsely idealistic views of the war that had prevailed in Europe: "because I did not *believe* the literature during and after the war, on both sides: in Germany *and* in England, it was very much the heroic thing, where enemies were friends like you never saw before."[17] To show the true horror of World War I, Ulmer turned to the Gothic tradition and shaped an unnerving parable of Europe in the aftermath of a monstrous conflict, a whole continent that seems incestuously turned in upon itself, in love with death, and headed toward an orgy of self-destruction.

Chez Poelzig is immediately recognizable as the haunted house of the Gothic novel cleverly transposed to a modern setting, a sort of Bauhaus version of Castle Dracula.[18] Beginning with Horace Walpole's *The Castle of Otranto* in the eighteenth century, the Gothic novel is typically set in a ruined castle, which symbolizes the waning power of the Old Regime. The crumbling of the castle shows that the aristocracy is in decay, and yet its walls are still powerful enough to imprison a young hero and/or heroine. The castle usually has a dungeon below, where unspeakable acts can take place, forms of torture hidden from the prying eyes of the outside world. Ghosts often walk the castle's corridors, reminders of ancestral crimes committed on the premises, and it may be filled with moldy tombs and surrounded by a melancholy graveyard. The haunted castles of the Gothic novel embody the nightmare of the European Enlightenment: a powerful image of the way the Old Regime crushed freedom, of a past that stubbornly refused to let go, of a world of death that would not make room for the living.

Ulmer manages to maintain the Gothic symbolism of the haunted castle in *The Black Cat,* while adding a few modern touches of his own. As seen from afar and in interior shots, Poelzig's creation is a model of modernist architecture, with sleek lines, geometric forms, and a number of up-to-date gadgets, such as an intercom system and digital clocks. But this triumph of modernist art literally and figuratively rests upon a dark foundation. As Werdegast describes it: "The masterpiece of construction built upon the ruins of the masterpiece of destruction, the masterpiece of murder. The murderer of ten thousand men returns to the place of his crime." Poelzig's architectural wonder conceals the dungeonlike vaults of the old Fort Marmaros. It is truly a haunted house, redolent of its master's crimes, suffused with "an atmosphere of death," as Werdegast explains. In one of the most famous lines in the film, when Poelzig learns that his telephone is not functioning, he says: "You hear that, Vitus? The phone is dead. Even the phone is dead." The dynamite that lies under the fort, threatening to blow it up at any moment, is an emblem of the psychological tension between Werdegast and Poelzig that figuratively is just waiting to explode in the course of the movie.

Gothic Archetypes

The dungeonlike corridors in the depths of the old fort conceal reminders not only of Poelzig's military crimes during the war but also of his sexual crimes since. As we have seen, he keeps the embalmed corpses of women (presumably sacrifices at earlier Satanic ceremonies) on display in glass cases in the rooms of the old fort. As he explains to Werdegast about his long-lost wife: "You see, Vitus, I have cared for her tenderly and well. You will find her almost as beautiful as when you last saw her." A frightening caricature of the modernist aesthete, Poelzig is obsessed with the female form: "I wanted her beauty always." The key element in Poelzig is his possessiveness; he prefers the embalmed woman to the living one, because only in that state can he make her completely his own and enjoy her in a state of perfection forever.[19]

There is something profoundly compulsive about Poelzig's behavior. He is fixated on the past and obsessively keeps coming back to it. As Werdegast realizes, Poelzig in building his home has deliberately returned to the scene of his crime and he also collects women like trophies. In his obsessions he descends from a long line of Gothic villains who represent the dead hand of the past trying to maintain its grip on the living. He is a kind of vampire who preys upon young women and can hardly wait to drain them of their blood and make them immortal in his possession.[20] At the deepest level of the movie, this is Ulmer's symbol of the way World War I drained the lifeblood out of European culture and fixated it on death. Werdegast is just as implicated as Poelzig in this world of death. He speaks of the Russian prison he has returned from as a place "where the soul is killed slowly." Poelzig hurls this claim back at him in one of his few sympathetic speeches: "You say your soul was killed and that you have been dead all these years. And what of me? Did we not both die here in Marmaros fifteen years ago? Are we any the less victims of the war than those whose bodies were torn asunder? Are we not both the living dead?" "The living dead" is a term used of vampires—the undead—and here we see how the Gothic symbolism of *The Black Cat* merges with the very real issue Ulmer treats in the film, the way World War I scarred the European psyche. Everyone in Europe is now a victim of the Great War, caught up in the poisonous atmosphere of death it spread throughout the continent. Poelzig goes on to challenge Werdegast: "We shall play a little game, Vitus. A game of death, if you like." In Ulmer's portrayal, postwar Europe has become the grim playing field for a grand—and gruesome—game of death.

The vampire motif of *The Black Cat* is linked to the motif of father-daughter incest, another one of the disturbingly Gothic elements in the film. Incest epitomizes the transgressive force of the Gothic, its implacable urge to go beyond all boundaries, especially the bounds of conventional law and morality. Incest generally comes in two forms in the Gothic, with opposed symbolic valences: brother-sister incest and father-daughter incest. Brother-sister incest is symbolically rebellious—it represents the revolt of the younger generation against the older, the breaking of a fundamental taboo in a quest for absolute happiness (the perfect union of like with like). One finds this symbolism throughout Romantic poetry and fiction, especially in the writings of Lord Byron, and the motif culminates in truly operatic fashion in the Siegmund-Sieglinde story of Richard Wagner's *Die Walküre*. Father-daughter incest reverses the symbolic thrust of brother-sister incest. It represents the unwillingness of the older generation to yield to the younger. The father who sexually possesses his own daughter is refusing to turn her over to the next generation and allow her a life of her own. If brother-sister incest represents all the revolutionary forces that were sweeping through Europe from the late eighteenth century on, father-daughter incest represents the Old Regime against which they were rebelling.

Percy Shelley's play *The Cenci* is a good example of the Romantic archetype of father-daughter incest. Filled with Gothic paraphernalia of dungeons and prisons, the play tells the story of Beatrice Cenci, an innocent young maiden who is raped by her father, the vicious Count Cenci. Symbolically linked with the Catholic Church through his alliance with the pope, the aristocratic Cenci is a perfect image of the Old Regime in all its oppressive power and obsession with stifling the live-giving forces of the young. Cenci is a kind of vampire, unnaturally prolonging his own vital force by preying upon his daughter.[21] By the same token, vampirism is symbolically a form of father-daughter incest, as is clear in the Dracula myth in its many incarnations. Count Dracula—another predatory aristocrat—represents an older generation that will not make room for the new. The vampire is an older man who exerts a hypnotic fascination over a young woman, thereby coming between her and the young man she has fallen in love with. Using the greater sophistication that comes with age, the aristocratic vampire makes the young boyfriend look callow by comparison and attracts away the young woman. Dracula comes to her at night and merges with her in her bed, mixing his blood with hers and thereby artificially prolonging his own life. The sexual symbolism of the vampire has long been recognized, and its political symbolism as well. It is no accident that in traditional vampire stories the monster is always an aristocratic figure: *Count* Dracula.[22] As an undead creature, centuries old, emerging out of a ruined castle to suck the blood of the young, the figure of the vampire sums up the Gothic nightmare of a revolutionary Europe haunted by frightening memories of its aristocratic past, a past that simply refuses to die.

The traditional vampire myth splits the ambivalent image a young woman has of her father into its two "pure" sides—the benevolent and the malevolent parent. A woman is likely to have mixed feelings about her father. Insofar as he nurtures her, she looks up to him, but insofar as he stands in the way of her independence in life—her marriage to a younger man—she fears him. The vampire is the "evil twin" in the father archetype, the parent who will not allow his children to flourish on their own. As is clear in Bram Stoker's original *Dracula* and in many of the film versions of the story, the myth typically pairs the vampire with an opponent who represents everything good about the older generation, a benevolent father figure. In Stoker's version, Abraham Van Helsing, though obviously not the same age as Dracula, still stands for the older generation, and he must use its greater wisdom not to prey upon the young but to nurture them and liberate their energies. In contrast to Dracula, Van Helsing does not show a sexual interest in the young women he is called upon to protect. Instead he labors to thwart the vampire's designs upon them and to free them from his spell. The enduring power of the vampire myth rests partly on the way it captures the intergenerational psychodynamics of family life.

Strictly speaking, *The Black Cat* is not a vampire story, but it seems reasonable to think that a movie coming out of Universal and starring Bela Lugosi might show the influence of *Dracula*. The pairing of Poelzig and Werdegast is modeled on that of Dracula and Van Helsing. Poelzig is the evil father archetype. He has married his own daughter, and he keeps Karen Werdegast imprisoned in his house. Evidently he will not even allow her out of the bedroom, and he kills her when he discovers that she has disobeyed him and crossed its threshold. Symbolically, for Joan Alison he plays the role that Dracula does for the young women in his story. Although frightened by him, Joan also seems fascinated by his aristocratic bearing and his sophistication (her husband offers Poelzig little competition in these areas). Clearly Poelzig means to possess her and prevents her from leaving his home. Thus it becomes necessary for Werdegast to help her, using the wisdom that comes with age to free her from Poelzig's spell (it is appropriate, then, that Vitus is a psychiatrist). The callow young man she loves, Peter Alison, has no chance of saving her on his own. Thus, in the symbolic pattern of *The Black Cat,* Werdegast at first sight seems to represent the good side of the parent archetype—during the film's crisis he addresses Joan as "dear child"—with Poelzig representing the evil side.[23]

The Black Cat complicates this simple opposition by suggesting that, deep down, Poelzig and Werdegast are mirror images of each other. Unlike Van Helsing in *Dracula,* Werdegast does at times display a sexual interest in the young woman he is supposed to protect. In the early scene in the train compartment, a dozing Peter Alison opens his eyes to catch Werdegast caressing his wife's hair. Werdegast hastily explains that she reminds him of his own wife, Karen. Since "Karen" is also the name of his daughter, one can say that in his attraction to Joan, Werdegast, like Poelzig, is confusing his daughter with his wife. In any case, he is showing interest in a woman young enough to be his daughter. Evidently, in the original shooting script, Werdegast was an even more ambiguous figure, explicitly battling with Poelzig to possess Joan.[24] Even in the film as it has come down to us, both Peter and Joan at one point or another regard Werdegast as in league with Poelzig and hence as their enemy. In his obsessiveness, he becomes a double for Poelzig. He is also fixated on the past, and by the end of the film Werdegast is just as crazed as his antagonist, and ultimately just as destructive.

Innocents Abroad

The genius of *The Black Cat* lies in the way it maps the Gothic psychodynamics of the family onto a political landscape. At the heart of the film stands a conflict between the older and the younger generations, and the older generation must destroy itself if the younger is to be freed. What is fascinating about the film is the way Ulmer identifies the older generation with Europe and the younger with America, thus creating an allegory of European-American relations in the post–World War I era. America is the child of Europe, but a child that needs to get free of its parents, or go down to destruction with them. Poelzig represents the Satanic fascination of the European past, the force of the undead trying to draw the youth of America into its vampiric grasp. Werdegast represents a more benign aspect of European culture, willing to let America go free. Poised between these two antagonists, the Americans are presented as naive and unsophisticated compared to the Europeans.[25] When Werdegast asks Joan Alison if she has ever heard of Satanism, she stares at him with a blank expression, as if to say, "What in the world are you talking about?" The Americans have evidently led sheltered lives and have been shielded from the kinds of shattering experiences the Europeans have undergone, especially in the war. In comparison with the world-weary Europeans the Americans seem like children. Implicitly drawing a contrast with his American guests, Poelzig reproaches Werdegast: "Come, Vitus, are we men or are we children?" Werdegast is capable of cold-bloodedly skinning alive a fellow human being; Peter Alison winces when he simply has to watch the doctor injecting his wife with a sedative. Although the Americans are genuinely frightened by what they see of the Europeans, in their ignorance and superficiality they tend to laugh off whatever seems foreign and strange to them. Unable to pronounce a German umlaut, Joan jokingly refers to Poelzig as "Mr. Pigslow."[26] But Hjalmar turns out to be nothing to laugh about. The Americans in the film may think that they are in a comedy—they are, after all, on their honeymoon—but they have in fact wandered into a tragedy, a deeply European tragedy that they, as Americans, are incapable of understanding. In a strange way, *The Black Cat* fits into the familiar American genre of "innocents abroad" (to use the title of one of Mark Twain's works). Already in the nineteenth century, American authors such as Nathaniel Hawthorne and Henry James were exploring the impact of European culture on Americans who travel across the Atlantic. Ulmer's trick was to reconfigure the "innocents abroad" theme by developing it in the context of a horror story out of the European Gothic tradition.

The most striking fact about the Americans in *The Black Cat* is the amount of time they spend unconscious. They are barely able to stay awake throughout most of the film. Both Joan and Peter fall asleep in the opening sequence in the train compartment. Joan is knocked out in the bus crash and must be carried unconscious to Poelzig's house. That night the Alisons are both shown sleeping, while the wide-awake Werdegast and Poelzig begin their cat-and-mouse game. Given a "powerful sedative" by Werdegast to help her rest, Joan seems to be sleepwalking when she first gets up and meets Poelzig. Speaking later of the bus crash, she says: "I don't remember anything after that." She faints twice in the course of the action; Peter is knocked unconscious twice, first by Werdegast's servant and then by Poelzig's major-domo. The suggestion seems to be that Americans are largely unconscious of what is happening in Europe. As an émigré to the United States, Ulmer may have wanted to give Americans a wake-up call about the European tragedy. His movie points to a genuine horror in Europe, a continent still playing out the feuds that sparked the First World War, making Europe a dangerous powder keg of violence just waiting to explode again.[27] *The Black Cat* suggests that, unfortunately, Americans would not recognize a European horror story even if they wandered right into the middle of it. With World War II breaking out in Europe barely five years after *The Black Cat,* Ulmer turned out to be truly prophetic about the potential for catastrophe.[28]

The contrasts Ulmer develops between Europeans and Americans are not all to the advantage of the latter. To be sure, the Europeans in *The Black Cat* are deeply neurotic, obsessive-compulsive, and self-destructive, not to mention downright evil and even Satanic, while the Americans are free, open, good-natured, and optimistic. But at the same time the Europeans are simply more interesting than the Americans. The Europeans are intelligent, cultured, and artistic, while the Americans are bland, prosaic, and more than a little bit obtuse. This contrast emerges clearly when Poelzig, Werdegast, and Peter Alison formally introduce themselves to each other. Poelzig is "one of Austria's greatest architects" and Werdegast is "one of Hungary's greatest psychiatrists." Alison's introduction starts off auspiciously but quickly collapses; he describes himself as "one of America's greatest writers—of unimportant books." Alison is in fact a writer of mass-market mysteries, and the film implicitly contrasts his cheap melodramatic stories with the genuine European tragedy that unfolds before his uncomprehending eyes.[29] Ulmer develops the European/American contrast along the lines of a high culture/pop culture contrast. The Europeans are consistently associated with high culture; they perform elaborate rituals in Latin to the music of J. S. Bach. Alison's roots, by contrast, are in American pulp fiction, and he seems bewildered by the rarefied aesthetic environment he encounters in Europe.

Confronted, for example, with the brilliance of Poelzig's architectural achievement in the modernist house, Alison says to Werdegast: "I suppose we've got to have architects, too, but if I wanted to build a nice, cozy, unpretentious insane asylum, he'd be the man for it." Alison's low assessment of Austrian modernism actually displays a good deal of American common sense. Poelzig *is* mad, and his house reflects his mania. Still, there is a strong element of cultural philistinism in Alison's failure to appreciate the subtleties of Poelzig's art. On a simple level, Hjalmar must show Peter how to use a stylish art deco radio (and what comes on is Schubert's *Unfinished Symphony*). On a more profound level, Alison proves blind to the depth of the evil all around him. Listening to talk of the black cat and its connection to deathless evil, Alison can only say: "Sounds like a lot of supernatural baloney to me." In another one of the film's most famous lines, Werdegast pointedly replies: "Supernatural, perhaps; baloney, perhaps not." Then, echoing Hamlet's famous words to Horatio, Vitus adds: "There are more things under the sun," calling attention to Alison's limited horizons. In Ulmer's vision, American innocence and optimism keep passing over into a dangerous ignorance and naïveté.

The contrast between Europeans and Americans is neatly summed up in the fact that Werdegast and Poelzig play chess, while Alison can merely claim that he "used to play a very good hand of poker." Ulmer emphasizes the cultural superiority of Europe by representing it in terms of Bauhaus architecture and Freudian psychoanalysis, two avant-garde movements that had come out of Europe and were being introduced into the United States in the 1930s, largely as a result of European émigrés like Ulmer himself. Psychoanalysis and modernism in architecture were still rather exotic phenomena for the kind of audience Ulmer could expect for *The Black Cat*, and he does a good job of connecting the two. Poelzig's house is at one and the same time a representative of modern architecture and a kind of Freudian symbol. The gleaming house up above, with its geometric structure, represents the rational ego; the dungeonlike fortress down below, with all its darkness and grim reminders of Poelzig's madness, represents the hidden depths of irrationality in the id.[30]

Coming from the world of the Austro-Hungarian Empire, Ulmer no doubt admired the extraordinary achievements of his compatriots in the fields of architecture and psychoanalysis.[31] Yet the complexity of *The Black Cat* can be seen in the way that Ulmer quite perceptively links both phenomena to the aftermath of World War I and even suggests that there is something potentially Satanic about them. The unprecedented new opportunities that arose for architects to rebuild Europe after World War I

Bela Lugosi (as Dr. Vitus Werdegast) and Boris Karloff (as Hjalmar Poelzig) in *The Black Cat* (1934). Directed by Edgar G. Ulmer. (Universal Pictures/Photofest)

were sadly linked to the unprecedented scale of the destruction the war had caused throughout the continent. In that sense, as we have already seen in Werdegast's description of Poelzig's house, modernist architecture rested on the ruins left by the Great War. Moreover, the radical character of the break modernist architects made with traditional styles and modes of building reflected their profound disillusionment with the whole of Western civilization. The cultural traditions of Europe had failed to halt the catastrophe of the Great War; many Europeans wondered at the time if perhaps these traditions had even contributed to it. The contempt that modernists in all the arts displayed for traditional culture was rooted in their sense that it had let Europe down in a crisis. That is why there was a strong strain of nihilism in European modernism, even in its architecture, which seemed concerned as much with tearing down the old Europe as with building a new one.[32]

The war similarly gave a new impetus to psychoanalysis. Could this new science account for the violence that had suddenly taken the whole continent of Europe by surprise? Surely there was something lurking undiscovered in the depths of the human psyche that people had been unaware of. Psychoanalysts began to probe beneath the surface of the human mind in an effort to uncover the hidden sources of violent behavior and war. It is no accident that Freud's *Group Psychology and the Analysis of the Ego* came out in 1921. With his theory of the primal horde, the Austro-Hungarian scientist was seeking, among other things, an explanation for the catastrophe that had just befallen Europe. The thrust of Freudian psychoanalysis was to suggest that irrational, aggressive impulses are always lurking just below the surface of the rational ego, even in ordinary, law-abiding citizens.

Appropriately as the work of an Austrian and a movie that features a psychiatrist, *The Black Cat* reflects this Freudian understanding of the human psyche.[33] Two respected professionals, a doctor and an architect, turn out to be monstrously mad, harboring murderous impulses. What is extraordinary about the Black Mass scene is the utter ordinariness of the participants. The men all appear to be respectable members of society; in their evening clothes, they look mostly like middle-class businessmen. The women look just as decent; we see nothing of the stereotype of the grotesque witch in the scene. As the participants in the Black Mass put on their robes, they could be getting ready for a college commencement. Ulmer's point seems to be that the most ordinary human beings can be hiding Satanic impulses in their breasts.[34] But this kind of psychoanalytic insight can itself be demonic. In seeking out the causes of evil and perversion, psychoanalysis gives us a glimpse into the abyss, and risks unnerving and disorienting us with its revelations of human depravity. A strain of nihilism thus links modern architecture and psychoanalysis in the film, symbolically reflected in the way that Poelzig and Werdegast form mirror images of each other. For much of the film they act like opponents, but eventually Werdegast gets caught up in his rival's cult.[35] Representing the new cultural aristocracy of modern Europe, architect and psychiatrist are both Satanic. That is how Ulmer carries the Gothic tradition forward into the twentieth century. In a strange way, Ulmer portrays European high modernism as rooted in the horrors of World War I and, as a result, bordering on the brink of madness, ready to plunge into a nihilistic abyss.

We come away from *The Black Cat,* then, with a very disturbing and conflicted response. We have sensed that, compared to Peter and Joan Alison, Werdegast and Poelzig have seen much deeper into human life. But we are not convinced that the Austro-Hungarians are better off for all their insights into the depths of human evil. They seem to have been corrupted by their encounter with evil, perhaps even driven insane. The Americans might be all the healthier for turning their backs on this glimpse into the heart of darkness. Early in the film Peter Alison has already sensed that something has gone terribly wrong with his honeymoon and vows never to leave North America again and expose himself to European horrors: "Next time I go to Niagara Falls." The epilogue to the film stresses the limited character of American experience, the way its horizons are closed off from the European experience of tragedy and remain confined to the commonplace and everyday. Returning on a train from his ordeal, Peter finds a newspaper review of his latest thriller, *Triple Murder:* "Mr. Alison has in a sense overstepped the bounds in the matter of credibility. These things could never by the furthest stretch of the imagination actually happen. And we would wish that Mr. Alison would confine himself to the possible, instead of letting his melodramatic imagination run away with him." Ulmer is obviously having fun with his audience here, using the cheap melodrama of Alison's fiction to set off the genuine European tragedy he has just portrayed in his movie.[36] Indeed, "there are more things under the sun" than the world of American popular fiction comprehends. By confining itself to the possible, which is to say the everyday, that fiction cuts itself off from the darker aspects of human existence that European culture has for centuries been daring to explore. As a novelist, Peter Alison is no Dostoyevsky.

Ulmer seems to be self-conscious about his own peculiar position—working in the pop culture genre of the horror movie while trying to tell a deeply serious tale of European tragedy. That may be why he chooses to thematize the subject of pop culture vs. high culture in his movie. He shows that, as Americans, his hero and heroine cannot understand the very story that Ulmer as a European has tried to tell. And yet in a sense he suggests that Americans would be better off turning away from the tragedy of Europe. The ability of Americans to build a better future seems to depend on their shutting themselves off from the tortured European past. Peter and Joan share a remarkable talent for forgetting, of going through the most horrific experiences and remaining unscathed and unscarred. At the end of what ought to have been a deeply traumatic experience for them, they are prepared to laugh it off and go on with their lives. In this respect they contrast sharply with the Europeans Werdegast and Poelzig, who go to their destruction precisely because they cannot forget the past and move on.

Under European Eyes

In the end *The Black Cat* is an oddly self-reflexive film and in that sense can be considered philosophic. As an American film made by a European that deals with the differences between America and Europe, it is a work that in effect meditates on its own origins. Ulmer was a European émigré making a film for the American market, and he drew upon everything that he learned from European cinema to do so. The film becomes strangely autobiographical, or at least self-referential, dealing with what it means to move between Europe and America. Working on the film made Ulmer acutely aware of his European cultural heritage, and yet he chose to portray how problematic that heritage had become by the 1930s for Americans, whose best hope lay in looking forward rather than back in history. The film is a kind of elegy to a European high culture that seemed to have killed itself off in the cataclysm of World War I and its aftermath. But it is also a tribute to Ulmer's new homeland, the United States, with all its optimism and moral decency, and what he hoped might be its immunity to the European disease of corrosive nihilism.

Ulmer's conflicted feelings about his own film surface in what was originally intended to be the ending of *The Black Cat:* "The film ends on a light note, but the ultimate in-joke never made the release print. When the Alisons hail a passing bus, the driver was scripted as being none other than Edgar Ulmer, disguised in white beard and goggles. Speaking in Austrian [*sic*], he eyeballs the couple and shakes his head contemptuously. 'Will you take us to Vizhegrad?' asks Peter. 'I'm not going to Vizhegrad,' replies Ulmer. 'I'm going to a sanitarium to rest up after making *The Black Cat* in fourteen days!'"[37] Here is cinematic self-reflexiveness with a vengeance—a moment straight out of Mel Brooks's bag of tricks, rather than F. W. Murnau's. With its postmodern archness, this epilogue would have broken the dark mood of the film in a way that the playful scene that really ends it does not.[38] Still, in this projected epilogue, we do catch something of Ulmer's self-consciousness about working in the world of American pop culture. Having grown up in the very different world of European high modernism, he is now in Hollywood making a crazy horror movie on an absurdly short shooting schedule, and it has driven him nearly crazy himself. We can feel both Ulmer's humorous sense of detachment from his work on the film and his concern that the pressures of filmmaking can lead a true artist to madness. Ulmer shows that he is aware that *The Black* Cat is merely a work of mass entertainment, and yet at the same time he hints at how obsessively he labored on it. His mixed feelings about being a European artist working in American pop culture seem to cry out in this would-be comic epilogue.[39]

Ulmer is not unique in his ambivalent view of America from a European perspective. Many European observers over the years have shared his sense that democratic America has purchased its freedom from the nightmares of Europe's aristocratic and conflicted past only at the expense of its cultural development. In perhaps the best analysis ever written of the United States, Alexis de Tocqueville, writing in the nineteenth century in his *Democracy in America,* argues that Americans will have a difficult time equaling European cultural achievements in the arts and sciences.[40] The European tradition of dwelling upon America's lack of high culture continued unabated into the twentieth century, in such movements as the Frankfurt School critique of mass entertainment in the United States as a soul-destroying culture industry.[41]

To focus on a single extreme example: in Martin Heidegger's thought, America functions as an image of everything that Europe is not. It may seem bizarre to link a horror movie like *The Black Cat* with the author of *Being and Time,* and yet the symbolic geography of Heidegger's philosophy bears a curious resemblance to the imaginative map of Ulmer's film. Like Ulmer, Heidegger sees Europe as poised between two hostile and uncomprehending world powers, Russia to the east and America to the west.[42] And also like Ulmer, Heidegger sees Europe as tragically on the brink of perishing of its own self-destructive tendencies: "This Europe, in its ruinous blindness forever on the point of cutting its own throat, lies today in a great pincers, squeezed between Russia on one side and America on the other. From a metaphysical point of view, Russia and America are the same; the same dreary technological frenzy, the same unrestricted organization of the average man."[43] Heidegger's equation of Russia and America may seem odd, but it rests on the idea that these two gigantic nations became the bastions of the common man and antiaristocratic leveling in the twentieth century, and thus threatened to undermine centuries of authentic European culture. Heidegger's vision is actually far more extreme than Ulmer's, and yet in Werdegast's account of World War I and his Siberian imprisonment, *The Black Cat* does present Russia as an even more immediate threat to European culture than America; its prison system has destroyed the soul of a cultivated central European like Werdegast.

Heidegger dwelled upon the dual threat to Europe from the East and the West:

We have said: Europe lies in a pincers between Russia and America, which are metaphysically the same, namely in regard to their world character and their relation to the spirit. What makes the situation of Europe all the more catastrophic is that this enfeeblement of the

spirit originated in Europe itself. . . . All things sank to the same
level. . . . Intelligence no longer meant a wealth of talent, lavishly
spent, and the command of energies, but only what could be learned
by everyone. . . . In America and in Russia this development grew
into a boundless etcetera of indifference and always-the-sameness.
. . . Since then the domination in those countries of a cross section
of the indifferent mass has become . . . an active onslaught that
destroys all rank.[44]

Heidegger spoke these words originally in a lecture delivered at the University of Freiburg in the summer of 1935, that is, roughly one year after
Ulmer created *The Black Cat*. As different as the German philosopher and
the Austrian/American filmmaker undoubtedly were, when they looked at
the world in the 1930s, they seem to have shared a common sense of European culture in peril.[45] Both Heidegger and Ulmer saw the decaying of the
aristocratic culture of Europe as proceeding hand in hand with the rise of a
democratically leveling culture in the great non-European world powers of
the day. With Heidegger in mind, we begin to find something ominous in
the way Ulmer portrays the blandness of his Americans in *The Black Cat*. On
the meta-level in the movie, American pop culture is obliterating European
high culture—the mass-produced mystery novel is taking the place of the
European high Gothic.

The European ambivalence toward the New World is encapsulated in a
brief poetic tribute to America written by Johann Wolfgang von Goethe in
1827 called "To the United States":

America, you're better off than
Our continent, the old
You have no castles which are fallen
No basalt to behold.
You're not disturbed within your inmost being
Right up till today's daily life
By useless remembering
And unrewarding strife.

Use well the present and good luck to you
And when your children begin writing poetry
Let them guard well in all they do
Against knight- robber- and ghost-story.[46]

Drawing upon the same Gothic conventions, Goethe contrasts Europe with America in exactly the terms Ulmer uses in *The Black Cat*. Goethe certainly seems to be celebrating the fledgling United States precisely for the way it differs from Europe. With its castles in ruins, Europe is the land of the dead past; for Goethe, America is the land of the living present. Europe remains in the grip of unproductive memories and "unrewarding strife." Cut off from the nightmares of the European past, America will have the freedom to shape the future. But a hint of condescension is mixed with Goethe's admiration for the United States. When he thinks of Americans, he thinks of children. He hopes that they will be spared from the nightmare of ghost stories (*Gespensterge-schichten*) as well as tales of knights (*Ritter*) and robbers (*Räuber*). Yet Goethe's friend and colleague Friedrich von Schiller was famous for a play called *Die Räuber*, and what is Goethe's own masterpiece, *Faust*, if not the greatest of all *Gespenstergeschichten*? The European imagination had in fact fed itself for generations precisely on tales of knights, robbers, and ghosts. Goethe's brief ode to the United States thus quietly sounds a cautionary note. The absence of castles in America points to something lacking in its imaginative horizons. Without antique monuments—a meaningful past and symbols rooted in tradition—how will America find nourishment for its artistic imagination?

Drawing upon European sources of inspiration for an American horror movie, Ulmer was perhaps troubled by the same question. He suggests that Americans might do well to sever their cultural ties to Europe, but at the same time he demonstrates exactly how important those ties have always been to the flourishing of culture in America. We think of Hollywood as an American institution, and yet a look at the film community in the 1930s shows it populated by boatloads of European directors, cinematographers, screenplay writers, actors and actresses, and technicians, without whom the movie industry as we know it would have been impossible. Ulmer hoped to warn Americans against their cultural links to Europe, and yet in *The Black Cat* he introduced them to strange new European imports, such as Bauhaus architecture and Freudian psychoanalysis. Along with all the other European émigrés who directed horror movies in the 1930s, he helped make the avant-garde cinematic techniques of the German expressionists part of the Hollywood mainstream. In the end Ulmer's project in *The Black Cat* is internally contradictory—to create a very European movie to argue for the cultural independence of America. Fortunately for him and us, this self-defeating quest resulted in a horror movie masterpiece, an unusually thoughtful product of pop culture that philosophically reflects on the relation of pop culture to high culture.

Notes

My epigraph is taken from Gary D. Rhodes, "'Tremonstrous' Hopes and 'Oke' Results: The 1934 Reception of *The Black Cat*," in *Edgar G. Ulmer: Detour on Poverty Row,* ed. Gary D. Rhodes (Lanham, MD: Lexington, 2008), 303. Laemmle, the founder and head of Universal Pictures, was responding to questions about why *The Black Cat* did not follow the Edgar Allan Poe story on which it claimed to be based.

1. For a concise account of the European Gothic tradition and its transformation in nineteenth-century American fiction, see the chapter "Charles Brockden Brown and the Invention of the American Gothic" in Leslie A. Fiedler, *Love and Death in the American Novel* (Normal, IL: Dalkey Archive, 1997), 126–61.

2. For an overview of Universal's contribution to the horror movie genre, see Tom Weaver, Michael Brunas, and John Brunas, *Universal Horrors: The Studio's Classic Films, 1931–1946,* 2nd ed. (Jefferson, NC: McFarland, 2007); and John T. Soister, *Of Gods and Monsters: A Critical Guide to Universal Studio's Science Fiction, Horror and Mystery Films, 1929–1939* (Jefferson, NC: McFarland, 1999).

3. See, for example, Stefan Grissemann, *Mann in Schatten: Der Filmmacher Edgar G. Ulmer* (Vienna: Paul Zsolnay, 2003), 67; Gregory William Mank, *Karloff and Lugosi: The Story of a Haunting Collaboration* (Jefferson, NC: McFarland, 1990), 56, 81–82; Chris Steinbrunner and Burt Goldblatt, *Cinema of the Fantastic* (New York: Galahad, 1972), 81, 87–88; Don G. Smith, *"The Black Cat,"* in *Bela Lugosi,* ed. Gary J. Svehla and Susan Svehla (Baltimore: Midnight Marquee, 1995), 67–68, 71; and Weaver, Brunas, and Brunas, *Universal Horrors,* 95.

4. See Smith, *"Black Cat,"* 65; and Mank, *Karloff and Lugosi,* 80.

5. See Smith, *"Black Cat,"* 64–65; and Mank, *Karloff and Lugosi,* 80.

6. Like all commentators on the film, I treat *The Black Cat* as the creation of Edgar Ulmer. But as is the case with almost all movies, especially one coming out of a Hollywood studio, *The Black Cat* was a collaborative effort. On the role of Ulmer's screenplay writer, George Carroll Sims (pen names: Peter Ruric and Paul Cain), see Dennis Fischer, *"The Black Cat,"* in *Boris Karloff,* ed. Gary J. Svehla and Susan Svehla (Baltimore: Midnight Marquee, 1996), 94–95. Due to a series of accidents, studio intervention in the making of *The Black Cat* was initially minimal, and Ulmer had an unusual degree of artistic freedom in originally shaping the film. On this subject, see Fischer, *"Black Cat,"* 97. Universal did, however, intervene after Ulmer produced the rough cut, and forced him to recut the film and to reshoot certain scenes. Taking into account all these factors, critics nevertheless regard *The Black Cat* as the work of Ulmer and assume that it reflects his peculiar artistic interests and obsessions. See, for example, John Belton, *The Hollywood Professionals,* vol. 3, *Howard Hawks, Frank Borzage, Edgar G. Ulmer* (London: Tantivy, 1974), 149.

7. See Paul Mandell, "Enigma of *The Black Cat,*" in *The Cinema of Adventure, Romance and Terror,* ed. George E. Turner (Hollywood: ASC, 1989), 184.

8. See ibid., 192–93.

9. On the score, see Mank, *Karloff and Lugosi,* 56, 80; Mandell, "Enigma," 193–94;

Weaver, Brunas, and Brunas, *Universal Horrors,* 93; and Alison Peirse, "Bauhaus of Horrors: Edgar G. Ulmer and *The Black Cat,*" in Rhodes, *Edgar G. Ulmer,* 283. Ulmer's love of classical music is evident throughout his films, most famously in *Carnegie Hall* (1947). One of Ulmer's lesser films, *Isle of Forgotten Sins* (1943; also known as *Monsoon*), is redeemed only by its musical score, which is filled with quotations from Richard Wagner's operas; its deep-sea divers discover an underwater treasure of gold to the tune of the Rheingold motif from Wagner's *Das Rheingold.* Typically, Ulmer turns a B-movie into a rewriting of Wagner's Ring Cycle. For more on Ulmer and classical music, see my essay "Film Noir and the Frankfurt School: America as Wasteland in Edgar Ulmer's *Detour,*" in *The Philosophy of Film Noir,* ed. Mark T. Conard (Lexington: University Press of Kentucky, 2006), 149–50, 159n23.

10. Mank reports that on the set of *The Black Cat* Ulmer's nickname was "the aesthete from the Alps" (*Karloff and Lugosi,* 47). Ulmer's daughter remarked in an interview: "My mother always tells the story that when she married him, their honeymoon was like three weeks of her being locked in a room with him, and with him educating her! Even though she had had a very fine, 'normal' American education, it was nothing like his European culture." See Tom Weaver, "Her Father's Keeper: Arianné Ulmer Cipes," *Video Watchdog* 41 (1997): 41.

11. For the "clashing cultural dynamics" of *The Black Cat,* see Christopher Justice, "Edgar G. Ulmer: The Godfather of Sexploitation?" in Rhodes, *Edgar G. Ulmer,* 33. For a general study of Ulmer as an émigré and of the theme of exile in his films, see Noah Isenberg, "Perennial Detour: The Cinema of Edgar G. Ulmer and the Experience of Exile," *Cinema Journal* 43 (2004): 3–25.

12. I have transcribed all quotations from *The Black Cat* from the DVD version available in Universal's *The Bela Lugosi Collection* (2005).

13. On the issue of the shock value of *The Black Cat* and the role of censorship in its production, particularly Universal's initial benign neglect and later intervention in reshaping the film, see Mank, *Karloff and Lugosi,* 55, 70, 79; Mandell, "Enigma," 181–82, 184–85, 188; and Fischer, "*Black Cat,*" 91–92, 97. Ulmer had to meet with the infamous Hollywood censor Joseph Breen before going ahead with the film. On this point see David J. Skal, *The Monster Show: A Cultural History of Horror* (New York: Faber & Faber, 1993), 178; and Mark A Vieira, *Sin in Soft Focus: Pre-Code Hollywood* (New York: Harry N. Abrams, 1999), 175. Even with the cuts and reshooting ordered by Universal, *Variety* called the screen version of *The Black Cat* "a truly horrible and nauseating piece of sadism" (quoted in Fischer, "*Black Cat,*" 110). When the film was shown later in Great Britain, it was censored even further, with the devil worshipers improbably refashioned into "sun worshipers" (Fischer, "*Black Cat,*" 112).

14. Although Karen Werdegast is technically only Poelzig's stepdaughter, the incestuous implications of their marriage are very strong.

15. See Skal, *Monster Show,* 180.

16. See Grissemann, *Mann in Schatten,* 80; Skal, *Monster Show,* 177; and Dion Tubrett, "The Devil's Contract: The Satisfaction of Self-Destruction in Edgar G. Ulmer's *The Black Cat,*" in Rhodes, *Edgar G. Ulmer,* 297–98.

17. Peter Bogdanovich, *Who the Devil Made It* (New York: Alfred Knopf, 1987), 576.

18. Ulmer himself said of *The Black Cat:* "It was very much out of my Bauhaus period" (Bogdanovich, *Who the Devil Made It,* 576). See also Grissemann, *Mann in Schatten,* 70; and Bret Wood, "Edgar G. Ulmer: Visions from the Second Kingdom," *Video Watchdog* 41 (1997): 28. On architecture in the film, see Mandell, "Enigma," 186, 193; and Peirse, "Bauhaus of Horrors," 278–81. Mank claims that Poelzig's house was in fact inspired by a Frank Lloyd Wright creation, the Ennis-Brown House at 2607 Glendower Avenue in the Hollywood Hills (*Karloff and Lugosi,* 59).

19. Ulmer's fullest study of the aesthetic temperament, and its potential for horror, is *Bluebeard* (1944), the story of an artist who feels compelled to murder the beautiful models he paints. In its portrait of an artist living in poverty, forced to work for a dealer who makes more money than he does from his work, *Bluebeard* may be Ulmer's most autobiographical movie, an allegory of his own career in the film business. Steffen Hantke, "Puppets and Paintings: Authorship and Artistry in Edgar G. Ulmer's *Bluebeard,*" in Rhodes, *Edgar G. Ulmer,* 190, discusses the tensions "between the economic necessity to serve the culture industry on the one hand, and artistic ambitions on the other" in *Bluebeard.* For more on the relation of *Bluebeard* to *The Black Cat,* see Grissemann, *Mann in Schatten,* 195–207.

20. Mank reports that the original shooting script of the film speaks of "Poelzig's embalming room, where he immortalizes the bodies of his women after having immortalized their souls in other, perhaps gentler ways" (*Karloff and Lugosi,* 63).

21. On Count Cenci as a vampire, see James B. Twitchell, *The Living Dead: A Study of the Vampire in Romantic Literature* (Durham, NC: Duke University Press, 1981), 79–92.

22. For a detailed study that links Stoker's Dracula specifically to the Anglo-Irish aristocracy, see Michael Valdez Moses, "The Irish Vampire: *Dracula,* Parnell, and the Troubled Dreams of Nationhood," *Journal X* (Autumn 1997): 66–111.

23. Thus this time Lugosi got to play the Van Helsing part to Karloff's "Dracula." Determined to change his screen image, Lugosi insisted on playing a "good guy" in *The Black Cat.* See Grissemann, *Mann in Schatten,* 68; and Mank, *Karloff and Lugosi,* 53.

24. On the differences in the original script, see Mank, *Karloff and Lugosi,* 69; Mandell, "Enigma," 188; and Fischer, "*Black Cat,*" 91–92, 104, 106.

25. On the characterization of the Americans in the film, see Tubrett, "Devil's Contract," 291–93.

26. According to Mank, the movie originally contained a breakfast scene in which David Alison, like the typical Ugly American, "insults the house, Poelzig, the Hungarian language, Hungary, the food, and the servants" (*Karloff and Lugosi,* 69).

27. See Skal, *Monster Show,* 178.

28. I may seem to be giving Ulmer too much credit for prophetic powers and political seriousness in *The Black Cat.* But Mandell reports that in Ulmer's original draft of the story, a character named Frau Goering was to be included in the Black Mass scene, described as "to be played by a man, the dark fuzz on her lip suggesting

Hitler's moustache" ("Enigma," 190). This detail casts a new light on *The Black Cat* and suggests that it may have been more of a political allegory than people have supposed. As a Jewish émigré from the German-speaking world in Europe, Ulmer was undoubtedly aware of what was happening in Berlin in 1934. That fact may add a new layer of significance to Ulmer's story of Europeans haunted by their defeat in World War I, seeking revenge for the wrongs done to them, and turning to a Satanic cult leader for salvation—and ultimately being destroyed in the process. The connections to Hitler in *The Black Cat* have been noted by several critics; for example, Grissemann quotes J. Hoberman, echoing a famous book by Siegfried Kracauer and describing *The Black Cat* as "from Caligari to Hitler in one lurid package" (*Mann in Schatten*, 82). See also Tubrett, "Devil's Contract," 293.

29. As Fischer points out, the author of the screenplay of *The Black Cat*, George Carrol Sims, wrote for Hollywood under the pen name Peter Ruric, but also wrote mystery stories under the pen name Paul Cain ("*Black Cat*," 94–95). On Sims/Ruric/Cain, see also Mandell, "Enigma," 183.

30. Cf. Belton, *Hollywood Professionals*, 154. Cf. Fiedler on the symbolism of the upper and lower levels of the Gothic castle (*Love and Death*, 132).

31. There are undocumented claims that Ulmer studied architecture in his youth in Vienna. *The Black Cat* even contains an architectural history in-joke; the Karloff character is named after the well-known German architect Hans Poelzig. See Isenberg, "Perennial Detour," 4, 10. As for Ulmer's knowledge of psychoanalysis, his wife reports that Ulmer and Karloff used to talk about the subject on the set of *The Black Cat* and casually mentions: "Edgar was a Jungian." She adds that Lugosi "mistrusted the Krafft-Ebbing conversations Boris enjoyed with Ulmer" (Mank, *Karloff and Lugosi*, 67–68). Ulmer later said of his film *Strange Illusion* (1945): "I was fascinated at that time with psychoanalysis, and this story was about a father-son relationship" (Bogdanovich, *Who the Devil Made It*, 596).

32. For general reflections on this subject, see Massimo Cacciari, *Architecture and Nihilism: On the Philosophy of Modern Architecture*, trans. Stephen Sartarelli (New Haven, CT: Yale University Press, 1993).

33. For a reading of *The Black Cat* in terms of Freud's concept of the death instinct, see Tubrett, "Devil's Contract," 289–300.

34. The ordinariness of the cult members comes across in the screen version of the movie; the shooting script, by contrast, called for them to be "as odd and freakish as possible—all to have the suggestion of some kind of abnormality about them. Members, for the most part, of the decadent aristocracy of the countryside" (Mank, *Karloff and Lugosi*, 71). See also Mandell, "Enigma," 190.

35. This aspect was emphasized more strongly in the original version of the script. See Mandell, "Enigma," 188.

36. Throughout *The Black Cat* "melodrama" functions as a negative pole. Earlier in the film Poelzig reproaches Werdegast: "Of what use are all these melodramatic gestures?" Contrasting high culture with pop culture, Ulmer seems intent on distinguishing his tragic story from vulgar melodrama.

37. Mandell, "Enigma," 192; see also Mank, *Karloff and Lugosi,* 78.

38. On postmodernism in the film, see Grissemann, *Mann in Schatten,* 77.

39. Cf. Stefan Grissemann's comment on the Kino DVD documentary *Edgar G. Ulmer: The Man Off-Screen* (2004): "He loved European culture, especially high culture, which brought strange dissonances into his trivial American films."

40. For Tocqueville's view of culture in the United States, see part 1 of book 2 of *Democracy in America,* especially chapters 9–19.

41. For an excellent survey of the way European philosophers and intellectuals have viewed America, see James W. Ceaser, *Reconstructing America: The Symbol of America in Modern Thought* (New Haven, CT: Yale University Press, 1997). I explore Ulmer's relation to the Frankfurt School at length in my "Film Noir" essay. I argue that *Detour* (1945) presents a more negative view of America than *The Black Cat* does, precisely because, in Frankfurt School fashion, Ulmer measures it against the standard of European high culture, for example, contrasting jazz unfavorably with classical music, much the way Theodor Adorno did. The theme of Europe vs. America recurs throughout Ulmer's career. *Carnegie Hall* once again sets up a contrast between European classical music and American jazz but offers a more hopeful outcome, a synthesis of the two musical traditions in a Gershwin-like rhapsody that the hero is able to perform in the venerable concert hall at the end of the film. On this subject, see Tony Tracy, "'The Gateway to America': Assimilation and Art in *Carnegie Hall,*" in Rhodes, *Edgar G. Ulmer,* 211–23. One of Ulmer's last and most peculiar films—his 1958 contribution to the "nudie" genre, *The Naked Venus*—also turns on the differences between European and American culture, this time much to the disadvantage of the latter. In France people appreciate the finer things in life, including classical music, painting, and nudity, whereas Americans, in Ulmer's view, are enmeshed in puritanical attitudes that are destructive of all true art. On this subject, see Justice, "Edgar G. Ulmer," 31–34.

42. For a detailed analysis of Heidegger's view of America, see Ceaser, *Reconstructing America,* 187–213.

43. Martin Heidegger, *An Introduction to Metaphysics,* trans. Ralph Manheim (Garden City, NY: Anchor, 1961), 31.

44. Ibid., 37–38.

45. Nietzsche is undoubtedly the common link in their thought. For Nietzsche on the perilous state of Europe, particularly the menace from Russia, see, for example, section 208 of his *Beyond Good and Evil.*

46. Johann Wolfgang von Goethe, "To the United States," trans. Stephen Spender, in *The Permanent Goethe,* ed. Thomas Mann (New York: Dial, 1953), 655. For the German original, see *Insel Goethe: Werkausgabe,* ed. Walter Höllerer (Frankfurt: Insel, 1970), 1:224–25.

From Domestic Nightmares to the Nightmare of History

Uncanny Eruptions of Violence in King's and Kubrick's Versions of *The Shining*

John Lutz

> The past is never dead. It's not even past.
> —William Faulkner, *Requiem for a Nun*

> The tradition of all the dead generations weighs like a nightmare on the brain of the living.
> —Karl Marx, *The Eighteenth Brumaire of Louis Bonaparte*

> JACK TORRANCE: Mr. Grady, you were the caretaker here.
> DELBERT GRADY: I'm sorry to differ with you, sir. But you are the caretaker. You've always been the caretaker.
> —*The Shining*

Early in Stanley Kubrick's *The Shining*, Dick Hallorann assures the apprehensive Danny Torrance that there is nothing in the hotel that can actually hurt him and explains that the terrible events of the past can leave behind a trace of themselves that is visible only to those who shine. As it turns out Hallorann is profoundly mistaken. In an ironic twist, he *overlooks* the one thing in the Overlook Hotel that will eventually kill him, Danny's unstable, alcoholic father who, in the final shot of the film framing the photograph of the Fourth of July celebration in 1921, proves to have always been there. Hallorann's mistake is based on the assumption that the past has no power over the present. Nonetheless, both Kubrick's film and King's novel each investigate the complex ways in which the past acts upon—indeed, lives on in—the present. In King's novel this past manifests itself through Jack's growing abuse of Wendy and Danny, an abuse that is ultimately revealed to have its origin in Jack's victimization by his own father. In Kubrick's film the scope of victimization is much broader and encompasses the forms of systematic violence inflicted by American institutions upon oppressed and exploited groups. In effect, in Kubrick's adaptation of the novel the frightening, evil world perceived by the victim of child abuse undergoes an allegorical transposition to the nightmarish violence lying hidden in the foundations of American society. In both the novel and the film the vehicle for depicting this hidden violence is what Freud described as the uncanny, or that which "belongs to the realm of the frightening, of what evokes fear and dread."[1]

Kubrick's overt interest in Freud's work on the uncanny has been commented upon by Diane Johnson, who collaborated with Kubrick on the screenplay. Johnson notes how she and Kubrick sought explanations in the works of Freud in general, and his essay on the uncanny in particular, for the key elements that make something frightening.[2] Although it has been commented upon less frequently, some of the most terrifying moments in the novel—the jiggling handle of the door of Room 217 once Jack has locked it, the entity in the concrete ring in the snow-laden playground—conform equally to Freud's description of the uncanny. These episodes can be connected, as in Freud's analysis, with something familiar that has been repressed but returns as a terrifying element.[3] The woman in Room 217, "long dead and reclining in her bath, a bar of Lowila in one stiffening hand as she waited patiently for whatever lover might come," has a clear connection to Jack's submissive and abused mother, just as the child entity Danny encounters in the concrete ring with its head split open, "crawling after him in the dark, grinning, looking for one final playmate in its endless playground" evokes the history of child abuse lurking beneath the appearance of normality in the Torrance family.[4] In each case, the past is, to paraphrase William Faulkner's frequently quoted assessment of history, neither dead nor past but a concrete material force constantly threatening to emerge in the present. A similar process is at work in Kubrick's film, where evil is consistently represented as "a disembodied, vague state of cosmic affairs" and "the world as an evil and forbidding place" where violence can erupt unexpectedly at any moment.[5] As Brigitte Peucker points out in her analysis of the uncanny in Kubrick's film, "The ghost materializes and is revealed to have a body; Kubrick's uncanny is decidedly corporeal."[6] Indeed, Kubrick's use of the uncanny is concerned with rendering the past corporeal and registering the ways in which the nightmare of history continually impinges upon and defines the present. Taken together, both King's novel and Kubrick's film adaptation explore psychological, historical, and economic traces of the uncanny. These three interrelated aspects of the uncanny are woven together thematically through the narrative of domestic abuse, the postcolonial narrative of American expansion at the expense of nonwhite victims, and the desire for power and control that underlies commodification and the social hierarchies that reinforce it.

King's Inverted Family Romance

In his comments upon the process of translating works of literature to the screen, Kubrick suggests that the most adaptable novels are ones that have an overt concern with the inner lives of their characters.[7] Since King's novel focuses on the inner life of its three central characters as well as the inner life of the family they comprise, Kubrick undoubtedly found it ideal for adaptation. From the very first line of the novel, when Jack inwardly assesses Stuart Ullman as an "officious little prick" (3) while outwardly flashing his "big wide PR smile" (4), King invites the reader to consider the disjunction between the inner and outer worlds of his characters and privileges the inner one as the most significant indicator of identity. Like his father, Danny, too, experiences a profound gap between his inner and outer life. On the surface he appears to be a normal young boy playing with his toys. Nonetheless, his inner life is shot through with anxieties and fears focused upon the marital ambivalence of his parents and the hidden tension between them to which his ability to "shine" gives him privileged access. Danny's anxieties are clearly centered upon his unpredictable, abusive father whose alcoholism, professional failures, and self-doubts have initiated a crisis in the family that is subject to repression but continually returns in the periodic reminders of the episode in which Jack dislocated Danny's shoulder. At the same time the novel provides numerous examples of how Danny's gift of insight initiates a process of learning about the world beyond his family that contributes to his ongoing psychological development. This process includes an element of estrangement from his parents as he encounters other adults like Dick Hallorann, with whom he shares the gift of shining.

Indeed, in many ways Danny's experiences at the hotel conform to the period of a child's development that Freud characterized by the term "family romance." In this developmental stage, "the child's imagination is occupied with the task of ridding himself of his parents, of whom he now has a low opinion, and replacing them by others, usually of superior social standing." Freud goes on to note that this activity usually manifests itself in daydreams in which the child aims to replace the real father with a more distinguished one. Freud viewed this imaginative recasting of the family not as an indication of the child's desire to actually replace the father but as "an expression of the child's longing for the happy times gone by, when his father seemed to him the strongest and most distinguished of men, and his mother the dearest and loveliest of women."[8] In other words, the family romances of children represent a desire to return to the past when they were still capable of completely idealizing their parents. Even though the novel's depiction of Jack and Wendy's relationship before the birth of Danny points out that the roots of their marital problems existed from the very beginning, from Danny's perspective this ideal moment is clearly the period before his father dislocates his shoulder. However, as the subsequent events in the hotel will indicate, the ideal past to which Danny wishes to return is not what it seems. Rather than rediscovering the good qualities of his real father through his imagination, he discovers a monster, an ogre whose future violence Danny glimpses early in the novel when Jack arrives home in his Volkswagen and Danny sees "a short-handled mallet, its head clotted with blood and hair" (49), beside him on the front seat. In this sense King's novel fails to conform to Freud's pattern of family romance. Although it quite obviously explores the motif of father-mirroring and the father-lost-and-regained obsession apparent in some of King's other works,[9] *The Shining* represents an inverted family romance in which the daydream of the more distinguished father is replaced by the nightmare of the monstrous one. In this connection it is extremely relevant that the replacement father whom Danny eventually discovers is not someone higher on the social scale but the African American cook, Dick Hallorann. At the end of the novel, after giving Danny fatherly advice about how to get on in the world, Hallorann sits on a dock with Wendy and Danny as Danny reels in a fish. In this closing image the family unit is restored. However, in an interesting variation on the pattern of family romance, the father with the good qualities proves to be someone who, in the larger frame of American society, occupies a lower social status rather than a more distinguished one.

Dealing consistently with the theme of duality and doubleness, King's inverted family romance constructs numerous uncanny doubles who reflect the inner lives, ambivalent feelings, violent impulses, and frustrated hopes of its central characters. In his essay on the uncanny Freud points out that the duplicating, dividing, and interchanging of the self represent one source of the uncanny. Freud emphasizes that one can find embodied in the double "all the strivings of the ego that were frustrated by adverse circumstances, all the suppressed acts of volition that fostered the illusion of free will."[10] This description is particularly apt in reference to Jack, whose frustrated hopes as a writer and blocked aspirations to a higher social and economic class not only are directly linked to the appearance of psychological doubles like his father and Delbert Grady but also prove to be the foundations of the violent rage directed at his wife and son. As Thomas Allen Nelson points out, the "novel associates Jack's lapses into murderous rage with a pattern of father/son doubling, with his own father's frustration and drunken failures, and with a latent wish to punish his wife and son for his inadequacies as a man and incompetence as a writer/teacher."[11]

The connection between Jack's frustrated ego and his own past as a victim of child abuse is rendered explicit in the novel when his father's voice communicates with him on the CB radio, encouraging him to kill his wife and son:

> —kill him. You have to kill him, Jacky, and her, too. Because a real artist must suffer. Because each man kills the thing he loves. Because they're always conspiring against you, trying to hold you back and drag you down. Right this minute that boy of yours is in where he shouldn't be. Trespassing. That's what he's doing. He's a goddam little pup. Cane him for it, Jacky, cane him within an inch of his life. Have a drink, Jacky my boy, and we'll play the elevator game. Then I'll go with you while you give him his medicine. I know you can do it, of course you can. You must kill him. You have to kill him, Jacky, and her, too. Because a real artist must suffer. (341)

The reference to the cane evokes the episode described in the text when Jack's father beats his mother into unconsciousness with his cane, and although it is never overtly stated, it is implied that this is the weapon that Jack's father used to discipline him as well. In this passage all the elements of domestic abuse and the ambivalent feelings that it evokes in its victim and perpetrator alike are present. The voice of Jack's father commands him to kill his wife and son in order to enforce a form of masculine, paternal authority rooted in male domination while also suggesting that it will help fulfill his artistic aspirations. While urging him on to commit brutal violence, his father's voice simultaneously promises to reward him with the love that he never gave him. In effect, this episode presents the reader with a portrait of the child victim transformed into the adult abuser. The voice of Jack's father represents one of his uncanny doubles, a powerful trace of the past provoking feelings of frustration, helplessness, and rage that will materialize in an eruption of violence directed at his wife and son.

Danny's supernatural guardian, Tony, represents yet another uncanny double that functions as a kind of father figure for Danny as well as a source of guidance that enables him to overcome the evil forces at work in the Overlook. Tony provides one of the only sources of stability in Danny's crumbling world. When his father comes to murder him and Danny intimates that it is not really his father but a manifestation of the evil force that "had accrued, as secret and silent as interest in a bank account" (639), Tony materializes before him and is revealed as an incarnation of himself in the future: "And now Tony stood directly in front of him, and looking at Tony was like looking into a magic mirror and seeing himself in ten years, the eyes widely spaced and very dark, the chin firm, the mouth handsomely molded. The hair was light blond like his mother's, and yet the stamp on his features was that of his father, as if Tony—as if the Daniel Anthony Torrance that would someday be—was a halfling caught between father and son, a ghost of both, a fusion" (639–40). In the complete image of Tony, Danny is provided with an ideal image of self. The characteristics that he exhibits are wholly positive ones and exude a confidence and competence that ultimately elude Jack. Just as Jack and his father represent a ghostly fusion, so do Jack and Danny mirror each other since Danny is also a victim of his father's violence. Jack's victimization by his own father plays a central role in his gradual corruption. However, the supernatural forces that inhabit the Overlook Hotel, forces frequently referred to by the former caretaker Delbert Grady as the "management," are of equal importance in the process by which the feelings of inadequacy, helplessness, and rage bequeathed to him by his abusive father are turned toward violence.

As a perpetrator of violence against his own wife and two daughters, Grady represents yet another one of Jack's ghostly doubles, but the frustration upon which Grady attempts to capitalize is connected with Jack's declining financial status and failure to achieve upward mobility for himself and his family. When Grady informs Jack of his son's attempt to enlist the aid of Dick Hallorann, he offers him an opportunity for advancement in the Overlook's hierarchy:

> "And the manager puts no strings on his largesse," Grady went on. "Not at all. Look at me, a tenth-grade dropout. Think how much further you yourself could go in the Overlook's organizational structure. Perhaps . . . in time . . . to the very top."
> "Really?" Jack whispered. (535–36)

Grady's offer elicits the larger social and economic frame contributing to Jack's frustrated ego and exacerbating the suffering caused by his fractured and divided self. Dominated as a child by the masculine power and abusive paternal authority of his father, he confronts a similar form of evil in the supernatural, impersonal hierarchy of the hotel. The management offers Jack the opportunity to take his father's place. In this way the novel establishes the continuity between the private world of domestic abuse and the public world of American corporate power. Abusive paternal authority is equated with the exercise of social control by the management. This comparison is given further emphasis later, when Jack attacks Wendy with the roque mallet and insists that he will show her "who is boss around here" (564). By the same token, when Grady taunts him after Jack has been locked in the pantry by Wendy and Danny, he suggests that this "hardly sets [Jack] off as being of top managerial timber" (582). In effect, Jack chooses a course of action in which he has to prove his worth to the management of the hotel, a position that represents a mirror reflection of his relationship with his abusive father. As such, it comes as no surprise that when he goes after Dick Hallorann, he is motivated by the desire to show the hidden authority of the Overlook that he is "of *managerial timber*" (633). Just as Jack's relationship with his father was characterized by a victimizer/victim paradigm, so, too, does he find himself in a relationship of domination and submission with the management of the hotel. Offered the opportunity to raise himself in the corporate hierarchy, Jack is willing to sacrifice Danny (and Wendy) as his "ticket of admission" (581) to greater power and affluence. However, there is a duality here as well since his betrayal of his son also entails a betrayal of the victim within himself. From a divided, conflicted figure who struggles to keep the violent legacy of his past at a distance, Jack is transformed into a brutal monster obsessed with power. He becomes a faceless "company" man, mindlessly doing the bidding of the invisible bureaucratic forces occupying the hotel.

Can You Find the Indians?

In the novel Danny's awareness of these hidden forces finds expression by reference to a visual puzzle commonly given to children as a game. When Danny becomes aware that things are not in their proper place, he imaginatively compares the hotel to a picture in which one must find the hidden Indians:

> But now things had been misplaced. Things were missing. Worse still, things had been *added,* things you couldn't quite see, like in one of those pictures that said CAN YOU FIND THE INDIANS? And if you

strained and squinted, you could see some of them—the thing you had taken for a cactus at first glance was really a brave with a knife clamped in his teeth, and there were others hiding in the rocks, and you could even see one of their evil, merciless faces peering through the spokes of a covered wagon wheel. But you could never see all of them, and that was what made you uneasy. Because it was the ones you couldn't see that would sneak up behind you, a tomahawk in one hand and a scalping knife in the other. (291)

Basing his assessment of the evil lurking in the hotel upon a familiar visual puzzle, Danny unconsciously makes use of a quite common stereotypical, racist image of Native Americans in order to understand the uncanny threat of violence that he senses closing in around him. Interestingly, the image of the evil, merciless brave prepared to inflict ruthless violence upon his unsuspecting victim reverses the historical relationship between white settlers and Native Americans by transforming the victims into the victimizers. This represents another device by which King emphasizes the intergenerational legacy of domestic abuse that transforms the victim into the tyrant. However, an equally fascinating aspect of this passage concerns how Kubrick makes use of it in his film version of *The Shining* to allude to the genocide of Native Americans during the founding of the United States. Although Diane Johnson mentions Kubrick's interest in the extermination of Indian peoples, and many critics have noted the Native American motifs and images in the film, none have pointed out the connection between the reference to the visual puzzle in the novel and Kubrick's use of it in the film.[12] In effect, Kubrick takes Danny's imaginative understanding of the uncanny evil lurking in the hotel in terms of a visual puzzle and creates a visual puzzle of his own that transforms the "merciless brave" in the novel into the victim of merciless American expansion. The images of Native Americans in the film serve as an elaborate visual puzzle for the viewer, an uncanny trace of violence that represents not Native Americans as agents of evil, but the inability of America to acknowledge or come to terms with the genocide of Native Americans.

Just as in the visual puzzle in King's novel, so, too, in the film "Indians" constantly lurk in the background of the camera's frequently elaborate tracking shots, emerging only when, as in Danny's description, the viewer "strains and squints" to see them. Soon after Jack and Wendy arrive at the hotel and Stuart Ullman gives them a tour of the premises, he mentions that the Overlook Hotel was built on an old Indian burial ground. Ullman also notes that the builders were rumored to have repelled some Indian attacks during construction. When the tour passes through the Colorado Room, Wendy notices the Native American motifs on the walls and floor. Ullman points out that they are authentic Apache and Navajo designs. As the tour moves behind the central staircase—where Wendy will later confront Jack with a bat—and the camera tracks the party from the opposite side of the staircase, a portrait of a Native American is barely visible on the wall opposite the fireplace behind the stairs. When Dick Hallorann shows Wendy the food locker, a can of Calumet baking powder with a Native American chief logo is clearly visible behind him. When Wendy and Danny enter the maze and Jack seems to observe them as he hovers above the model in the Colorado Room, Wendy's hair is braided in a distinctively Native American style. When the first evidence of Jack's instability begins to emerge and he throws the tennis ball against the wall in the Colorado Room, the wall has four traditional Navajo figures painted on it. When Wendy is beginning to feel isolated and uses the CB to contact the Ranger station, she is wearing a yellow jacket with Native American motifs. In his conversation with the bartender, Lloyd, Jack alludes to "White Man's Burden," an allusion to "Rudyard Kipling and the Victorian notion of Europe's duty to civilize the 'uncivilized' nonwhite world" that conjures the period in which the Overlook was built.[13] Finally, when Jack is locked in the food locker, the Calumet cans appear once again in the background.

Most of these images are offered in a context that suggests the repetition of acts of violence. However, unlike King's novel, where the repetition of the past hinges almost exclusively upon domestic abuse, Kubrick's film maintains the core elements of domestic violence but widens the scope of the past to incorporate European and American history. While serving as an explicit focus of Jack's assault with the tennis ball, the Overlook's Navajo and Apache designs and furnishings also serve as a reminder of America's exploitation of Native Americans in the use of their cultural and religious symbolism for the purposes of decoration.[14]

At the same time, the picture of the Native American on the wall behind the staircase in the Colorado Room is located directly beneath the site at the top of the staircase where Wendy will later confront Jack with a bat. The implicit comparison between the genocide of Native Americans and the misogynistic violence Jack inflicts upon Wendy is given further emphasis by the two identical fireplaces: one behind and one at the top of the staircase. Wendy is literally standing in the same place as the Native American in the portrait below her. The violence that Jack attempts to inflict upon her signifies the enduring presence of patriarchal repression and its link to the doctrine of Manifest Destiny associated with white notions of masculinity and power. Indeed, it is in the very passage below her, behind the staircase, where Stuart Ullman informed her and Jack that "all of the best people" in the century have stayed at the Overlook. In this context Jack's efforts to "correct" Wendy and Danny represent an attempt to assert his male authority and power. As Philip Kuberski aptly puts it, for Jack the Overlook hotel represents an "opportunity to recover the lost territory of American masculinity; it is a rich man's hotel from an age of rich men, from the age of unrestricted capital expansion, before women's suffrage, the income tax, civil rights and other indignities."[15] In assaulting Wendy, Jack repeats the history of American territorial expansion in an attempt to assert his masculinity and dominance.

At the same time the mention that the hotel was built on an Indian burial ground and Indian attacks were repulsed during its construction participates in Kubrick's critique of the forms of patriarchal, racist, and class domination that have informed the original creation and reproduction of American social and economic institutions. As David A. Cook eloquently notes in his assessment of Kubrick's film, "*The Shining* is less about ghosts and demonic possession than it is about the murderous system of economic exploitation which has sustained the country since, like the Overlook Hotel, it was built upon an Indian burial ground."[16] Perhaps one of the most subtle allusions to the systematic murder of Native Americans and the forms of institutional domination that have arisen upon it occurs in the food locker when the can of Calumet baking powder appears behind Dick Hallorann's head along with other brand-name goods. Significantly, this is the first time that Dick communicates with Danny telepathically. The eerie music in the background deliberately evokes the uncanny in association with the appearance of the Calumet can in order to allude to Native American genocide. On the one hand, the use of the word *Calumet* and the Native American chief as a brand-name logo comment upon the exploitation of Native American culture for the purposes of commodity production and exchange. This idea is given further emphasis later in the film when multiple cans of Calumet baking soda appear on the shelf alongside other commodities when Jack is conversing with Delbert Grady. On the other hand, the word *calumet* itself has a great deal of significance, since a calumet is an elaborately designed pipe serving as a token of universal peace among the Illiniwek. Historically, the calumet was first presented in 1673 to Father Jacques Marquette, who founded Michigan's first European settlement. Thus, the word not only furnishes a link to the early European incursions into Native American territory (the mention of the Donner party represents another such allusion) but is also a profoundly ironic allusion to the betrayal of Native Americans through the violation of treaties often ratified by sharing a peace pipe. Finally, the racist character of such betrayals finds one of its most powerful expressions in the murder of Dick Hallorann, who will be killed on the site of a Navajo circle design in front of the cashier's cages.[17] This detail provides yet another historical trace of violence that emphasizes the continuity between the genocide of Native Americans, the enslavement and oppression of African Americans, and America's rapid growth in the nineteenth and twentieth centuries as an economic power.

Violence and the Illusion of Mastery

Consistently throughout the film, Kubrick forges links between various victims of oppression in order to focus attention upon how the assertion of white male violence lies at the foundation of American society. The link between the oppression of Native Americans and the oppression of women emerges through the consistent comparisons made between the two that take place in the context of Jack's fantasies of complete masculine freedom, paternal authority, and sexual license. One of the film's most startling and enigmatic evocations of this triad of desires occurs when Danny and Wendy enter the Overlook's maze and Jack is depicted demonically looking down at the exact replica of the maze in the Colorado Room. As he looks down at the maze from a vantage point implying the seemingly omnipotent power of his gaze, Wendy and Danny eventually arrive at its center. As noted above, Wendy's hair is braided in Native American fashion. Jack's vantage point overlooking the maze suggests a position of complete mastery and rational control over his wife and son and evokes one of the symbolic dimensions of the hotel's name. Nonetheless, this perception of absolute power is ironically undercut by Jack's eventual demise in that very same maze and Danny's escape from it. In this sense the hotel is aptly named, since it simultaneously points in opposite directions. The word *overlook* suggests both a position of commanding height that grants one the capacity to see an entire landscape and the act of missing something that has significance—that is to say, the name of the hotel suggests both complete and incomplete acts of perception. Furthermore, Jack's estimation of his ability to master his environment is fundamentally connected to the institutional hierarchy of the hotel. This connection is made initially with the living managers of the hotel and later with its supernatural overseers.

When Jack arrives at the Overlook Hotel for his interview, he is immediately introduced to a formal chain of command in which he must operate. As Randy Rasmussen notes, "Stuart Ullman's office is a modest statement of collective authority" and the "small American flag on his desk places Ullman, the hotel, and Colorado within an even larger institutional framework."[18] Geoffrey Cocks also takes note of the flag and points out the eagle behind Ullman's desk and the fact that his transposed initials are "U.S."[19] Adding further emphasis to Ullman's identification with American political authority, a significant portion of the interview takes place with the camera tightly focused on Ullman and the window behind him. This viewpoint, along with the other allusions to American government, resembles a typical presidential address from the Oval Office. At the same time a clear continuity exists between the living management of the hotel and its supernatural inhabitants: Jack's gradual corruption by the unseen residents of the hotel is facilitated by his desire to join the ranks of the wealthy guests who have vacationed there. As Greg Smith argues, if Jack wants to join the 1921 Fourth of July party, "he will have to shed his enlightened liberal schoolteacher/writer personality and adopt the racist views seen as constituting a valid claim to authority by wealthy, white, pre-Depression and pre–World War II American societal circles."[20] The continuing legacy of this viewpoint finds expression in the way Jack is manipulated to enforce a racist and sexist ideology that serves a set of class interests that are inimical to him and his family. The invisible management of the hotel is not unlike the frequently faceless directors of financial interests or corporations responsible for large-scale economic exploitation. In effect, Jack is offered admission to the ranks of the ruling class if he adopts the managerial/paternalistic standpoint intended to keep women, nonwhites, and unruly children in their place.

In Jack's descent into madness, the film presents the viewer with a mirror image of the lower/middle-class conservative white male filled with misdirected rage at minorities and women and faithfully serving the interests of the very group working against his well-being and happiness. Even though he will not benefit personally, the supernatural management of the hotel gradually moves Jack to embrace the misogynistic and racist attitudes of the wealthy white elite. The ghostly management's ideology, conveyed most forcefully by Delbert Grady's reference to Hallorann as a "nigger cook," mirrors the dominant ideological attitudes of those managing American domestic, foreign, and economic policy. The extent to which Jack instantly finds the Overlook "homey" testifies to the uncanny presence of repressed violent impulses within him as much as it signifies his aspirations to join the class it represents and his willingness to become an agent of paternalistic, racist repression. All of Jack's efforts are clearly directed at exerting mastery and control over his wife and son.

However, there is a consistent aspect of play and playacting to Jack's violence that may seem to undercut its seriousness. Caldwell and Umland, attentive to this aspect of Kubrick's film, argue for "a cohesive metaphor of *play* which is far more significant than critics have been willing to acknowledge." They point out that the hotel is comparable to "an enormous playground with limitless opportunities for play" but conclude that "Kubrick's manipulation of the play metaphor in *The Shining* obviates the film's aesthetic force and therefore undermines any 'serious' intent."[21] Although Caldwell and Umland make a convincing argument for the central significance of the metaphor of play in the film, they fail to consider the ways in which play may be a deadly serious activity. Applying the Freudian psychoanalytic framework that Kubrick consulted when writing the screenplay, one cannot fail to note Freud's most well-known exploration of children's play, the description of young Hans in *Beyond the Pleasure Principle* and the *fort/da* game he develops to compensate for his mother's absence. On several occasions Freud witnessed this young boy taking a wooden reel with a string attached to it and throwing it over the edge of his cot. When he threw it over the edge and it disappeared, he would exclaim, *Fort!* the German word for "gone." When he reeled it back in he would cry out *Da!* or "there." Freud interprets this game as the young child's "great cultural achievement—the instinctual renunciation (that is, the renunciation of instinctual satisfaction) which he had made in allowing his mother to go away without protesting."[22]

In Freud's account, the game represents a form of compensation for loss that cannot be explained by reference to the motive of pleasure, since the loss of the mother was not pleasurable. Freud concludes that the child had another motive, explainable by reference to the existence of an instinct for mastery. Freud remarks, "At the outset he was in a *passive* situation—he was overpowered by the experience; but, by repeating it, unpleasurable as it was, as a game, he took on an *active* part. These efforts might be put down to an instinct for mastery."[23] In short, Freud discovers an underlying motive for play that is quite serious and, indeed, all important—the attempt to compensate for the original loss of the mother and return to a state of primary narcissism. Interestingly, several critics have pointed out that the interior of the hotel serves as a metaphorical representation of the interior of the mother's body.[24] Furthermore, the relationship between play and the playing or exchange of roles that constantly takes place in the hotel in connection with doubling consistently returns to forms of patriarchal domination. These forms of domination are shown to be grounded in egoistic eruptions of sexual violence in which members of oppressed groups are

Jack Nicholson (as Jack Torrance) in *The Shining* (1980). Directed by Stanley Kubrick. (Warner Bros./Photofest)

coded as feminine. At the same time this doubling process is responsible
for generating uncanny reversals in which the violent pursuit of mastery
proves to be profoundly self-destructive. Jack's dual role as a protector of
his family and a source of narcissistic violence against them points to the
justifying paternalistic values of patriarchy even as it uncovers their uncanny
roots in the desire for mastery.

In the final analysis, Jack's pursuit of mastery and control represents a
self-destructive illusion. His fantasies of power turn out to be secretly directed and controlled by hotel management. Jack's past—America's past—ultimately masters him, and he becomes a willing pawn of history. There is
perhaps no more powerful evocation of Jack's illusion of mastery than his
final pursuit of Danny in the hedge maze. As he is reduced to an inarticulate,
raging monster, all of the remaining vestiges of Jack's humanity fall away
before he is transformed into a frozen figure trapped in the labyrinth of his
own self-destructive desires. As Cynthia Freeland points out in connecting
this moment with the uncanny, "the traditional masculine virtues have
been perverted into abusive power as Jack merges with evil."[25] However, in
taking for granted that these traditional masculine virtues must undergo a
process of perversion, Freeland overlooks the real force of Kubrick's critique

of patriarchy as well as the subtlety of his use of the uncanny to comment on paternalistic ideology. Kubrick's critique is far more radical. The traditional masculine virtues Freeland alludes to do not need to undergo a process of perversion because they *already are* the ideological representation of the real forms of power and domination they help to perpetuate. Jack's violence merely represents the uncanny mirror reflection of masculine virtue in practice. Reason, control, and the command of language constitute the defining illusions of the patriarchal worldview and are progressively exposed as ideological distortions of real history and its brutal repetitions of the past. One of the most powerful messages of the film involves the revelation that so-called masculine virtues are indistinguishable from the abusive exercise of power in practice. This revelation points far beyond the scope of events at the Overlook Hotel to a critique of European and American history and the Enlightenment values that inform it.

The Nightmare of History

The concern with organized institutional forms of violence and power informs the uncanny subtext of *The Shining* and, as others have pointed out, it represents a common focus in Kubrick's films.[26] The repetition of the past finds representation in the film in ways that are both overt and metaphorical. Nevertheless, in every case these repetitions suggest passivity or helplessness before the onslaught of history. One of the most obvious examples of repetition revolves around Jack's efforts to repeat the actions of the former caretaker Delbert Grady. At the same time Danny's uncanny encounters with the ghosts of Grady's daughters explicitly connect the repetition of history with violence. Furthermore, in his enigmatic encounter with Grady in the bathroom adjoining the Gold Room, Jack accuses Grady of being the caretaker and is told that he has *always been* the caretaker. Significantly, this encounter ends with Jack becoming convinced that he must "correct" Wendy and Danny. Soon after this real or imagined conversation, Jack sets out to kill Danny and Wendy, but only after repeating many of the same lines spoken by the ghosts of the hotel. This repetition of language signifies Jack's imprisonment within the nightmare of history and emphasizes his subjection to powers beyond his control or understanding.[27] Jack's manuscript supplies a significant indication of his growing alignment with inhuman forces depriving him of all individual agency. The repetition of the same line—All work and no play makes Jack a dull boy—registers his entrapment within an ideological system reinforcing patriarchal, class, and racial domination and links his attempts at mastery to the narcissistic motives of play discussed above. To the degree that the manuscript emulates a wide variety of poetic and written forms of expression, it dramatizes a complete emptying of content from literary form that renders it meaningless. Subject to the commands of history, Jack's personality undergoes a parallel emptying that dramatically points out how his unconscious allegiance to the past has destroyed his creative potential.

In effect, the haunting presence of history materializes and drives him to replace the possibility of fulfilling meaningful work or self-realization with a meaningless repetition of the past. As Thomas Allen Nelson points out, the manuscript "resembles a horizontal labyrinth . . . [suggesting] fate and psychological entrapment [and] associates Jack's madness with an image of reduction and repetition."[28] Jack's madness signifies the materialization of history and, on a symbolic level, the supernatural forces that nurture his growing instability function concretely in the film as historical ones.[29] If Jack's repetition of the same text points to his own progressive dehumanization into a figure whose narcissistic motives can be manipulated to transform him into an agent of brutal violence, the film, along with its historical subtext, points to the role of modern institutions in reproducing both domestic and global nightmares. Just as the Overlook Hotel is haunted by unseen evil and Jack Torrance is hunted by hidden forces bent upon his family's destruction, so, too, are the seemingly benevolent faces of political, economic, and cultural authority shown to be stalked by an uncanny double inflicting untold violence and harm upon the powerless. As Linda Holland-Toll points out, "It is not the idea that Jack is a monster which is so discomforting; it is that Jack Torrance reflects so many people in the society, who would not like to think of themselves as monsters, and who, indeed, to all appearances, are not monsters."[30] Holland-Toll is speaking of King's novel; however, her insight can easily be applied to the Jack Torrance in the film, who initially no more appears to be a monster than do the monstrous institutions that Kubrick aims to unmask and expose.

These monstrous institutions show themselves in the form of concrete traces of the past. This past is registered not only in literal historical references but also in the untold numbers of photographs that line the walls of the Overlook. In this sense Jack's joining of the ranks of those who populate the hotel's photographs is entirely appropriate, since it signifies the way in which the past exerts its concrete influence on the present. Indeed, Brigitte Peucker observes the degree to which *The Shining* is "haunted by photography."[31] To the extent that photographs are a means of recording the past and assigning it a place and meaning, Kubrick uses photography as a metaphor for the helplessness and passivity of human beings before the onslaught of history. The elaborate tracking shots of the camera, coupled with the vast visual puzzle or spatial labyrinth represented by the interior of the hotel, construct an uncanny space that frequently gives his characters a false assurance of being able to master it before their actual experiences violently shatter their illusions and demonstrate the degree to which it masters them. In this respect Kubrick's characters may not be unlike the members of his audience, who, provided with a story ostensibly about the mental breakdown of an isolated man and the collapse of his family, are actually given a tale about the hidden brutality of their own institutions, an uncanny fable mirroring their own pursuit of mastery and their own subjection to the nightmare of history.

Notes

My epigraphs are taken from William Faulkner, *Requiem for a Nun* (New York: Vintage, 1975), 80; Karl Marx, *The Eighteenth Brumaire of Louis Bonaparte* (New York: International Publishers, 1991), 15; and *The Shining*, dir. Stanley Kubrick (Warner Brothers, 1980).

1. Sigmund Freud, *The Uncanny*, trans. David Mclintock (New York: Penguin, 2003), 123.

2. Diane Johnson, "Writing *The Shining*," in *Depth of Field: Stanley Kubrick, Film, and the Uses of History*, ed. Geoffrey Cocks, James Diedrick, and Glenn Perusek (Madison: University of Wisconsin Press, 2006), 58.

3. Freud, *The Uncanny*, 147.

4. Stephen King, *The Shining* (New York: Pocket, 1977), 382, 433–34. Subsequent page references to this work will be given parenthetically in the text.

5. Cynthia A. Freeland, *The Naked and the Undead: Evil and the Appeal of Horror* (Boulder, CO: Westview, 2000), 215.

6. Brigitte Peucker, *The Material Image: Art and the Real in Film* (Stanford, CA: Stanford University Press, 2007), 108.

7. Greg Jenkins, *Stanley Kubrick and the Art of Adaptation* (London: McFarland, 1997), 23.

8. Sigmund Freud, "Family Romances," in *The Uncanny*, 38, 40.

9. Joseph Reino, *Stephen King: The First Decade, Carrie to Pet Sematary* (Boston: Twayne, 1988), 36.

10. Freud, *The Uncanny*, 142, 143.

11. Thomas Allen Nelson, *Kubrick: Inside a Film Artist's Maze* (Bloomington: Indiana University Press, 1982), 199.

12. Johnson, "Writing *The Shining*," 59.

13. Randy Rasmussen, *Stanley Kubrick: Seven Films Analyzed* (London: McFarland 2001), 263.

14. Frank Manchel, "What About Jack? Another Perspective on Family Relationships in Stanley Kubrick's *The Shining*," *Literature/Film Quarterly* 23, no. 1 (1995): 72.

15. Philip Kuberski, "Kubrick's Caretakers: Allegories of Homeland Security," *Arizona Quarterly* 63 (Spring 2007): 5.

16. David A. Cook, "American Horror: *The Shining*," *Literature/Film Quarterly* 12, no. 1 (1984): 2.

17. Nelson, *Kubrick*, 217.

18. Rasmussen, *Stanley Kubrick*, 236.

19. Geoffrey Cocks, "Death by Typewriter: Stanley Kubrick, the Holocaust, and *The Shining*," in Cocks, Diedrick, and Perusek, *Depth of Field*, 203.

20. Greg Smith, "'Real Horrorshow': The Juxtaposition of Subtext, Satire, and Audience Implication in Stanley Kubrick's *The Shining*," *Literature/Film Quarterly* 25, no. 4 (1997): 302.

21. Larry W. Caldwell and Samuel J. Umland, "'Come and Play with Us': The Play Metaphor in Kubrick's *Shining*," *Literature/Film Quarterly* 14, no. 2 (1986): 106, 111.

22. Sigmund Freud, *Beyond the Pleasure Principle* (New York: Norton, 1961), 14.

23. Ibid., 15.

24. See Peucker, *Material Image*, 111. Peucker argues that the corridors of the hotel can be viewed as corporeal passages for the transport of blood, and the hotel as the body of the mother. Similarly, Robert Kilker, who views the film as a vehicle for a subtle misogyny based in the fear of the abject, interprets the winding road leading to the Overlook as an umbilical cord to a monstrous feminine from which Jack cannot free himself. See Robert Kilker, "All Roads Lead to the Abject: The Monstrous Feminine and Gender Boundaries in Stanley Kubrick's *The Shining*," *Literature/Film Quarterly* 34, no. 1 (2006): 57–58.

25. Freeland, *The Naked and the Undead*, 225.

26. See Cocks, Diedrick, and Perusek, *Depth of Field*. In their introduction the editors point out that many of Kubrick's films "confront in particular the unprecedented organization of power and violence among people and states that dominated much of the first half of the century" (8).

27. Pat J. Gehrke and G. L. Ercolini, "Subjected Wills: The Antihumanism of Kubrick's Later Films," in Cocks, Diedrick, and Perusek, *Depth of Field*, 111, 117.

28. Nelson, *Kubrick*, 228.

29. Cocks, "Death by Typewriter," 200–201.

30. Linda J. Holland-Toll, "Bakhtin's Carnival Reversed: King's *The Shining* as Dark Carnival," *Journal of Popular Culture* 33 (Fall 1999): 137.

31. Peucker, *Material Image*, 107.

"Hot with Rapture and Cold with Fear"

Grotesque, Sublime, and Postmodern Transformations in Patrick Süskind's *Perfume*

Susann Cokal

Jean-Baptist Grenouille, antihero of Patrick Süskind's international best seller *Perfume: The Story of a Murderer,* is "one of the most gifted and abominable personages in an era that knew no lack of gifted and abominable personages" (Süskind 2001, 3). He is smart, talented, and completely amoral, shunned by his fellow humans from the moment he's born. He commits crimes that shock the community with their apparent purposelessness, killing a total of twenty-six virgins (or, in the film version, fourteen women of varied sexual experience) and inadvertently leaving a trail of other bodies behind. He is a monster. He is a parasite. He is also the greatest creative genius of his era.

From birth, Grenouille has an uncanny power to sicken and terrify people. "I only know one thing," says his wet nurse: "this baby makes my flesh creep because it doesn't smell the way children ought to smell" (Süskind 2001, 11). Specifically, "the bastard himself, he doesn't smell" (10). In his odorlessness, Grenouille is (perhaps paradoxically) disgusting—and because of it (also somewhat paradoxically), he will eventually show a deep capacity for the sublime experience of speechless awe dear to eighteenth-century philosophers. Without the scent markers that might weave him into the social fabric, he grows up free of manners, morals, or compunctions about hurting others to get what he wants. He is an olfactory blank slate who reinvents himself by robbing others of their own odors.

Perfume has been described as "a very cleverly constructed and well-told, but essentially trivial, horror story with fantastic elements and just a whiff of the conventional detective novel" (Durrani 1999, 228). But it is so much more. Both the 1985 novel and the 2006 movie undertake a philosophical meditation on expression and perception, using as their subject the ineffable (to some people trivial) sense of smell rather than the more often privileged sense of sight. Smell is particularly suited to the horror genre, which depends on shaking up the innermost part of our beings. It is the most primal sense, the one that develops first and stays with us; it can provoke visceral experiences—vomiting, shudders, joy—even more immediately than sight and sound, for example, can do. Grenouille himself thinks of it as an ultimate power: "For people could close their eyes to greatness, to horrors, to beauty, and their ears to melodies or deceiving words. But they could not escape scent. For scent was a brother of breath" (Süskind 2001, 155). If we live, if we breathe, we find it almost impossible not to perceive odors.[1]

All-pervasive and inevitable, able to disgust, amuse, and delight, smell is fertile territory for both the disgusting grotesque and the uplifting sublime, two categories that have intertwined during the postmodern era. Through a misshapen, eerie character who both undergoes and provokes sublime olfactory experiences, Süskind explores the nature of aesthetics and artistic creation. In this way, as Edith Borchardt has noted, "Süskind parodies Kantian theories of the origins and nature of knowledge by exploring the idea that the highest aesthetic abstraction can be achieved through the most primitive of the senses" (1992, 99). Ultimately, Grenouille's crimes are the transgressive acts of an artist and a sort of unwitting natural philosopher attempting to forge a subjectivity. That his crimes destroy and deconstruct beauty in order to create something sublime is part of the book's ultimate horror, as *Perfume*'s readers (or moviegoers) hover between feelings of revulsion and the hope inspired by beauty.

Both horror and the sublime put us in touch with something beyond our ordinary lives. In her influential book *Solitude and the Sublime,* Frances Ferguson notes that any aesthetic experience involves an interplay between internal and external stimuli, with the effect registered on the body (1992, 6). That effect is perhaps most intense with the sublime, a category of experience that strikes wonder and terror into the beholder; it so palpably approaches the divine that it transcends physical form and leaves the perceiving subject. A response to a phenomenon beyond mere beauty, it is usually located in nature: a mighty waterfall, the Grand Canyon, a mountain range. The sublime was of particular interest during the Age of Reason, which (much like our own period) sought to define and explain what lies beyond reason itself. Describing the postmodern version of that experience, Jean-François

Lyotard elaborates: "The soul is . . . dumb, immobilized, as good as dead" (1993, 251). In any era the sublime is shocking.

Here is Grenouille's first encounter with the sublime, embodied in a young Parisian girl discovered cleaning plums:

> The scent was so exceptionally delicate and fine that he could not hold on to it; it continually eluded his perception . . . his very heart ached. He had the prescience of something extraordinary—this scent was the key for ordering all odors, one could understand nothing about odors if one did not understand this scent, and his whole life would be bungled, if he, Grenouille, did not succeed in possessing it.
>
> He was almost sick with excitement. . . .
>
> Grenouille felt his heart pounding, and he knew that it was not the exertion of running that had set it pounding, but rather his excited helplessness in the presence of this scent. He tried to recall something comparable, but had to discard all comparisons. (Süskind 2001, 38–39)

Though the novel doesn't say so explicitly, this is a textbook description of the sublime experience, whether from the Enlightenment or the postmodern era. The encounter is extraordinary, unlike anything else; it makes him feel sick and helpless. It is, in a word, overwhelming, and it hints at some realm beyond our mortal earth; by touching the divine, it provides a potential organizing principle for our entire world. So when Grenouille strangles this girl and sniffs to heart's content, experiencing "pure bliss," he feels as if he has finally been born: "for until now he had merely existed like an animal with a most nebulous self-awareness. But after today, he felt as if he finally knew who he really was: nothing less than a genius" with a "higher destiny: nothing less than to revolutionize the odiferous world" (43). It is through the sublime that he begins to develop both an inkling of a self and an aspiration to be more than that little self alone, and the category will continue to organize his attempted transformation.

The movie version (directed by Tom Tykwer) takes this passage a step further and, in a voice-over, explicitly calls the scent emitted by this first virgin "sublime." Courting its audience, the film also uses more conventions of traditional horror: an early murder of a household pet, Baldini's cat; a display of dead bodies; a torture scene after Grenouille's arrest; and attempts to make us sympathize with Grenouille. Tykwer softens Grenouille's criminality and makes the strangling an accident, coming about as Grenouille tries to hush the girl. In either case, sublime bliss—or the awareness of its potential—leads to a crime in which Grenouille will attempt to create himself first as a being conscious of itself, then as a god conscious of all things. The sublime will frighten Grenouille more deeply later on; for now it is dangerous primarily for the person who evokes it.

The grotesque is often a jollier category, though it can invoke a shudder of its own. It depends almost wholly on the physical—the ugly, misshapen, scatological—and produces a feeling of comedy as often as one of revulsion. As we'll see, in Süskind's eighteenth century everyone and everywhere, from palace to marketplace, is grotesque. That's because everyone stinks—hyperbolically, exaggeratedly, superabundantly, amusingly. Everyone, that is, except for the misshapen main character, Grenouille, and the virgins on whom he preys. Grenouille, who is capable of sublime perception, is a grotesque figure par excellence: small, scarred, ugly, and freakishly without odor. He is variously compared to a toad (that's what his name means), a tick (for example, Süskind 2001, 21, 33), a monster (17), and a mere thing (13). He can eat next to nothing—spoiled meat (20), bats (132)—and is able to survive all manner of diseases, including dysentery, cholera (20), and a near-fatal bout of anthrax (32). His very abhorrence allows him to become the greatest artist who ever lived, and his various apprenticeships to a tanner, a perfumer, and a distiller of essential oils give him the science he needs to create complex emotional responses.

Postmodernists love the grotesque body because it doesn't fit preconceived ideas of perfection—it keeps changing, becoming something else. Flowing through much postmodern art is a mortal fear of everything falling into place; hence the pastiche and bricolage that are hallmarks of the era. If an artist were to find the perfect form, he or she would have nothing more to express. The grotesque fascinates because it offers contact with another plane of existence. It is one way of reaching beyond ordinary, anodyne life, as it stirs the senses and creates excitement. Geoffrey Galt Harpham has written that the word itself "designates a condition of being just out of focus, just beyond the reach of language. It accommodates the things left over when the categories of language are exhausted" (1982, 3).

In designating the unrepresentable, in eluding language and definition, the grotesque is related to the sublime. What the two categories have most fundamentally in common is excess. Both transgress boundaries, whether through an exaggeration of body or a surplus of beauty; they bring us into contact with something beyond our ordinary experience. In *Perfume* that something beyond consists in the systematic crimes that Grenouille commits in order to make one transcendent perfume, an "angel's scent" (Süskind 2001, 154) that will make him universally loved. Coldly cunning in their use of the perfumer's science, horrifying in their apparent purposelessness, these murders produce the greatest and most ephemeral experience of divinity our little world has ever known, bearing out Lyotard's claim that sublime art makes "a world apart . . . in which the monstrous and the formless have their rights because they can be sublime" (1993, 249). The two categories braid together here and produce a story unsettling in its own genius, asking and answering a question particularly relevant to the postmodern era: How is it possible for an artist such as Grenouille (or Süskind) to reconcile revulsion, awe, and uplifting beauty?

Everybody Stank

In *Perfume* everyone, even the charismatically aromatic virgins, inhabits a grotesque world. As the first page informs us, "there reigned in the cities a stench barely conceivable to us modern men and women. The streets stank of manure, the courtyards of urine, the stairwells stank of moldering wood and rat droppings. . . . People stank of sweat and unwashed clothes; from their mouths came the stench of rotting teeth, from their bellies that of onions, and from their bodies, if they were no longer very young, came the stench of rancid cheese and sour milk and tumorous disease" (Süskind 2001, 3). This description alone would be enough to brand *Perfume* a work of horror. But these are not unusual bodies, like Grenouille's; these bodies belong to ordinary citizens, nobility, even the king and queen. When Grenouille concocts a perfume that will let him pass as human, he uses old cheese, cat dung, sardine oil, and other "ghastly" ingredients (150). As the category's great theorist, Mikhail Bakhtin, has written, "Exaggeration, hyperbolism, excessiveness are generally considered fundamental attributes of the grotesque style" (1984, 303). Grenouille reveals humanity's inherent repulsiveness: to be human, in *Perfume,* is in itself to be grotesque. Even those virgins would end up reeking if Grenouille didn't kill them first.

Grenouille's talent for discerning scent is itself a kind of grotesque feature, going beyond human and even typical animal ability to become another bodily exaggeration. No one, not even the perfumer Baldini, quite realizes how sensitive Grenouille's nose is; they think it's good, certainly, but they don't realize it is supernaturally so.[2] When his last and most desirable victim flees the carnage with her father, for example, Grenouille is able to follow her to a distant inn simply by smelling the traces in the air.

Grenouille's ability to sift out scents becomes even more exaggerated in the film version of his life, and therein lies much of his grotesque identity. As the newborn infant lies on the midden heap where his mother has thrown him—the nastiest spot in the nastiest marketplace in literary history—his luminous little nose quivers, catching scents of fish, rotting food, human breath. It is for smell alone that he seems to suck in enough breath of his own to make himself heard and draw people to his rescue.

The film, in fact, puts the greatest burden of grotesquerie on Grenouille's sense of smell and his brute determination to find olfactory pleasure. The actor who plays him, Ben Whishaw, is quite handsome, with dark curls and a sculptured face. Only a layer of dirt marks his unsavoriness; he is generally much more appealing to look at than the black-toothed peasants, potbellied nobles, and scarred workers who surround him. Without the novel character's physical imperfections, his keen nose and willingness to kill become even more important to the definition of his character. Still, as we have seen, the film tries to soften the viewer's distaste for its protagonist by making his first crime (the murder of the plum girl) an accident. Grenouille is a murderer, but a handsome and even understandable one.

Neither does Grenouille simply smell things; he lusts for smell. That lust is the same as a Rabelaisian gluttony or a Boccaccian priapism. His nose is his sexual organ; he is never tempted to rape or even make love to any of his victims; he merely wants to sniff them. All of his desire has been located in his nose—which makes him even more terrifying to the people of Grasse when he starts killing off their daughters: "Strangely enough, this knowledge only increased the sense of horror, for everyone had secretly assumed that the girls had been ravished. People had at least known the murderer's motive. Now they knew nothing at all" (Süskind 2001, 197). A sexual crime is understandable; an unexplained one suggests that the perpetrator is beyond human, or at the very least beyond human comprehension. The murderer thus becomes an unknown quantity, truly a monster. Of course, if the townspeople knew that the girls are being killed in order to be coldly and scientifically distilled into a perfume, they would be even more horrified at the nature of the violation. (I will discuss his scientific method below.)

It may at first seem ironic that Süskind uses the word "grotesque" to describe Grenouille's own lack of body odor: "It was grotesque" ("Es war grotesk" [Süskind 1985, 154]) that "he, Grenouille, who could smell other people miles away, was incapable of smelling his own genitals not a handspan away!" (Süskind 2001, 135).[3] In this case, "grotesque" refers not to ugliness but to the unsettling effect of the uncanny, which Freud defines as something familiar made strange, therefore frightening and repulsive: "the 'uncanny' is that class of the terrifying which leads back to something long known to us, once very familiar" (2004, 75).[4] The uncanny comes associated with a sense of malevolence: "We also call a living person uncanny," Freud writes, "usually when we ascribe evil motives to him. But that is not all; we must not only credit him with bad intentions but must attribute to these intentions capacity to achieve their aim in virtue of certain special powers" (91). Grenouille's odorlessness and his superhuman ability to detect scents make him a primal figure of horror. And he is aware of his own selfish evil: "He was not out of his mind . . . he wanted to do it [create the "superhuman . . . angel's scent"] because he was evil, thoroughly evil" (Süskind 2001, 155).[5]

Grenouille even horrifies himself. Once he finds a mountain cave and grants himself time and solitude to craft an imaginary sense-world based on past experiences, he smells himself and experiences the same feeling of uncanny defamiliarization that made his first wet nurse's flesh creep. Lying in his imaginary castle of scent memories, he tries to smell the odoriferous trace he himself leaves—and finds nothing: "Virtually drowning in himself, he could not for the life of him smell himself! . . . As this became clear to him, he gave a scream as dreadful and loud as if he were being burned alive" (Süskind 2001, 134). This terror is, finally, what brings him out of the cave, where he decides to create his "angel's scent." He dimly starts to realize that without a personal smell he is not a subject as other people are. (His lack of subjectivity helps to explain the unusually strong presence of an expository narrative voice in the novel and of voice-over in the film.) Trying to complete his angel's scent, he will incidentally fashion what philosophers might call a sort of self—creating subjectivity by composing the proper fragrance to mimic it. But Grenouille doesn't truly think in terms of a self; he sees the world in shades of presence and absence, transcendence and revulsion. For an illuminating exploration of solipsism and self in *Perfume*, see Jurich 1996. Jurich acknowledges that "Grenouille's olfactory organ is virtually his only self—intellect, feeling, soul" (87). She compares Grenouille to Dracula and the child in the horror film *The Bad Seed*.

The term *grotesque* was coined to describe the exaggerated figures painted on the walls of Roman grottos or caves (Bakhtin 1984, 31–32). It's appropriate, then, that when Grenouille emerges after seven years in his cave, he could be the textbook illustration of the term:

> He looked awful. His hair reached down to the hollows of his knees, his scraggly beard to his navel. His nails were like talons, and the skin on his arms and legs, where the rags no longer covered his body, was peeling off in shreds.

The first people he met, farmers in a field near the town of Pierrefort, ran off screaming at the sight of him. But in the town itself, he caused a sensation. By the hundreds people came running to gape at him. (138)

His already scarred and misshapen body has become even stranger, allowed to grow beyond usual boundaries and social norms: the long hair and nails, the peeling skin—no wonder some townspeople say he's "not really a human being, but . . . some kind of forest creature" (Süskind 2001, 138). This spectacle is alarming, but it is also irresistibly attractive, particularly to those used to living in urban centers where norms are constantly defined and reinforced.

This creature may seem an unlikely vehicle for supreme experiences of beauty, but his lack of personal odor makes him a blank slate on which to inscribe new identities. The grotesque body is a creative and destructive physical shapelessness, a formless lump of clay tied to both birth and death. Bakhtin describes it as "a body in the act of becoming. It is never finished, never completed; it is continually built, created, and builds and creates another body . . . the essential role belongs to those parts of the grotesque body in which it outgrows its own self, transgressing its own body, in which it conceives a new, second body" (1984, 317). Bakhtin is writing about the bowels and phallus here, but the same holds true of Grenouille's talents. In Grenouille's case, olfactory shapelessness enables evil artistry. With no odor of his own, he can easily assume any smell, and thus any identity, he himself can create. By applying one mixture or another, he can eventually make himself smell like an ordinary, inconspicuous human (Süskind 2001, 182) or one who inspires sympathy (183)—and, ultimately, like a god who might provoke a passionate sexual orgy or a cannibalistic carnival in which he himself is destroyed in perverted image of the Catholic Mass. He transcends his own bodily limits to create the impression of new bodies.

Only one of the emotional responses expected of the grotesque is a kind of benevolent disgust; another is laughter. As Bakhtin has written, "The cosmic, social, and bodily elements are given here as an indivisible whole. And this whole is gay and gracious" (1984, 19). Grenouille, however, is rarely comic; although the narrative voice's detachment provides the distance needed to turn tragedy into comedy, the most we achieve is a certain irony—amusing, perhaps, and certainly biting, but not "gay and gracious." The recipe for a human odor is grotesque here, and it may provoke a laugh or two; but the laughter comes at our own expense, ultimately more disgusting than amusing. The comic elements of grotesquerie get plowed into the overall unsettling effects of the uncanny and sublime.

Fatally Wonderful, Terrifyingly Celestial

The uncanny episode in the cave is actually one of the first intimations that Grenouille might reach the sublime, for both experiences feed on fear: in one case the fear of something half recognized and not quite right, and in the other the overwhelming terror of an encounter with awesome power. As the story progresses it peels back layers of sublime experience and explores numerous dimensions of the category. Grenouille must pass through that uncanny period in the cave before he decides to create perfumes that will not merely smell beautiful and create the illusion of humanity, of belonging, but also connect with the divine.

Even in the eighteenth century, when the concept of the sublime had its heyday, opinions were not unanimous as to what exactly constitutes it. Süskind is, moreover, playing here with multiple forms: eighteenth-century ideas, particularly influenced by Immanuel Kant, and a somewhat more complicated postmodern sense (after all, he is writing in the postmodern era). Most theorists agree that the sublime is on a register far above that of mere pleasure in beauty. Beauty allows the subject to feel superior, even by the act of judging the beauty, but the sublime is humbling. We see that notion in *Perfume:* The girls who fascinate Grenouille, particularly Laure, are beautiful—though their lovely faces and bodies aren't what attract him. Just as Humbert Humbert's nymphets are otherworldly daemons rather than simply pretty little girls (Nabokov 1989, 17), Grenouille's sublime virgins are more than merely good to look at. After he kills the Parisienne, it's just a few hours before "he could no longer recall how the girl . . . had looked, not her face, not her body" (Süskind 2001, 44). What he remembers is "the best part of her," her fragrance.

When he smells Laure and recognizes her sublimity, he meditates on the sensory confusion that comes from a heavenly odor: "People will be overwhelmed, disarmed, helpless before the magic of this girl, and they will not know why. And because people are stupid and use their noses only for blowing, but believe absolutely anything they see with their eyes, they will say it is because this is a girl with beauty and grace and charm. . . . And none of them will know that it is truly not how she looks that has captured them, not her reputed unblemished external beauty, but solely her incomparable, splendid scent!" (Süskind 2001, 171–72).[6] Smell may be primal and therefore scarcely considered in contemplations of beauty; but it can also fool the other senses, and therein lies some of its otherwordly power.

Beauty is tied to the world, but the sublime elevates the person who experiences it. Edmund Burke wrote that we register aesthetic power and "know" objects through their effects on our bodies; aesthetic pleasure then arises from, as Frances Ferguson puts it, "the satisfactions that one can have in objects as extensions of one's relations with other human beings" (1992, 4) Thus for the English theorist the sublime is empirical and tied to social relationships. In Germany, Kant took a different stance, arguing that since objects lack consciousness, aesthetic experience depends on communication with intentionlessness, as found in nature—so his is an asocial, antiempirical vision: "It must be nature, or be thought of as nature" (Kant, *Critique of Judgment,* quoted in Ferguson 1992, 38)—that is, beyond human control.[7]

It would seem natural to assume that since *Perfume* is a German book, rooted in the German tradition of pure reason, Kant's model would be dominant in Süskind; and in fact, given Grenouille's detachment from the world he inhabits, the antiempirical source of sublimity seems the most apparent. But it's important to remember, as Ferguson points out, that while early critics saw sublime moments as a chance for the individual to become "a metonymy of his culture"—a representative of collective experience—modern critics posit the sublime as a moment in which subjectivity can be constructed (1992, 38). And, contradictory as it may seem, that is precisely how Süskind transforms Grenouille from a grotesque type into (occasionally) a modern rational creature: through experience of the irrational sublime.

In the movie the perfumer Baldini describes a fragrance's potential for the sublime. Early in Grenouille's apprenticeship Baldini tells him that most perfumes are made up of twelve notes or essences, though the ancient Egyptians believed in a thirteenth note that would "bring out and dominate the others." He tells a story of an amphora in a pharaoh's tomb that, when opened, released a scent "of such subtle beauty and yet such power that for one single moment every person on earth believed they were in paradise." In that sample twelve essences were identified, but the thirteenth eluded everyone. Although Baldini dismisses the story as a legend, it serves as a model for the movie Grenouille's own masterwork. We thus expect that he will slay thirteen girls to make his perfume in addition to the Parisienne with the plums.

In the novel Grenouille's first explicitly acknowledged sublime experiences come in the mountain cave where he lives alone for seven years, uncorking imaginary bottles of remembered scents (remember, the novel does not use the word *sublime* to describe his encounter with the plum girl). While his first memories are eminently nasty—for example, "the stench of raw, meaty skins and tanning broths" or "the collective effluvium of six hundred thousand Parisians" (Süskind 2001, 124), he avenges the assault on his "patrician nose" with the memory of distilled water. The first time the word *sublime* is used it comes in a context of highly pleasurable violent rage: "Ah! What a sublime moment! ["Ah! Welch sublimer Augenblick!" (Süskind 1985, 142)]. Grenouille, the little man, quivered with excitement, his body writhed with voluptuous delight and arched so high that he slammed his head against the roof of the tunnel, only to sink back slowly and lie there lolling in satiation. It really was too pleasant, this volcanic act that extinguished all obnoxious odors, really too pleasant. . . . It imparted to him the wonderful sense of righteous exhaustion that comes after only truly grand heroic deeds" (Süskind 2001, 124–25). The orgasmic nature of the experience needs no comment. Significantly for this discussion of the sublime, it combines "voluptuous delight" and pain, an overabundance of pleasure and a sense of heroism. Although banging his head against the tunnel roof might remind Grenouille of his physical limitations—and thus the boundaries of his own existence—he has an overwhelming physical experience that produces a sense of mental and emotional expansion. If this is how he feels when rehearsing scents all by himself, imagine what creating new scents for an unsuspecting world can make him feel.

When he encounters his next and most sublime virgin, Laure, Grenouille is more open to the experience than in Paris, and even more frightened because he partially recognizes it. Standing in the streets of Grasse, he catches "a fatally wonderful scent," one that turns him "hot with rapture and cold with fear" (Süskind 2001, 169) because "to have found that scent in this world once again brought tears of bliss to his eyes—and to know that it could not possibly be true frightened him to death" (170): Laure's aroma is not yet ripe, but already it is "terrifyingly celestial" (171). This is a transformative experience with a world beyond nature as he knows it—beyond civilization, too; for if finding the scent a second time is impossible, then he must be in touch with something beyond the possible. Hence the fear: there is something greater at work than Grenouille himself. And hence, too, the final inspiration for his angel's scent.

Up to this point the sublime has been found in nature, particularly the girls' natural smells. As we've seen, this is typical of philosophical conceptions. Even as he undergoes that sublime experience with Laure, Grenouille feels himself capable of dominating it and becoming the "omnipotent god of scent" of which he dreamed upon coming down from the mountain (Süskind 2001, 155). "No," he thinks, "he wanted truly to possess the scent of this girl behind the wall; to peel it from her like skin and to make her scent his own" (172). That is, his original experience may be sublime, but he hopes to gain mastery over human souls by breaking his own bliss down into the merely beautiful, then rebuilding it as something apparently natural but even better than nature. And in this he succeeds—though not in the way he first envisions.

Before Laure, the novelistic Grenouille kills two dozen other virgins of Grasse and perfects his technique for acquiring their scent. With all those odors blended together in a "diadem of scent" and Laure's odor "at its sublime acme" (Süskind 2001, 193), his careful creation of the one ultimate perfume enables him to wield power over human response and even human nature. Those who smell this concoction experience it not as a heady artificial scent, like the elixirs he makes for Baldini, but as a natural phenomenon, a body odor that belongs to him and changes according to emotion and situation. He thus composes or "writes" an apparently authentic but actually fictive body through his perfume, and those who catch a whiff fall in love. But he remains himself, the malevolent, ugly little tick, and ultimately he will want to destroy himself as a hateful example of grotesquerie.

With Professional Circumspection, Not Really a Human Being

After leaving the cave Grenouille falls into the hands of the Marquis de La Taillade-Espinasse, who fancies himself a scientist and uses Grenouille's spotted and scarred body as an example of a crackpot notion of the corruptive effects of gases on the body (Süskind 2001, 141). Silly as this idea is, and ugly as Grenouille's body looks, the episode contextualizes a world of theory and experiment in which Grenouille's scientific approach to robbing maidens of their scents seems to make some sense. He lives, after all, in the Age of Reason, and the rational is (hoped to be) supreme.

His years of apprenticeship have given him a coldly scientific approach to distillation, but when Grenouille begins to harvest human scents he has another uncanny experience. He takes the sheets of a dead sackmaker and performs an enfleurage (impregnating the scent in animal lard), only to find "the result was eerie: right under Grenouille's nose, the sackmaker rose olfactorily from the dead" (Süskind 2001, 187). The familiar is again defamiliarized, or encountered in an unfamiliar form that is unsettling even to the man who produced the effect. But this time the uncanny is the *desired* effect; though Grenouille disposes of the scent he's captured this time, he knows he's accessed that realm of fear and illusion and is well on his way to the sublime.

The murders themselves are "gruesome" (Süskind 2001, 194), partly in the attitude of their dispatch. Grenouille has found that a blow to the head is the most effective way to kill without tainting maidenly odor with the stink of fear. He takes the girls' hair and their clothes—at this point no one realizes he's also infusing their body odors—and he seems to have a magical ability to enter their homes undetected: "The murderer seemed impalpable, incorporeal, like a ghost" (197), and the lack of sexual perversion makes him all the more sinister. The townspeople guard their daughters fearfully, uselessly. They are relieved when, after twenty-four murders at home, a killer is caught in Grenoble.

The situation is, again, somewhat different in the film. As with the early plum girl, director Tykwer varies the motivation of some later murders; for example, Grenouille kills a prostitute in Grasse spontaneously, because she's been insulting him. He extracts her odor not so much because it's sublime as because it's there; when he finally stands over Laure (Laura in the movie), he hesitates, lowers his arm, meets her gaze with remorse; and the deathblow comes offscreen. In Tykwer's vision, then, he is a more commonly coded and understandable criminal—some of those women provoked him. And the first two girls who die in Grasse are not virgins but strumpets: that prostitute and a flower picker who's been flirting with a fellow laborer. The well-known convention that sexually active girls are prime targets for a villain makes some of the movie's cruelty more palatable and obscures a bit of Süskind's brilliance. Only later will Antoine Richis (Alan Rickman) mention that the killer wants not the girls' virginity but something as yet unknown. And in the sexual orgy in Grasse, Tykwer's Grenouille imagines making love to the Parisian plum seller and sheds a wistful tear—something the truly monstrous character of the book would never think of doing.

In both movie and novel only Antoine Richis remains vigilant and attempts to spirit his beautiful budding daughter away. "The murderer had opened his [Richis's] eyes," explains the novel's narrator, and now he alone has a sense of the victims' specialness and the murderer's intention: "For if one imagined—and so Richis imagined—all the victims not as single individuals, but as parts of some higher principle and thought of each one's characteristics as merged in some idealistic fashion into a unifying whole, then the picture assembled out of such mosaic pieces would be the picture of absolute beauty, and the magic that radiated from it would no longer be of human, but of divine origin" (Süskind 2001, 203). That higher principle is precisely the sublime of which Kant and Lyotard write; the beauty Richis imagines goes beyond earthly and participates in the divine. Thus, in an ironic way, Grenouille achieves his first sublime effect: he makes an anxious father realize what wonders his daughter offers, gives him intimations of the celestial and transcendent, and helps him reach a higher place in his own thinking.

To no avail. Antoine and Laure's flight only prompts Grenouille to act more quickly, and at last the novel's readers see how Grenouille works—getting a glimpse into the rational though still grotesque man of science he has become. "With professional circumspection" (Süskind 2001, 214), he prepares a "scent diagram" of the body by applying oil to a large linen sheet; after bludgeoning Laure's head, he wraps her in the cloth, cuts off her hair, and takes her clothes. Over the course of some hours her scent soaks into the linen, and Grenouille removes the cloth and scrapes her skin clean of oil. This is his proudest moment to date: "He was, now that he really considered it, a truly blessed individual!" and he thanks himself for being who he is (219).

Here Süskind's Grenouille becomes a horror antihero, a cousin to Hannibal Lecter or the sinister gynecologists in David Cronenberg's *Dead Ringers*. He has a method; he is calculating; but he is also, by ordinary worldly terms, insane. The movie makes this point earlier by showing his first victim from Grasse being infused in a giant alembic, Grenouille working casually around her. The film character doesn't express the same grandiose aspirations as the novelistic original; in a way, his "scent for scent's sake" approach may produce a more immediate shudder, but it won't have the lasting repulsive effect of that single-minded quest for subjectivity.

Thinking of himself as Grenouille the Great, he is much easier to capture; almost as if he is stupid, he doesn't try to escape arrest and sits quietly in jail, looking like "this mediocrity, this miserable nonentity, this cipher"—not a murderer at all (Süskind 2001, 227). His character is particularly opaque in the novel's trial scene, as if he has lost all sense of human subjectivity; he "received the verdict without emotion" and makes no last wish (229). This passivity and opacity are, of course, part of his simple plan. At his own scheduled execution he will try out his sublime perfume for the first time.

Pure Liquid, Boundless Fear and Terror

The film begins with the scene of Grenouille's sentencing, setting up a horror to come—an expectation that will be satisfyingly dashed when Grenouille pulls out his scent bottle. As the novel describes that would-be execution scene, adopting the spectators' point of view:

> And then a miracle occurred. Or something very like a miracle, or at least something so incomprehensible, so unprecedented, and so unbelievable that everyone who witnessed it would have called it a miracle afterwards if they had taken the notion to speak of it at all—which was not the case, since afterwards every single one of them was ashamed to have had any part in it whatever.

... The man in the blue frock coat who had just climbed out of the carriage *could not possibly be a murderer*. Not that they doubted his identity! (Süskind 2001, 235)

This miracle, an apparent manifestation of the divine on earth, renders the viewers sublimely speechless, awed and overpowered—exactly what Grenouille has been planning. Feelings overcome reason, and the spectators fall in love with him: "and they were unable, unwilling to do anything about it. It was like a fit of weeping you cannot fight down, like tears that have been held back too long and rise up from deep within you, dissolving whatever resists them, liquefying it, and flushing it away. These people were now pure liquid, their spirits and minds were melted; nothing was left but an amorphous fluid, and all they could feel was their hearts floating and sloshing about within them" (236–37). What they are experiencing are the by now well-established effects of the sublime, that overwhelming sense of something greater than the human phenomenal world.

With little to which to compare this feeling, the townspeople translate it into the sexual. If spirits and minds are now liquid, bodies experience the same sort of fluidity and boundarilessness—and Grasse undertakes an orgy. In short, "They all regarded the man in the blue frock coat as the most handsome, attractive, and perfect creature they could imagine. . . . It was as if the man had ten thousand invisible hands and had laid a hand on the genitals of the ten thousand people surrounding him and fondled them in just the way that each of them, whether man or woman, desired in his or her most secret fantasies" (Süskind 2001, 238). They begin copulating hysterically, "all topsy-turvy" and "infernal" (239).

That orgiastic confusion is, not coincidentally, related to the grotesque by way of the carnivalesque, also described by Bakhtin. Old-fashioned folk festivals such as Carnival included this element of a world turned upside-down, all hierarchies erased and a triumph of pleasurable rebirth: "it is a special condition of the entire world, of the world's revival and renewal" (1984, 7). In *Perfume* the scene is bawdy, comic, ridiculous—and poignant. It is the outcome of Grenouille's careful scientific method, brutal crime, and divine aspirations: a physically grotesque world brought into being by the sublime. As Geoffrey Galt Harpham has written, "Sex dramatizes the incongruity of the human: straining for sublimity, we ape the beasts" (1982, 10). Grenouille has redeemed his own grotesque body and made it a source of joy, if not of bliss . . . thereby making others grotesque.

But Grenouille is disappointed. While congratulating himself on becoming "in very truth his own God," experiencing "the greatest triumph of his life," he is overcome with terror. This is no sublime terror related to bliss: "He was terrified because he could not enjoy one second of it"; although he longed to be loved, he now finds he loves no one and takes no pleasure in love anyway (Süskind 2001, 240). After all, he can't help noticing that he is not among the writhing, delirious mass of bodies, simply standing over them and observing as any deity would. At that moment, he wants to "empty himself . . . to be like other people," but he experiences another uncanny encounter with his own odorlessness: "he was filled with boundless fear and terror" (241), such that he welcomes Richis, who is approaching to kill him. At least then he will be truly participating in the scene, not simply causing it. But even Richis falls at Grenouille's feet and asks for forgiveness and permission to adopt his daughter's murderer (242).

Disgusted with humanity and all too aware of his own power, Grenouille realizes he may control people but will never actually know himself: "though his perfume might allow him to appear before the world as a god—if he could not smell himself and thus never know who he was, to hell with it, with the world, with himself, with his perfume." Even that perfume is mean- ingless: "The only one who has ever recognized it for its true beauty is me, because I created it myself. And at the same time, I'm the only one that it cannot enslave. I am the only person for whom it is meaningless" (Süskind 2001, 252). This is his moment of greatest self-awareness, but he still hasn't achieved the subjectivity he's been seeking. He can't transcend his grotesque and uncanny body either. This is the tragedy of Grenouille and perhaps of the eighteenth-century philosopher and artist: he might encounter the sublime, might even reproduce its effects in an artwork that appears to come straight from heaven into nature—but he will always be aware of his own limitations, and he himself will never communicate directly with the divine.

There is a second orgy scene, in the very brief fourth section of the novel; in the film it takes about four minutes. It is a literal carnival, an orgy of a different order—even more topsy-turvy, but sinister rather than bawdy, motivated by despair rather than joy, and this time Grenouille is bodily in- volved. Disillusioned with the people of Grasse, Grenouille returns to Paris and the people among whom he was born, a pack of desperadoes near Les Halles. Here he douses himself with the bottle's entire contents and "all at once" is "bathed in beauty like blazing fire." If one drop made the citizens of Grasse express their joy sexually with each other, emptying the bottle cre- ates a siren song of scent calling the desperadoes to Grenouille's doom. The thieves, whores, and others first "fell back in awe and pure amazement" but are quickly "drawn to this angel of a man. A frenzied, alluring force came from him, a riptide no human could have resisted, all the less because no human would have wanted to resist it" (Süskind 2001, 254). Soaked in "angel's scent," he is literally their angel, and he frees them of inhibition.

This time, however, the throng's desires are not sexual: "They lunged at the angel, pounded on him, threw him to the ground. Each of them wanted to touch him, wanted to have a piece of him, a feather, a bit of plumage, a spark from that wonderful fire. They tore away his clothes, his hair, his skin from his body, they plucked him, they drove their claws and teeth into his flesh, they attacked him like hyenas" (Süskind 2001, 254). The imagery swoops from heavenly—the angel in his various parts—to the bestial hyenas, tearing Grenouille the Great down to the desperadoes' own savage level. In short order they devour him, hacking at his body with cleavers and axes, gobbling up his flesh until he's entirely gone. In a reversal of the usual order of progression, the sublime plummets to the grotesque, and a particularly shuddersome form that involves cannibalism. All that striving, all that wickedly inspired craftsmanship, and he ends on a more hideous and horrific note than he began. So much for sublime transcendence and aspiration. As in the Catholic Mass, this is the fate of a god: to be consumed by his devoted followers.

But in fact to the cannibals themselves there is a sort of redemption here: "They were uncommonly proud. For the first time they had done something out of love" (Süskind 2001, 255). With these lines, the final ones in the book, we return to the root of Grenouille's own longing and the fulfillment of his disappointed hopes. He wanted to be loved; now he is, completely and consumingly, even if he still cannot love himself. His own longing for the virgins' scent is echoed in the desperadoes' longing for him, and crime again has braided the grotesque and the sublime together. The one thing lacking now is Grenouille; his nascent, ill-formed humanity has completely vanished along with his body.

Conclusion: Grotesque Crime, Sublime Art, and a Frenzied, Alluring Force

Grenouille's story—starting with the body born uncanny and made misshapen over time, moving through a crisis of subjectivity and aspiration toward the sublime—is at heart the story of many a good horror novel or film. Horror works by exciting fear and sometimes pity through the grotesque, then building on that fear to create a sense of the sublime—often by destroying a beautiful woman or women along the way. The sublime experience of the horror reader or viewer may never truly approach the levels Grenouille reaches when smelling his virgins (or that the townspeople and desperadoes enjoy during their orgies), but the genre plugs into the same sense of transcendence, an evil supernatural force that can transport us out of this world into the nebulous beyond.

Taking a cue from Edmund Burke, Lyotard writes that when experienced through art, the sublime has a distancing effect for the subject: "Thanks to art, the soul is returned to the agitated zone between life and death, and this agitation is its health and its life" (1993, 251). Art is supposed to be stirring and upsetting; Grenouille's masterwork is this in spades. And it goes beyond beauty to stir the soul in an altogether more disturbing way, a way that can involve the ugliness of the grotesque. His crimes make him an author of both categories; he becomes "Grenouille the Great," the god-like persona he first dreams of in the cave and later assumes in that famous orgy scene. But, again, he never truly inhabits the divine; his aspirations have been narcissistic all along, aimed at making himself loved rather than at uplifting humankind.

To himself, such an artist can embody only the more ugly, perhaps laughable, aspects of the grotesque. His spirit now hovers between death (of his own body) and life (of the people who have consumed him), and he will never find that sublime bliss. In the end Grenouille's horror and his tragedy lie in being unable to experience his own creation as transcendently as others can. In trying to build up a self, he has lost the ability to appreciate his creation.

Notes

1. One exception here is the character Madame Gaillard, who has no sense of smell left (Süskind 2001, 22) and is therefore willing to raise him with her other foundlings. That lack partly explains why she alone of all Grenouille's hosts manages to live to old age: If she can't perceive Grenouille's lack of odor she can't be unsettled by it, and thus she will never inscribe him into history. She is narratively safe.

2. As the movie Grenouille (more articulate than the one in the novel) tells Baldini, he knows "all the smells in the world"; he has the "best nose in Paris." Tykwer paves the way for this assertion by showing Baldini (Dustin Hoffman) sniffing at a rival perfumer's most successful scent through his own prominent proboscis; he is completely unable to pick out the ingredients that Grenouille can assemble in a hasty rummage through Baldini's storeroom.

3. Elizabeth Guilhamon's otherwise helpful article "La caution du grotesque" maintains that Süskind uses the term only once, and later on ("Dieser Gedanke war natürlich von geradezu grotesker Unbescheidenheit" [1995, 209]). The article is nonetheless a useful overview of grotesque theorization and Süskind's use of under- and overstatement.

4. For a definition see especially Freud 2004, 74–76. In his odorlessness Grenouille is like the strange wooden doll Coppelia, who seems human in many ways but disturbs the viewer with subtle signs that she's an automaton. For a discussion of the uncanny in *Perfume* with a slightly different approach, see Woolley 2007.

5. The filmmakers don't show Grenouille's awareness of evil as explicitly—the nature of the medium and marketplace requires some sympathy for the main character—so they imply that if Grenouille is bad it is partly due to circumstances. The novel is less easy on its protagonist, and thus may come off as more disturbing.

6. Kant locates a certain type of the sublime in relations between the sexes: "A woman in whom the agreeableness beseeming her sex particularly makes manifest the moral expression of the sublime is called *beautiful* in the proper sense" (1991, 87)—that is, female beauty depends on embodying the sublime on earth. Kant also opposes sublime beauty and merely charming beauty, a distinction that Süskind plays with here.

7. For a deeper discussion of both philosophers' stance on nature and the sublime, see Ferguson 1992, especially 70–73. Kant, for example, thought that in order to be sublime in itself, a painting had to depict a sublime landscape.

Works Cited

Bakhtin, Mikhail. 1984. *Rabelais and His World*. Trans. Hélène Iswolsky. Bloomington: Indiana University Press.

Borchardt, Edith. 1992. "Caricature, Parody, Satire: Narrative Masks as Subversion of the Picaro in Patrick Süskind's *Perfume*." In *State of the Fantastic: Studies in the Theory and Practice of Fantastic Literature and Film*, ed. Nicholas Ruddick, 96–103. Westport, CT: Greenwood.

Durrani, Osman. 1999. "The Virtues of Perfume; or, The Art of Vanishing without Trace: Grotesque Elements in Patrick Süskind's *Das Parfum*." In *German Studies at the Millennium*, ed. Neil Thomas, 224–42. Durham, UK: University of Durham Press.

Ferguson, Frances. 1992. *Solitude and the Sublime: Romanticism and the Aesthetics of Individuation*. New York: Routledge.

Freud, Sigmund. 2004. "The Uncanny." In *Fantastic Literature: A Critical Reader*, ed. David Sandner, 74–101. Westport, CT: Greenwood.

Guilhamon, Elizabeth. 1995. "La caution du grotesque: Patrick Süskind's *Das Parfum*." In *Les songes de la raison: Mélanges offerts à Dominique Iehl*, ed. Claude David, 207–23. Bern and New York: Peter Lang.

Harpham, Geoffrey Galt. 1982. *On the Grotesque: Strategies of Contradiction in Art and Literature*. Princeton, NJ: Princeton University Press.

Jurich, Marilyn. 1996. "'Solus Solo': The Monster Self: Solipsism in *Peer Gynt, Grendel, Perfume*." *Para-doxa: Studies in World Literary Genres* 2 (1): 84–109.

Kant, Immanuel. 1991. *Observations on the Feeling of the Beautiful and Sublime*. Trans. John T. Goldthwait. Berkeley: University of California Press.

Lyotard, Jean-François. 1993. "The Sublime and the Avant-Garde." In *Postmodernism: A Reader*, Ed. Thomas Docherty, 244–56. New York: Columbia University Press.

Nabokov, Vladimir. 1989. *Lolita.* New York: Vintage.

Perfume: The Story of a Murderer. 2006. Screenplay by Bernd Eichinger and Andrew Birkin. Dir. Tom Tykwer. Perf. Ben Whishaw, Dustin Hoffman, Alan Rickman, Rachel Hurd-Wood. DreamWorks.

Süskind, Patrick. 1985. *Das Parfum: Die Geschichte eines Mörders.* Zurich: Diogenes Verlag AG.

———. 2001. *Perfume: The Story of a Murderer.* Trans. John E. Woods. New York: Vintage.

Woolley, Jonathan. 2007. "Home Truths: The Importance of the Uncanny for Patrick Süskind's Critique of the Enlightenment in *Das Parfum*." *German Life and Letters* 60 (April): 225–42.

Shock Value
A Deleuzean Encounter with James Purdy's *Narrow Rooms*

Robert F. Gross

> There is no more a method for learning than a method for finding treasures.
> —Gilles Deleuze, *Difference and Repetition*

The prospect of writing an essay on *Narrow Rooms* and the works of Félix Guattari and Gilles Deleuze is both inviting and challenging. Inviting, because this dynamic duo of French philosophy often investigated artworks as an important part of their philosophizing—the fictions of Franz Kafka, the music of Robert Schumann, the paintings of J. M. W. Turner, and the horror film *Willard,* to name only a few. Works of art, they asserted, had the power to challenge and break up deadening assumptions and habits not only of daily living but of philosophy as well. Great writers create "new forms of expression, new ways of thinking, and an entirely original language."[1]

Challenging, because Deleuze and Guattari were quite explicit about how art should *not* be used in philosophy. Art, they argued, should not simply be used to furnish examples that illustrated preexisting philosophical concepts. If I wrote an essay that used *Narrow Rooms* to explain Deleuze and Guattrai's concept of "de-territorialization," I would be paying them the compliment of showing admiration for the concepts they developed, but I would be completely betraying their idea of what philosophy is all about. For them, philosophy is meant to venture into the realm of the unthought, to force us out of comfortable and lazy reassertions and into the construction of new connections and concepts.

Moreover, Deleuze and Guattari rejected the widespread intellectual habit of "interpreting" works of art, which they dubbed "interpretosis."

The interpreter forces the artifact into the Procrustean bed of a preexisting system, whether Marxist ("It about class conflict"), Freudian ("It's about Mommy, Daddy, and me"), or any number of other critical schools. Interpretosis reduces the teeming, varied, "molecular" movements found in the work to simple "molar" oppositions—proletariat vs. bourgeois, mother vs. father, male vs. female, human vs. nonhuman, good vs. evil, and so forth. The goal of philosophy, science, and art is not to reduce experiences to mere oppositions but to render experience more complex, opening up new and vital possibilities for us. "Experiment, never interpret," urges Deleuze.[2] So to approach James Purdy's novel à la Deleuze and Guattari is to avail ourselves of the tools that they devised but also to accept the joyous challenge of realizing that we are not working within a closed system of thought but are using tools that open up on the world and lead to innovation and construction. Deleuze once said that he would like to teach a course the way Bob Dylan sang a song, with room for playfulness, clowning, and improvisation. For him and Guattari, learning was not learning to mimic but learning how to generate something new: "We learn nothing from those who say: 'Do as I do.' Our only teachers are those who tell us to 'do with me,' and are able to emit signs to be developed in heterogeneity rather than propose gestures for us to reproduce." Thought begins not with a preestablished method but with an encounter: "Something in the world forces us to think."[3] In this case the encounters are multiple: I encounter the writings of Deleuze and Guattari, and I encounter *Narrow Rooms,* with each forcing me to think. You, in turn, encounter my essay here as well as, I hope, encountering the writings of Deleuze, Guattari, and Purdy for yourself. No encounter should close in on itself—it should proliferate, leading to ever-new connections.

But when I say "I" encounter the work, I misrepresent the encounter, because Deleuze and Guattari see each of us as a multiplicity. I am not only an assemblage of fairly obvious roles and identifications (male, gay, U.S. citizen, Euro-American, son, teacher, scholar . . .) but a myriad of fugitive impulses, many of which may go unnamed or unidentified by me. The attractions and aversions that arise one moment, only to vanish the next, as I walk down the street reacting to weather, facades, passersby, and ads, are evidence that I am a creature far more various than the self-descriptors I just listed in parentheses. Not only do art and philosophy help me be aware of these molecular movements of multiplicity, they foster new ones as well, and that—for Deleuze and Guattari—is all for the best. Each one of us is a multiplicity, and so is the work of art.

The concept of multiplicity provides a very useful tool for revealing the brilliance of *Narrow Rooms*. While working in a genre that often achieves its effects and insights through strong and simple molar oppositions, Purdy complicates matters by presenting characters who are not confined to *being* opposed entities but who are caught up in complex *becomings* that reveal their multiplicities. In doing this he questions common ethical presuppositions in both the horror genre and our society and challenges us to come to a deeper understanding of both horror and love.

Narrow Rooms: **A Summary**

Before going any further, it may be useful for me to provide a quick summary of the novel to clarify the discussion that will follow. I warn you, however, that it is impossible for any précis to do justice to this knotty, complicated, and elliptical work, with its leaps back and forth in time, shifting points of view, deeply ambivalent character relationships, and multiple revisions of motivation as the story unfolds. Here goes:

Sid and Roy had shared an intense and conflicted relationship since adolescence. Roy grew up on the wrong side of the tracks and was obsessed with the star athlete, who came from one of the town's oldest and most respected families. Roy would do anything for Sid, and the two shared secret sexual encounters, but Sid kept Roy at arm's length in public, going so far as to slap him on graduation night when Roy demanded too much attention from him in public. Overcome with humiliation and rage, Roy used sex and drugs to gain a hold over the beautiful and patrician Brian, got Brian to seduce Sid, and set off a tumultuous affair that climaxed in Sid shooting Brian, an act that resulted in a three-year sentence for manslaughter.

When Sid returns from prison (and the novel begins), he gets a job as caretaker with the mysterious young invalid Gareth—another past lover of Brian's and victim of Roy's—and the two young men are soon involved in an intense sexual relationship. But Roy is still consumed with his plans for revenge on Sid, and Sid increasingly feels that Roy controls his destiny. After Roy rapes Gareth on Brian's grave one night and challenges the dead man to intervene in the unfolding revenge plot, Brian appears and commands Roy to have Sid crucify him on the barn door before Brian's dead eyes. When Sid arrives at Roy's, ready to submit to the man who has shaped his life, Roy reveals Brian's command and Sid acquiesces. Realizing that Sid had always loved Roy most, Gareth is outraged, driven to a jealous frenzy at the sight of his lover's and rival's tender lovemaking. When the police show up on the trail of Brian's corpse, Gareth provokes a shoot-out that proves fatal for him, Roy, and Sid.

Issues of Multiplicity: Resisting Binaries

As an example of this multiplicity at work in *Narrow Rooms,* let us look at a single character. Purdy has given him the name "Roy Sturtevant," but he is constructed out of a variety of heterogeneous descriptors. He is: renderer, scissors-grinder, Leatherstocking, valedictorian, booger, tormentor, prisoner, nailed man, coach, sweetheart, husband. Purdy further complicates our understanding of this "Roy-assemblage" through his similes: Roy as virtuoso violinist, angel, Indian, Roman statue, pacemaker, shark, and so on. Not only does each descriptor resonate differently in me as I encounter it, but a single descriptor can elicit a multiplicity of responses. One of the sobriquets most commonly applied to Roy is that of the "renderer," taken from his ancestor's occupation of boiling the carcasses of animals to render up fat. The image of Roy as renderer is linked to feelings of revulsion, fear, morbid fascination, and a masochistic desire to submit, but it is further complicated by Purdy's reminding us that the renderer's fat can be used to make soap. What at first summons up negative associations is made to carry positive associations as well; the renderer not only destroys but transforms and purifies. No one element of this assemblage effaces or subsumes the rest: Purdy challenges us to think of the complexity of renderer alongside that of valedictorian, angel, and nailed man. For an artist does not simply adopt a universal vision of human nature but constructs new images, some that may move outside what is commonly accepted as "human," such as the angel, shark, and pacemaker. The experience of encountering *Narrow Rooms* is different from that of encountering *Pride and Prejudice* or *Crime and Punishment* in part because Purdy constructs Jane Austen or Fyodor Dostoyevsky. He repeatedly makes violent connections that link opposing values: the civilized and the savage, the bestial and the spiritual, the destructive and the nurturing. The connections have the power to shock us into thought. For the "shock value" of *Narrow Rooms* lies less in the ostentatiously transgressive behavior of its characters (drug abuse, anal rape, illegal exhumation, self-laceration, crucifixion, and murder) than in the connections made between acts that are commonly held to be vicious and qualities commonly held to be virtues.

Even the cursory overview of the plot given above shows how Purdy's treatment of love here is distinctive. He does not separate the oppositions but weaves them together inextricably. To appreciate this achievement we can begin by contrasting it to an easily imagined schematic of a horror narrative at its most clichéd. Take a young, white, middle-class, heterosexual couple—the Lovers—and have them menaced by an Unspeakable Monster, which is eventually vanquished by Stalwart Male (Menaced Female may prove to be plucky but is more inclined to scream). The Lovers embrace. End of narrative. Here the oppositions are molar: Normalcy (configured as white, middle-class, and appropriately gendered in its behavior) vs. Monstrosity (which is none of those things). Love and the Human are kept clearly on one side of the dichotomy, Death and the Monstrous on the other. Nothing here forces us to think: clichéd oppositions structure the entire narrative.

Deleuze and Guattari challenge the notion that the artist creates out of a void. Rather, creation takes place against a thick expanse of clichés that suffuse the culture and threaten to subdue the artist from the start: "The painter does not paint on an empty canvas, and neither does the writer write on the blank page: but the page or canvas is already so covered with preexisiting, preestablished clichés that it is first necessary to erase, to flatten, even to shred, so as to let in a breath of air from the chaos that brings in the vision."[4] *Narrow Rooms* escapes the cliché of lovers vs. monster by combining the scenes of greatest horror with the most intense experience of intimacy between the lovers. Sid submits to the Renderer, only to learn that the terms of his submission are that he nail his master to the barn door and remove the nails at dawn, after having brought the corpse of Brian to witness the deed. Sid's "passive" act of submission consists of playing the "active" role of torturer to the "passive" Roy. The oppositions are totally confounded. The prospect of this horrific act reduces Sid to tears, vomiting, and a blood-curdling wail, but when the moment to act arrives he is astonished to discover how easy it is and soon finds himself reveling in the task: "Having put in the first nail he wanted to put in more, he had wanted as a matter of fact to cover entirely the scissors-grinder's body with nails so numerous that he would look like he was clothed in an iron suit composed of shiny little silver heads."[5] This surrealistic image, in which the bloody, vulnerable body is transformed (into armor? into an idol? a fetish figure?), gives us a Sid who is so at one with the command he has been given that he envisions himself surpassing the possible by fulfilling beyond the nth degree. It is in this moment of delirious, hyperbolic submission, in which the boundaries between master and slave disappear, that Sid first realizes that he loves Roy in the same way that he loved his high school diving coach, "who had also commanded him to accomplish the impossible" (157). Sid and Roy both submit fully to each other and to the command of Brian McFee, "whom they had both loved equally" (158).

Purdy multiplies the connections: tormentor to nailed man to lover to coach. The "horrifying" image of a naked man nailed to a barn door connects to the clean-cut, "All-American" image of a high school diver and his coach working together to surpass limitations. The connection renders the wholesome cliché unfamiliar and dangerous, investing it with male/male eros, sexualized submissiveness, and transgressive ambition. "Accomplishing the impossible" is suddenly no longer a lazy and thoughtless exaggeration of coach-talk from the sports world but an image revealed in all its vital extremity, existing simultaneously at the respectable core of American masculinity and beyond the pale. The insight is not unfamiliar to any reader of Deleuze and Guattari, for whom societies are not hermetically sealed, with clear divisions into inside and out. They are constantly springing leaks and generating lines of flight that confuse molarity.

Molecular Sexualities, Dangerous Becomings

Just as Purdy undermines the simple dichotomies that can structure the least thought-provoking examples of horror narrative, he also undermines, years before their appearance, the oppositions of the most sentimental variety of gay fiction. Instead of making his male "lovers" two men whose tender and totally unobjectionable affection for each other runs up against the heterosexist and homophobic structures of society, whether external or internalized (*Brokeback Mountain,* anyone?) and thus reiterating the molar oppositions of straight society, Purdy situates his novel on the fringes of that society. Unfolding primarily in a wilderness of cemeteries, decaying mansions, and deserted fields, Purdy's work does not focus on whether his characters are socially acceptable to the mainstream or not. Instead he focuses on the powerful and complex impulses that can be released through male/male eros.

Narrow Rooms subverts our casual, unthinking certainty that the effacement of boundaries in romantic love is necessarily distinct from the effacement of boundaries in monstrosity. Is there something perilous and potentially horrifying in the intensity that tramples down the boundaries between lovers, and is it perhaps, despite all our protestations, precisely what both lures us into and frightens us about intimacy? Does the feared-and-desired collapse release an experience of the chaos that underlies the tidy molar oppositions of sentimental romance, regardless of sexual orientation? Indeed, does the term "sexual orientation" reverberate as faintly oxymoronic, when the delirious movements of the sexual can be profoundly *dis*orienting?

Sid recollects a sexual encounter he had with Roy in the shower of their high school locker room. It was so intense and violently disorienting that he hurled Roy to the floor, kicked him, and fled into the crowded school corridor, naked. He recalls: *"I thought he would pull my guts and soul out of me he pulled so hard. I felt my cock had been swallowed by a shark. The pain and pleasure, confound him, was too much"* (91). The clichés of Freudian interpretosis would quickly substitute "castration" for shark, and soon Sid's panic would be diagnosed as castration anxiety from a *vagina dentate,* which has been displaced onto a male mouth, which is displaced onto a shark. The gay critic would be quick to reduce Sid's panic to internalized homophobia. A Deleuzean reading, however, would begin not by asking "What does it mean?" but "What does it *do?*" The event moves a male oral sex act into an encounter with a zone of oral/phallic intensity that is "becoming-shark." What clichéd thought would oppose as pleasurable (sex) and horrible (shark attack) is conflated and offers a complete evacuation of Sid's self—guts and soul—in becoming-shark.

Deleuze and Guattari are drawn to the becoming-animal as a way of challenging the anthropocentric limitations of humanism. The werewolf, the vampire, the animals of Kafka, the epic becoming-whale of Captain Ahab in *Moby Dick:* each provides the opportunity of a challenging encounter with the animal rather than the sentimental domestication of animals to corral them within the limitations of the human. Prior to the triumph of Western humanism, in which Man became the measure of all things, the sexual was frequently figured as the animal. Think of Ovid's *Metamorphoses:* Jupiter's becoming-swan, Io's becoming-cow, Actaeon's becoming-stag . . . These myths retain their vitality through the Italian Renaissance paintings of Titian, Tintoretto, and Veronese, and even make a comic appearance in Bottom's becoming-ass in *A Midsummer Night's Dream.* Since then, thinking about "human sexuality" (a revealing term) has tended to keep it safely confined to the limits of the human. *Narrow Rooms* traces what Deleuze and Guattari call "lines of flight" from that. The young men not only become-shark, they become-horse, become-forest-animal, become-cat, become-insect. While a moralizing, hierarchical interpretation might use these images to argue that the characters, in their life of drugs, sex, and violence, are "no better than animals," a Deleuzean reading sees these becomings as openings up to the possibilities of life beyond the so-called human.

While it lasts the saluchian blow job offers the possibility of Sid not being Sid—of not even being anyone. What if, Purdy suggests, sexuality is not constituitive of individual identity but profoundly disintegrative of it? Sid does not flee becoming-shark until after he has reached orgasm. The becoming of the sex act is totally consuming. It is only in the moment after that Roy returns to Roy and the panic and revulsion become violence and flight. A flight that carries its chaos out into the society . . . the football hero launched into the school corridors, delirious and buck-naked.

Purdy swiftly draws the curtain on what ensues.

Concepts of Philosophy, Sensations of Art

The moment of becoming-shark provides an excellent example of how Deleuze and Guattari view the workings of art. They define the task of philosophy as the construction of concepts; the task of art, the construction of sensations, which include percepts and affects. The division is not absolute, of course, although it is useful. The dialogues of Plato contain many artistic qualities; the plays of Tom Stoppard have many conceptual discussions. "Percepts" are sensations of perceptual material, but liberated from any individual perceiver. In literature we can encounter percepts without them being grounded in the perceptions of any individual character, thus attaining an impersonality. Consider the opening lines of *Narrow Rooms:*

> THE HUMAN EMBRYO *is curled up in a ball with the nostrils placed between the two knees.*
> *At death the pupil opens wide.* (1)

We encounter these two percepts without their being grounded in space or time. We have no character to whom we can ascribe them as their author, reader, or thinker. Human life is bracketed by two totally impersonal images: one prenatal and closed in upon itself; the other, at the moment of death, expansive. Life is posed between contraction and expansion, but what, finally, does the pupil open onto? Is the openness of vision a function of the end of vision, of nothingness? No character will quote or expatiate upon these opening lines. We may consider them differently after having read the entire novel and noted Sid's description of Roy as the "coach" and he as the "pupil": is life a process of overcoming constriction, whose completion is found at life's end? Are we to link this openness to Dr. Ulric's contemplation of Gareth's mother, Irene, as she enters the hospital room of her dying son, having "gone beyond grief into some other chamber that is reserved for those who have lost all hope, all hint of promise or benediction, and who have found a calm, if not a peace, in the acceptance of nothing" (190)?

This eloquent description is an example of what Deleuze and Guattari would call an "affect." It goes beyond simply stating what Irene may be feeling to the evocation of a feeling state that can be contemplated independently of her. The slow, measured tempo of the passage, the balance established between "lost" and "found," leading us to the final koanlike presentation of "the acceptance of nothing," all contribute to the solemn, almost sacred tonality of this affect. Purdy avoids using the conceptual term "nothingness," which would have given the sentence a slightly existentialist cast, preferring the more tense and ambiguous juxtaposition of "acceptance" with "nothing." For if I said in a casual conversation, "She accepts nothing," I would acknowledge "She doesn't accept anything" as an accurate paraphrase of what I had just said, but I would not acknowledge it as an accurate paraphrase of "She accepts nothingness." Purdy's "acceptance of nothing" hovers between the two statements without being resolved into either. Purdy presents the act of acceptance from that other chamber beyond grief to us with the comfort neither of total understanding nor of character identification to anchor to it. Purdy invites us, like Dr. Ulric, to contemplate this state without the facile pleasure of identification: we cannot have the sentimental pleasure of claiming we "feel her pain."

For a Deleuzean understanding of literature and film has nothing to do with the widespread belief that these arts make us better people by broadening our understanding of others through acts of identification. Identifications reduce multiplicities, encouraging us to see the world through a single set of eyes, usually one who flatters our vanity (the brave hero, the alluring heroine). By riveting ourselves to a single, fixed identity, our perception of molecularity dwindles down to clichés. We are better off engaging the text, moment to moment, in all its molecular becomings. Purdy helps us do this by discouraging a simple, vicarious identification with any individual character. He shifts from one set of thoughts to another, from dialogue and monologue to impersonal descriptions of nature. The experience of the novel refuses to be reduced to a single point of view—it is a world in flux. Similarly, for Deleuze and Guattari nothing is fixed; life is experienced through encounters of varying intensities. Two bodies, a barn door, a hammer and nails. Out of that, connections are made; events take place. HE—TO NAIL—BLOOD—TO SPURT—FORCE—TO DRIVE—HE—TO NAIL.

Through this charting of events, we see that Sid is not only acting but acted upon. He is driving nails but is also "driven by some force unknown to him" (156). Not an act of pure volition nor the result of hypnotic suggestion, a traumatic childhood, or a neurosis, the event of driving drives nails, blood, Sid himself, with all the impersonality of an infinitive verb. Deleuze and Purdy concur in not domesticating events to the mere confines of our selves. Our passions, loves, and even our deaths do not merely come from within us, they come to us from without as well, with a sometimes horrifying impersonality. How else do we feel the fatality of Tristan and Isolde drinking the love potion, or Macbeth encountering the witches? So too, here: the event cuts across boundaries, impersonal.

Impersonal, too, is the horror of the scene. Where does it reside? Purdy does not describe Roy's feelings as he is being nailed to the barn door, and Sid's sense of horror at the deed vanishes as he begins to execute it. The horror of the event exists independently of the thoughts of either character. It even exists independently of interjections on the part of the narrator. ("But, dare I describe the *horror* of the scene? What fiend so possessed them?") Indeed, affect of horror is intensified by the fact that the characters do not experience it. Horror, in *Narrow Rooms,* is something that we experience and move beyond, not vanquish. We as readers still experience horror as Sid leaves it behind, moving through exhilaration to love. By the final pages of the novel, Roy's body, emaciated, scarred from strokes with a straight razor and bleeding from his nail wounds, does not horrify Sid, who washes him, caresses him, and sucks on his penis.

The love that lies beyond the horror shows itself to be even more impersonal than the horror. Sid realizes that this love is not simply focused on Roy, or on his identification of Roy with the Renderer or Scissors-Grinder. It is a love that is one with a night of savage sex with a multiple murderer one night in the prison shower years ago, and carries him back eons to an "'eternal' lover, or husband, or sweetheart" (179). To be true to love in this novel is not to be true to beauty, brains, patience, or any of the "good points" that might render someone lovable in our common cultural understanding. It is not even to be true to a discrete individual. It is to be true to an impersonal eros beyond revulsion or horror. The emptying-out of self that had so transfixed Sid in the shower with Roy and horrified him afterward triumphs.

Deleuze and Guattari rejected the widespread understanding of love as merely a bond between two people. "What a depressing idea of love," wrote Deleuze, "to make it a relation between two people, whose monotony must be vanquished as required by adding other people."[6] The intensity of love in *Narrow Rooms* spawns multiplicities: Roy sends Brian to Sid in his place; Brian takes to Gareth after his rejection by Sid; Roy reinstates Sid in Gareth's bed. None of these moves cancel out the intensity—rather, they augment it. Ungenerous actions, on the other hand, usually spring from an inability to overcome a sense of self, and manifest themselves in acts of possessiveness, as though love carried with it a proprietary interest. When Irene fires Sid as Gareth's caretaker because she finds the two of them in "almost unconscious bliss" as they enjoy oral sex together, she is sufficiently self-aware to know that her reaction is fueled by "jealousy and envy" (57). She persists in dismissing Sid, however, even though she knows her son has improved under Sid's care. Similarly, Gareth's possessiveness leads him to be "sickened and thrilled" (181) by the sight of his lover and rival in each other's arms. Pride, usually in the form of social snobbishness, creates barriers that would prevent encounters. Sid's brother Vance is revolted by the thought that his brother has taken a job that requires him to look after Gareth's most intimate needs, finding it a humiliation. Gareth, in turn, is disgusted by Sid's attraction to a social pariah like Roy. Sid's growth throughout the novel is a result of his profound humility, his belief that there is nothing beneath him after his experience in prison. In Deleuzean terms, possessiveness and pride are "blocks" to the novel's intense "flows."

Ultimately, the intensity of these flows is so great that it ruptures its social confines and becomes an international media event. What we had been imagining as an isolated event in a rural backwater is broadcasted to the radios of the town and soon to television sets "all over the world" (185). From the little we learn of this transmission, it is clear that the report is not altogether accurate; the role of Brian, for instance, has been lost in the telling. But although it is distorted, it cannot be silenced. It blasts through any remnant of the closet, momentarily breaking down oppositions of center and margin, public and private, insider and outsider. With the speed and delirium of Sid bolting naked from the locker room, the story of Roy and Sid streaks through the world independently of them in an event that will prompt, in turn, new encounters and multiplicities.

The Joy and Horror of Becomings

The flows of intensities in the novel are generated, first and foremost, through encounters with Roy. A social outcast as far as the old families of Revolutionary War stock are concerned, he bears the stigma of being the descendant of a renderer. His body is gaunt, his hands are covered with cuts, his nails are black, and he has not taken a bath in a decade. When he finally does bathe, the bath water becomes brown with mud and dead vegetation. Drugs and sex flow through him, as do feelings of humiliation and rage. His body has become a vehicle of memory. He has scarred his face where Sid struck it, and he lacerates his body at the places that have enjoyed contact with Sid's body. Roy is the locus of horror, both in his treatment of himself and others, and yet he is also the bearer of gifts, including marijuana, sexual pleasure, and dolls.

A Marxist critic in the throes of interpretosis could easily construe the novel as a tract on class conflict of molar identities, with the decadent rural aristocracy, trapped in their vast, decaying mansions filled with heirlooms and outsize furniture, falling under the erotic and financial control of the scarred yet hypervirile Worker. But if we ask what this interclass eros does instead of what it means, we can contemplate Worker becoming-aristocrat, Landowner becoming-slave. The becomings are not symmetrical but release molecular flows. Landowners hold onto patrician markings even as they submit; the Worker may be becoming-Landowner but holds onto his marginality. The erotic creates new forms of intensity, mutations across class lines that call the very lines into question. Roy cuts his face with a razor where it was slapped—Sid emerges from jail with his body scarred from razor cuts—Roy takes a razor to himself. Roy, Sid, and Irene all grow thinner as the novel progresses, as if an impersonal leanness cuts across assemblages, rendering the fat off their bones.

Becoming-rendered, the event that elicits the greatest horror both in readers and characters, becomes the most desired of all becomings. What is the violence that the achievement of impersonality requires? Possible connections beyond the limits of the book present themselves: to the practices of medieval flagellants, the sufferings of courtly lovers, and the private rituals of anorexia and cutting in contemporary society.

Narrow Rooms situates horror at the core of all its becomings. Does not any becoming worthy of the name elicit some fear of loss or dissolution that must be confronted? For Purdy, horror is not to be vanquished or evaded but embraced. While horror is often configured or understood in our culture as an impulse that turns us away from encounters, Purdy constructs an acceptance of horror as an expansion of our possibilities.

In this acceptance Purdy reveals a striking similarity to Deleuze and Guattari, who admired the philosophies of Spinoza, Nietzsche, and the Stoics, all thinkers who urged a fundamentally joyful acceptance of whatever may befall us. This affirmative stance of *amor fati* strengthens our ability to live creatively, open to encounters and experiments. The pseudo-tragic attitudes that stress loss, absence, mourning, and melancholia, on the other hand, reduce our capacity for living. For Deleuze and Guattari, all art worthy of the name opens us up to the possibilities of life. One of the advantages of art, they observed, is that it can give us the insights of the drug addict without our taking drugs ourselves, the perceptions of the schizophrenic without suffering from schizophrenia.

From this Deleuzean point of view, the art of horror contains joy, an expanded sense of encountering and contemplating the extremities of fear and revulsion: "Yes, the essence of art is a kind of joy, and this is the very point of art. There can be no tragic work because there is a necessary joy in creation: art is necessarily a liberation that explodes everything, first and foremost the tragic. No, there is no unhappy creation, it is always a *vis comica.*"⁷ The joy of constructing and linking sensations goes beyond the emotions of any of the characters in *Narrow Rooms* or any sense of loss or horror we may feel at their violent deaths. The creation of art transcends the horror of its subject matter.

As Irene holds Gareth, whose face is described as at once "handsome" and "nothing but rivulets of blood" (191), her eyes seem opened wide and able to take in both beauty and horror, and Purdy invites us to do the same as his novel reaches its conclusion. As imaginative inhabitants of that other chamber, perhaps we overcome the revulsion inherent in horror by not denying it. *Narrow Rooms* both evokes horror and challenges us to deepen our understanding of its profundity and importance.

Notes

My epigraph is taken from Gilles Deleuze, *Difference and Repetition,* trans. Paul Patton (New York: Columbia University Press, 1991), 165.

1. Gilles Deleuze, *Masochism: Coldness and Cruelty,* trans. Jean McNeil (New York: Zone, 1991), 16.
2. Gilles Deleuze and Claire Parnet, *Dialogues II,* trans. Hugh Tomlinson and Barbara Habberjam (New York: Columbia University Press, 2002), 48.
3. Deleuze, *Difference and Repetition,* 23, 139.
4. Gilles Deleuze and Félix Guattari, *What is Philosophy?* trans. High Tomlinson and Graham Burchell (New York: Columbia University Press, 1991), 204.
5. James Purdy, *Narrow Rooms* (New York: Carroll & Graf, 2005), 157. Subsequent page references to this work will be given parenthetically in the text.
6. Deleuze and Parnet, *Dialogues II,* 101.
7. Gilles Deleuze, "Mysticism and Masochism," in *Desert Islands and Other Texts, 1953–1974,* ed. David Lapoujade, trans. Michael Taormina (Los Angeles: Semiotext(e), 2004), 134.

Making Monsters

The Philosophy of Reproduction in
Mary Shelley's *Frankenstein* and the
Universal Films *Frankenstein* and
The Bride of Frankenstein

Ann C. Hall

Philosophical inquiries. *Bride of Frankenstein. Son of Frankenstein. Abbott and Costello Meet Frankensein.* FrankenBerry breakfast cereal. Mary Shelley's novel *Frankenstein* has bred a number of offspring, and some, like her monstrous character, are far from perfect. And while some are imperfect, misshapen creatures, it is difficult to ignore the novel's focus on reproduction as well as its tendency to spawn offspring. The novel is so fecund for many reasons. A cynic might conclude that there are so many interpretations, so many versions, because there is so much money to be made, so many careers to be crafted, that anything really goes.

But a careful reader will notice immediately that despite the differences of critical opinion, the novel highlights the perils of reproduction by its ambiguous presentation of the creator and the monster. There is, for example, equally compelling evidence to suggest that (1) the novel sympathizes with Victor; (2) the novel sympathizes with his creation; (3) the novel does not sympathize with either; and (4) the novel sympathizes with both.

Add to this interpretive maelstrom those who use biographical details to interpret the text, and we have further difficulties.[1] Such readers use reproduction to interpret this novel of reproduction, seeking to understand the work through its conception, both emotional and intellectual. Evidence abounds for biographical interpretation. Mary Shelley's tortured relationship with her father, William Godwin; the death of her extremely talented mother, Mary Wollstonecraft, in childbirth; the difficulties Mary Shelley had conceiving children and bringing them to term, losing many babies before their birth or shortly thereafter. And then there is the issue of the intellectual influences that helped her to conceive the monstrous story: Plato, Rousseau, Godwin, and her mother's feminist philosophies.[2] To carry the reproductive metaphor regarding the critical reception of the novel further, *Frankenstein* has helped to spawn the feminist literary criticism movement, as some critics have used the novel to demonstrate the power of female writers and female interpretation.[3]

Clearly, the critical climate mimics the reproductive anxiety that terrorizes the pages of the novel and two of its more popular offspring, the 1931 Universal film and its sequel, *The Bride of Frankenstein* (1935). In the novel, the two films, and the scholarship, reproduction represents anxiety rather than the usual stereotypical responses: love, joy, new life. Examining the novel and the two Universal films through the work of philosopher/psychoanalyst Luce Irigaray, it is clear that these anxieties are not limited to Shelley's life and personal matters. Instead, there is a cultural anxiety over reproduction, one that stems from the role of women in a patriarchal culture and, ironically, their role in reproduction.

One of the strengths of the work of Luce Irigaray is that she questioned the history of philosophy in her work *Speculum of the Other Woman* from a feminist perspective, arguing, in general terms, that representation itself in philosophy and in art reflects a desire to return to the womb, a desire to re-present reproduction for men in particular. In *Speculum* she interrogates the philosophical principles that are the foundation of the Western tradition and modern social constructions of self, gender, and identity. Her project is similar to Virginia Woolf's interrogation of the British Library and the study of literature in *A Room of One's Own;* Irigaray interrupts the seamless nature of Western philosophical inquiry, inserting a feminist perspective—essentially, she is like a precocious student in a history of philosophy lecture asking the questions no one wants to hear, let alone answer. Taking the speculum, a culturally defined female instrument, she enters the world of philosophy beginning with modern times and ending in Plato's cave, the ultimate womb for Western culture. And through her travels, journeys, and investigations, she demonstrates that the speculum, the female tool, will not reflect, will not re-present, partriachy and its own desires to return to the womb.

The speculum, the mirror, serves as a metaphor for the place of the feminine in patriarchy, and through her journey to the center of philosophy, Irigaray concludes that the mirror will not reflect. It will not, once again borrowing from Virginia Woolf's *A Room of One's Own,* reflect the image of man at twice his natural size (1957, 36). Of course, what is at stake here is more than an academic or rhetorical matter. At stake is the entire question of identity. To paraphrase Freud's famous description of penis envy: We see identity. We know that we are without it. And we realize that we must have it.[4] For many, like Freud, Jacques Lacan, Jacques Derrida, and Luce Irigaray, the determining symbol of identity is in fact the penis, or what some prefer to call the phallus, with all its symbolic and cultural power. But for Irigaray and others, the penis/phallus is just a lure, a misleading and ultimately unsuitable symbol upon which to hang identity hats. For it, like the speculum in the cave, will disappoint. To choose the phallus or the mirror as a means to determine identity is ultimately a fantasy, a trick. But despite the repeated indicators to the contrary, many continue to search for something, that other that will fulfill them, making them feel whole, complete, help them find the perfect identity. What Irigaray, Lacan, and Derrida hope to demonstrate is that this goal is impossible. Identity is always a misshapen, half-formed creature, full of desire, seeking completion.

Tied to this pursuit is language and the question of interpretation. In a brilliant move, helping to rescue the works of Sigmund Freud from oblivion, Jacques Lacan (1977, 30–114) answers the question How do we know what the unconscious communicates or means? His answer is We know because it is structured like language. Trouble is, this conclusion does not necessarily mean clarity. As Elizabeth Grosz explains in her feminist introduction to Lacan: "Instead of Freud's lucidity and concern to make psychoanalysis accessible and scientifically accessible, Lacan cultivates a deliberate obscurity; where Freud attributes the powers of discourse to the unconscious, Lacan explains what its 'language' consists in, what its effects on the discourses of consciousness are" (1990, 13). Given the rather unstable nature of the psyche and identity, how can interpretation occur? Another philosopher answers this question succinctly in his landmark essay " Structure, Sign and Play." According to Jacques Derrida:

> There are two interpretations of interpretations, of structure, of sign, of play. The one seeks to decipher, dreams of deciphering a truth or an origin which escapes play and the order of the sign, and which lives the necessity of interpretation as an exile. The other, which is no longer turned toward the origin, affirms play and tries to pass beyond man and humanisim, the name of the man being the name of that being who, throughout the history of metaphysics or of the ontotheology—in other words, throughout his entire history—has dreamed of full presence, the reassuring foundation, the origin and the end of play. (1978, 292)

Not only does this solution reflect our desire for "an answer," it also accounts for the dynamic nature of language, identity, and desire. Most important, what this solution offers is not relativism, a popular misreading regarding the importance of deconstruction. Instead, there is a certain kind of humility in the face of the reality of identity, language, and desire. We desire succinct, rigid, interpretations, whole and complete creatures, but what we live with are the unformed, misshapen texts and identities that are constantly being rewritten and reformed. For Derrida, Lacan, and Irigaray, this state of affairs is not entirely disconcerting, for this linguistic and psychological reality affords language and life the opportunity for new life, new ideas, and new uses of languages, the play of signification. From this perspective the novel serves as a metaphor of the human condition—monstrous creatures desiring fulfillment whose journey toward completion, albeit torturous and painful, entertains and creates.

In Irigaray's work the novel also serves as a metaphor for gender relations. Like Mary Shelley, Irigaray is indebted to male "father figures" for her philosophical insights, but through her interactions with them she, like Shelley, breeds her own, revolutionary offspring, one that challenges the patriarchy that also spawned her work. The cave, for example, the open wound from which philosophical inquiry emerges, represents maternal origins for Irigaray. It has, of course, been re-presented negatively in order to valorize the importance and autonomy of the patriarchy. And while there may be some idealization of the maternal, the patriarchy, the masculine subject, denies indebtedness to the mother, proposes individualization, and reproduces sameness. No difference, that is, femininity, is allowed:

> In other words, man does not get out of the "maternal waters" here but by freezing the path that would lead back to her, he gazes at himself, re-producing himself in that paraphragm. That hymen that will divide his soul with its mirroring surfaces just as it divides up the Universe. The search to perpetuate self-identity stops all contact dead, paralyzes all penetration for fear one may not find oneself always and eternally the same inside. . . . One never need pay off the debt, either in the past or in the future, if one can only attain the ideal of sameness, which of course defies deterioration of any kind. Alone at last. Fully equivalent to its being, based on none other, repeating being, close to himself alone. (Irigaray 1985a, 351)

The male desire for sameness, for reproduction not of new life but of the same life—himself—deadens. Within the constraints of this patriarchal stranglehold, where the woman serves as mirror but is not recognized in servitude, there is nothing: "She herself knows nothing (of herself). And remembers nothing" (Irigaray 1985a, 345). She is told to remain silent, to "keep still": "Indifferent one, keep still. When you stir, you disturb their order. You upset everything. You break the circle of their habits, the circularity of their exchanges, their knowledge, their desire. Their world. Indifferent one, you mustn't move, or be moved, unless they call you. If they say 'come,' then you may go ahead. Barely. Adapting yourself to whatever need they have, or don't have, for the presence of their own image" (Irigaray 1985b, 207–8). And yet her difference continues to appear, to disturb, to disrupt, to offer an alternative to the straight and narrow, the reproductive sameness, the persistence of phallocracy. There is feminine plurality, jouissance, which is a constant threat because, Irigaray notes, when women speak together, lips to lips, the result is multiplicity, more—oneness, connection without sameness, without slavish adherence to patriarchal expectations and models, in other words, sameness: "Open your lips: don't open them simply. I don't open them simply. We—you/I—are neither open nor closed. We never separate simply: a single word cannot be pronounced, produced, uttered by our mouths. Between our lips, yours and mine, several voices, several ways of speaking resound endlessly, back and forth. One is never separable from the other. You/I: we are always several at once" (209). There is a "way out" of the patriarchal oppression, a "way out" that embraces the maternal waters, the cave, the darkness, the layers of earth, reproduction, and multiplicity. It is a "way out" that Shelley also shares, a journey that reminds us of the origin, the maternal. In this way Shelley communicates her own views about reproduction, views that challenge the patriarchal construct of motherhood and speak volumes, not necessarily in a new language, such as Irigaray envisions, but in a language that highlights the multiplicity of the female experience, ironically in a way similar to the Derridean concept of interpretation—using the language of men to indict the language of men through a narrative about men trying to be women.

The novel *Frankenstein* establishes the ambivalent longings of the human condition through one of the relatively representative characters in the text, Robert Walton. Admittedly, he is an adventurer, exploring areas of the world that others only dream about, but he is an everyman—he had challenges in his childhood; he longs for fame and fortune; and he writes to his sister in the hopes of fostering at least one connection with another human being. The static representation of his sister could describe the role of women throughout the entire novel—at home, waiting, getting messages from the menfolk. At the same time, however, the novel challenges such a conclusion by demonstrating that all men, even the innocuous Walton, have trouble with real intimacy, real relationships.

Walton expresses his ambivalence when it comes to intimacy. On the one hand, he longs to "satiate his ardent curiosity" regarding new lands, hoping to be the first man to cross virginal territory (Shelley 1992, 26),[5] but then he also longs for a companion, someone with whom he may share his discoveries, triumphs, and tribulations. He alludes to Coleridge's poem *The Rime of the Ancient Mariner* and supposes that his love for adventure, the "marvellous," has been influenced by his reading of modern poetry. That may be, but the reference to Coleridge may also remind us that the tale of the woeful mariner was told to those who needed to hear it—in other words, everyman. We, like Walton and the wedding guest in Coleridge's poem, need to hear Frankenstein's story, a story about one man's herculean efforts to establish his own isolated, complete identity. For now Robert serves as a liaison between the tale of Frankenstein and Shelley's readers, perhaps protecting the story, perhaps highlighting the verisimilitude of the story, but more likely establishing a reliable witness and commentator on the events we are about to discover.[6] Walton's prayers, he thinks, are answered by the appearance of Frankenstein, a man whose sensibilities, again he thinks, are not as brutal as those of the deckhands on the ship. We, of course, learn a new level of brutality through the Frankenstein tale.

Ironically, Frankenstein admits that the noblest of human desires is the desire for intimacy: "we are but unfashioned creatures, but half made up" (Shelley 1992, 36). The other, then, serves to perfect and fulfill us. He even admits that he had such a friend but confesses that he lost that friend—without ever identifying who that singular person was—and says his life and the time of intimacy is over. Walton's kindness, however, inspires Frankenstein to tell his tale, to once again engage in an intimate act. At this point it appears that Frankenstein's words are true—intimacy involves making people better than they are singularly. And perhaps this is the hope of every writer. By communicating stories, engaging in a level of textual intimacy between author and reader, a new level of intimacy occurs that betters both.

Appropriately, Frankenstein's monologue begins with his birth, his childhood, and his school days. We learn about his family, his mother's sacrifice to save Elizabeth, the young woman who was raised by his family, from illness, and Frankenstein's own feelings for Elizabeth. Again, as is the case with Walton, Frankenstein is not driven by the need to connect with his family or the woman he loves. He is not inspired by a desire for wealth or by altruism, but by the "glory" that would attend his discovery, which will "render man invulnerable to any but a violent death" (Shelley 1992, 45). Frankenstein's words mimic Walton's: "Treading in the steps already marked, I will pioneer a new way, explore unknown powers" (51). Again, the ambivalence regarding intimacy is expressed in intellectual terms. As one of his teachers remarks, even those scholars who were wrong light the way. Frankenstein, like it or not, is dependent on others, but his desire for independence is powerful, so much so that he struggles to connect with anyone. And while Frankenstein clearly appreciates the compassion he sees in his beloved Elizabeth and his friend Clerval, he does not seem impressed enough to model his behavior upon them, the very people supposedly there to make him better as a result of their intimate connection with him. Instead he throws himself more deeply into the study of science and finally into his project, to become like a god—powerful, isolated, and aloof, the ultimate designation in terms of identity.

Rather than genuinely interacting with those around him, Frankenstein uses his friends, as well as Walton, as mirrors for his own desires. Through them he constructs a whole and complete identity, a performance that casts him into the role of God—not just a better man than he once was, but God, the divine creator. As Irigaray mentions, this role is one for "Everyman": "Completeness of one who is self-sufficient: this is the destiny to which the souls are called who have donned the nature of the living being most able to honor the Gods. This superior condition is the lot of the sex which, subsequently, will be called masculine" (1985a, 322). Frankenstein imagines what his life will be like with this creature: "a new species would bless me as its creator and source, many happy and excellent natures would owe their being to me" (Shelley 1992, 55). Of course, he is also aware he is overreaching. He realizes he is neglecting his family. He even chastises himself regarding this overindulgence, noting that "a human being in perfection ought always to preserve a calm and peaceful mind" and wonders about the destruction his passionate behavior will cause (57). It is important to remember, however, that these comments are made by Frankenstein the elder, not Frankenstein the younger. The elder has learned that his earlier behavior has not resulted in the positive results he had envisioned, but he still constructs a fantasy of identity—calmness and peace will result in power. At the time, however, he is still enamoured with a creature who will call him not just father but creator.

Of course these illusions are shattered with the birth of the creature, a birth so horrific of a creature so ugly that Frankenstein compares him to a creature from Dante's hell and flees the laboratory, thereby abandoning the creature he had hoped would adore him. Frankenstein turns to Clerval for support and conveniently sickens, thereby relinquishing any responsibility for the creature and his whereabouts. His creature will not mirror him, do him homage, bring him fame; in other words, the creature will not reflect, will not serve as the other whom Frankenstein had so hoped he would create.

At this point in the novel Frankenstein commits a number of cowardly and self-serving acts. Like the prodigal son, he returns to his family repentant, and it appears that perhaps he has learned that his egomaniacal quest to make a name for himself has led to nothing. Despite the fact that he is surrounded by his kin, he is still essentially self-absorbed. He discovers that his younger brother has been murdered. And because he is so self-absorbed, so convinced of his own uniqueness, it never occurs to him that his creation would behave exactly like him and try to return to his creator. Through a series of discoveries, Frankenstein realizes that the creature has not only killed his younger brother but has framed Justine for the crime. In a quick and unfair trial, the jury finds her guilty. Rather than admit the truth Frankenstein decides to keep his secret. And after the verdict he feels no compassion for Justine, only his selfish sense of self: "The tortures of the accused did not equal mine; she was sustained by innocence, but . . . fangs of remorse tore my bosom, and would not forgo their hold" (Shelley 1992, 79). And while innocence may hold value for the woman in Victor's view, it does not save her from a shameful death.[7] Frankenstein's response is to once again flee from the companionship and family that he says he so craves: "Solitude was my only consolation—deep, dark, deathlike solitude" (83). He retreats into himself further, only to be disturbed by the very creature he is hoping to avoid. Through this meeting we learn that the creature, too, seeks intimacy with others, but his attempts at connection are undermined, at least initially, by his horrific features rather than by his own selfishness. Through the course of his maturation, however, he learns that selfishness is the way of the human world. There are one or two exceptions, but for the most part, it is a winner-take-all world. And so, ironically, the creature becomes exactly like Frankenstein, monomaniacal. He, too, demands a mirror that will reflect his identity in a whole and complete way. He demands that Frankenstein create a mate for him.

Initially Frankenstein acquieces, but during a reflective moment in the lab he realizes that by creating a female version of the creature, more problems—and not just for him—would ensue. In one of his first moments of compassionate feeling, Frankenstein realizes that his actions have consequences beyond his personal life: "Had I a right, for my own benefit, to inflict this curse upon everlasting generations?" (Shelley 1992, 140). This moment, similar to the one experienced by Coleridge's mariner, might signify a turning point for the good doctor. For the first time he thinks of the human race, not just himself, but then almost immediately he returns to self-absorption: "I shuddered to think that future ages might curse me as their pest" (141). According to Irigaray, reproduction in patriarchy reflects Frankenstein's shift. Reproduction is about relationships among men, all about power, and concerns only the reproduction of patriarchal reputation. Thus it could be suggested that this shift in Frankenstein's attitude, from compassion to selfishness, reflects reproduction within patriarchy. It is not about reproduction. It is about re-producing the masculine image. It is about control and perpetuating the status quo.

When the creature confronts Frankenstein, moreover, there appears to be more than compassion for future generations at stake. The problem for Frankenstein is that the monster is like him, like all of us, actually, drawn to others for intimacy and support, but he is also drawn to others for a sense of power and domination. When the creature says, "You are my creator, but I am your master—obey" (Shelley 1992, 142), this repressed anxiety is articulated. Frankenstein is not afraid of the offspring as much as he is afraid that his creature will be able to usurp his power by creating creatures of his own. While the creature is exactly like Frankenstein, the monster will not reflect his creator's vision of himself; the creature will want to create a vision of his own, an identity of his own, and "father" offspring. Such usurpation must not occur, so he must be destroyed, in this case through eradication of the species.

Frankenstein is still so blinded by his own power that he presumes he will be able to marry Elizabeth and escape the monster's wrath and revenge. Of course, none of this works. Frankenstein leads the very person who could promise some level of intimacy into danger and certain death, perhaps out of fear of any connection on an equal level. Though many lament the lackluster characterization of Elizabeth and other female characters in the novel, their roles are consistent with Irigaray's philosophy of the other/female in a patriarchal culture. The role is to reflect, never to act. Elizabeth is just a prop in Victor's identity fantasy. What is interesting about the novel is that another male, admittedly a deformed, misshapen, and now for all intents and purposes castrated creature serves as the other, the oppressed, the female in Victor's patriarchal fantasy. Once Elizabeth is out of the way, Frankenstein and the creature can begin their real relationship, the one in which Frankenstein destroys the creature and saves the future, thereby reproducing his role as creator/god.

It is telling that the final scenes are presented on ice, reflective surfaces. With Frankenstein, the creature, and now Walton all trying to establish their own identities, it is clear that such a pursuit is futile and illusory. The search for a complete identity is slippery business, subject to many changes and the dynamic nature of life. And though Frankenstein is not an entirely admirable character, neither is the creature at the end of the tale. Both are obsessed with power and self. It is ironic, then, that when Frankenstein dies, the creature takes his body to the North Pole, perhaps offering a vivid symbol for the quest for identity—the pursuit of a stable, static identity results in or can only be death, never life, with its constant change, shifts, and interrelationships.

Irigaray uses the metaphor of frozen water to illustrate the oppression of women in patriarchy. Ice is an apt metaphor, for the patriarchy seeks to control and order, while the feminine serves as a threat. It is interesting to note, then, that the final scenes of the novel take place on ice. The men have attempted to live lives without women, without recognizing their indebtedness to the "maternal waters," so they are left with the frozen, dead mirror of ice. The novel, then, serves as a cautionary tale. We see the destruction wrought by the men who would be women and who would deny women, their difference, and their reproductive abilities.

The Universal 1931 version, of course, is a very loose adaptation of the novel, but the question of identity still prevails.[8] What makes us who we are? The brain? How we are treated as children? How people see us? Judging from the opening images, eyes swirling in the background as the credits roll, the film suggests that sight and spectacle have an important role in the film and its issues. The focus on the visual, the spectacle is an interesting phenomenon because the use of sight in what Lacan and subsequently Irigaray call the mirror stage is essential. As psychoanalysis demonstrates, the visual is the primary sense for establishing identity and gender.[9] The role of the camera is noteworthy as well, and it might be argued that many of these early Universal films are as much about the importance of film and the camera as they are about the stories they tell. For new film audiences, performers are seen in a way they have never been seen before. Information is presented in new ways. And here we see identity as represented in the human form and face—ironically, in this case, through a terribly disfigured monster—presented in a way that we have never seen before.

One of the first trompe l'oeil is the gravedigger. During the funeral services the camera pans across the graveyard, with its predominantly Catholic symbols, and lingers on a well-dressed man. Once the graveside services are complete, however, the man takes off his coat and hat, and it is clear that the coat may be the best piece of clothing he has. The vest and the backside of his garments are tattered, torn, worn, and darned in places. Thanks to the camera, we discover that things are not always what they seem. People, in particular, are not who they appear to be. The camera demonstrates that this man's identity is not whole and complete; there are literally holes in his persona.

In many ways the entire film struggles for completion and consistency but never quite achieves this end. Victor is not the mad scientist. There is another brother, Henry, who works on his creature. The patriarch Frankenstein is a baron who sounds more like a loveable farmer, while his sons sound like they have been trained in Britain. And the town is a mishmash of eastern European peasants. Thus, whereas the novel attempts to establish some connection with the characters and the plot, the film seems to make every effort to highlight the unusual and remarkable, once again establishing the importance of the camera, but not necessarily the story it is to film. We, after all, rely on the camera to show us these spectacles, things we have never seen before.

In another distancing move, the film version provides the good doctor with a sidekick who ultimately makes the error that will condemn the creature to a life of violence and pain by bringing Henry the brain of a criminal, not a normal person. As a result the creature is born morally flawed and ugly, a relationship the film constantly highlights. Beauty makes virtue. Since the creature cannot stand to look at himself, he has no understanding of his identity. And since the human characters in the film cannot stand to look at him, he is nothing to anybody—a monster. But the audience, again thanks to the intervention of the camera, the ultimate instrument of sight and identity, can look at the creature. We want "to look," "to see," and we need the camera to help us fulfill that desire. In one of the final moments, the film illustrates the mirror and its effects on identity through a scene in the windmill during which Henry and his creature look at one another through a spinning wheel, a wheel reminiscent of one of film's precursors, a zoetrope, simply a spinning wheel with stationary pictures inside that created the illusion of motion, motion pictures. As the creator and creature look at one another through this mechanism, it is clear that because they see each other, they are similar. Again, the film underscores the importance of the camera. Without it, you cannot see; without it, you are not you.

The final scene reunites Henry and Elizabeth, and once again, the camera's power is underscored. Here, however, it illustrates a private moment. The two are reunited, but here, as throughout the film, the role of the female is complicated but ultimately invisible. There are no mothers in the film, only fathers who care so deeply about their children that they will risk everything to save them. Unlike most of the women in the novel, Elizabeth in the film is free to leave the confines of her home. She leaves the house, helps bring Henry home, nurses him back to health, and is even a helpmate to the doctor and Victor Clerval. At one point Victor even proposes to Elizabeth in his friend's absence, but Elizabeth remains true to "her man." In this film, then, a film in which women are either victims or absent, the role of women is to mother their men, not their children.

Henry's infantile state is emphasized by the fact that he cannot complete what he started at all or without help. After creating the monster his doctor-teacher sets about destroying the monster, but he is taken by surprise and killed. And in the end when Henry attempts to kill the creature, he is thrown from the windmill. That leaves the villagers, that loyal and obedient mob so frequently resorted to in the Universal arsenal of horror pictures. Through their loyalty to one another, as well as their loyalty to the baron, they apparently destroy the creature and return the world to normalcy. In this way the film presents the question of identity in much simpler terms: you are who we say you are. The paternal, the Frankensteins, and the camera define selfhood. And in the end we are rewarded with another image of reproduction, in this case Elizabeth nursing her soon-to-be husband to health, not a challenge to patriarchal sameness but a monument to its reproduction.

In *The Bride of Frankenstein,* the camera presents its amazing power once again. Thanks to the camera, the opening scene presents a re-creation of the moment of re-creation of the novel. That is, the film shows Mary Shelley conceptualizing her novel. Lord Byron, Percy, and Mary Shelley sit around a fire, Bryon trying to bait Mary regarding her creation, her story. Mary stands her ground and appears to have the upper hand, an important point, given the double casting of Elsa Lanchester as both Mary and the bride. Such casting might lead some to conclude that the film implies that Mary is the monster, but in the scenes that virtually "bookend" the film, a woman disagrees with a man and defends her own views, thereby creating a refreshing representation of female independence and autonomy.

The film begins with the realization that the monster did not die, and he is on the loose. In one scene the monster learns about friendship through his relationship with a blind man. Here, as opposed to some great works of literature, as indicated in the novel, the monster learns about social activities, friendship, fine dining, sharing cigars, and drinking with companions. He learns to speak in a rudimentary fashion. But there is a moral here. The blind man clearly cannot see the monster, so he is deluded regarding the monster's identity, so much so that the old man thinks that the monster has been sent in answer to his prayers for a companion. Once again, identity and sight are linked. The camera presents truth.

With the serendipitous arrival of some local hunters, the blind man is saved from his monstrous friendship and the creation is on the move again. This time he meets a scientist, Dr. Pretorius. Here, however, the film illustrates the power of the camera to create fantasies through the wonderful miniaturization scenes in the doctor's office. The scenes also underscore Pretorius's power—he, for example, restrains the lewd king from violating the queen.

Perhaps because of this power, perhaps because he is accustomed to deformity, Pretorius welcomes the creature into his home and toasts to "a new world of gods and monsters." And while Pretorius is clearly driven by ambition, his curiosity also motivates his research. But like the earlier Frankenstein in the novel, he will go to any lengths to complete his project. He holds Elizabeth hostage while Henry and he complete the bride of Frankenstein. As in the novel and the earlier film, male characters control the creation of the female and reproduction in general. Unlike the male creature, who was created through a criminal brain (which is never mentioned in this version), the female in this film relies heavily on a heart,which, as Caroline Picart notes, carries "on the cliche that men think and women feel" (2002, 53). Female characters in both the novel and the 1931 film play supporting roles.

Here, however, in a stellar performance by Elsa Lanchester, female desire is finally represented, not, tellingly, via words but through a scream and a visual response—again highlighting the power of the camera over the story. In this scene the bride refuses her bridgegroom. Female desire is portrayed and highlighted. Men may want to reproduce. Men may want women to do as they say. Men may want to be reflected at twice their natural size, but in this brief moment the film shows that women will say no to these matters. There is female power here, and though it is exercised in negation, it is there nonetheless. For Caroline Picart (2002), the moment represents female desire as monstrous and terrifying, and she faults the film for representing female desire and sexuality in this way. For Radu Florescu, the moment is much lighter, "a cunning slice of macabre comedy" (186). Truly the moment is an important one, and to laugh in the face of patriarchy's promises is one of the few nonsexual powers available to women since Sarah laughed at the reproductive news from the angel of God. For Irigaray, this position of laughter and negation is a powerful one, and it makes change, though perhaps not clearly or immediately. But what the bride indicates is her own unwillingness to be defined by patriarchy. And though change does not occur through the

Colin Clive, Elsa Lanchester, Boris Karloff, and Ernest Thesiger in *Bride of Franken-stein* (1935). Directed by James Whale. (Universal Pictures/Photofest)

expression of female desire, it is enough to cause us to pause, and the image of Elsa Lanchester responding in this way has become a pop icon.

Female desire. Female power is frightening, but that does not mean that it does not or cannot exist within the confines of the patriarchy. There are moments when "two lips" come together, when women in their mul-tiplicity, diversity—and, by patriarchal standards, their perversity—exist, thrive, and threaten. As Irigaray advises all women: "Women, stop trying. You have been taught that you were property, private or public, belonging to one man or all. To family, tribe, State, even a Republic. That therein lay your pleasure. And that, unless you gave in to man's, or men's, desires, you would not know sexual pleasure. That pleasure was, for you, always tied to pain, but . . . such was your nature. If you disobeyed, you were the cause of your own unhappiness" (1985b, 203). Opening our mouths may be enough to make change happen, to challenge, to usurp.

In the final scenes of the film the relationship between the other and identity, specifically the reliance of the subject on the other to define iden-tity, is clearly articulated. When the monster realizes that he cannot have his bride, he realizes he cannot exist. And while this may signify that the female must be destroyed because she will not cooperate as expected, the scene also suggests the important role the other, the repressed, the oppressed plays in the identity fantasy of the subject.

As the castle explodes around them the monster tells Pretorius to leave: "We belong dead." On the one hand, he appears to sacrifice himself, saving Dr. Pretorius, and perhaps the rest of humanity, by choosing suicide. In this way the monster becomes the Frankenstein of the 1931 film and the novel, the master creator who saves the world for the future. On the other, the act is clearly motivated by his loss of identity. Without a bride, the monster is nothing. He has but a bit of power and that is to destroy himself and the mirror that will not reflect. Almost as if to resurrect the prominence of patriarchy, the film concludes with the explosion of the tower, a strangely orgasmic conclusion. All, we presume, is taken care of. The conclusion suggests that if women control reproduction, they cause problems for male performance, so they must be destroyed, but such a response also indicates the incredible power the female mirror, the female creation still wields in a patriarchal landscape. And, of course, the phallic tower is destroyed in the end, and it is the bride we remember, the bride who entertains, interests, and challenges audiences.

Notes

1. As Smith notes, "One aspect of Frankenstein's critical history, then, is this tendency not to examine the novel in its own right" (1992a, 189). A quick look at studies by recent critics illustrates that even the most complex theorists tend to use biography. See, for example, Gilbert and Gubar 1984; Ellis 1974; Poovey 1996; Moers 1996; and Johnson 1996.

2. See, for example, Levine 1996; Sterrenburg 1974; and Lipking 1996. Lipking argues that the entire work may be understood by one reference to the first page of Rousseau's *Emile.*

3. Gilbert and Gubar's *Madwoman* (1984) was one such important work. They not only demonstrated the utility of feminist criticism, they also highlighted the need to include female authors in the canon, leading the way for further developments in feminist criticism, today a rich and diverse field.

4. Freud's line is infamous: "She has seen it and knows that she is without it and wants to have it" (1963, 188).

5. All references to the novel are from the 1831 edition, edited by Johanna Smith, which for many is the definitive edition. For a discussion of the changes between the 1812 version and the 1831 version, see Smith 1992b, 14–15.

6. The use of the embedded narrative in horror novels is commonplace. See Bram Stoker's *Dracula*, Henry James's *Turn of the Screw,* and Emily Brontë's *Wuthering Heights,* among others.

7. Note the priest's abusive role in Justine's coerced confession: "Every since I was condemned, my confessor has besieged me; he threatened and menaced, until I almost began to think that I was the monster he said I was" (Shelley 1992, 80).

8. For a close analysis of the changes, see Picart 2002, 25–99.

9. As noted above on the female child's experience with seeing the penis, Freud's theory relies on sight. For the boy, the sight of the female genitals is equally disturbing, but perhaps in a different way: "The observation that finally breaks down the child's unbelief [the male child's denial regarding castration and finally the conclusion of the Oedipus complex] is the sight of the female genitalia. . . . With this, however, the loss of his own penis becomes imaginable, and the threat of castration achieves its delayed effect" (1963, 178). For Lacan, the "mirror stage" requires seeing the self in the mirror, and Irigaray also uses the mirror and the mirror stage to interrogate patriarachal principles. Such emphasis offered an important tool for film studies, and so many film theorists have looked to psychoanalytic principles for film criticism, particularly the visual construction of meaning, the unconscious participation in film, and so on. The most notorious essay is Laura Mulvey's "Visual Pleasure" (1989), but a quick look at film criticism in general demonstrates the important role psychoanalytic theory plays therein.

Works Cited

Derrida, Jacques. 1978. *Writing and Difference.* Trans. Alan Bass. Chicago: Chicago University Press.

Ellis, Kate. 1974. "Monsters in the Garden: Mary Shelley and the Bourgeois Family." In *The Endurance of "Frankenstein": Essays on Mary Shelley's Novel,* ed. George Levine and U. C. Knoepflmacher, 123–42. Berkeley: University of California Press.

Florescu, Radu, Alan Barbou, Matei Cazacu. *In Search of Frankenstein.* Boston: New York Graphic Society, 1975.

Freud, Sigmund. 1963. *Sexuality and the Psychology of Love.* Ed. Philip Rieff. New York: Collier.

Gilbert, Sandra, and Susan Gubar. 1984. *The Madwoman in the Attic: The Woman Writer and the Nineteenth-Century Literary Imagination.* New Haven, CT: Yale University Press.

Grosz, Elizabeth. 1990. *Jacques Lacan: A Feminist Introduction.* New York: Routledge.

Irigaray, Luce. 1985a. *Speculum of the Other Woman.* Trans. Gillian C. Gill. Ithaca, NY: Cornell University Press.

———. 1985b. *This Sex Which Is Not One.* Trans. Catherine Porter. Ithaca, NY: Cornell University Press.

Johnson, Barbara. 1996. "My Monster/My Self." In *Frankenstein,* by Mary Shelley, ed. Paul Hunter, 241–49. New York: Norton.

Lacan, Jacques. 1977. *Ecrits*. Trans. Alan Sheridan. New York: Norton.

Levine, George. 1996. "Frankenstein and the Tradition of Realism." In *Frankenstein*, by Mary Shelley, ed. Paul Hunter, 208–13. New York: Norton.

Lipking, Lawrence. 1996. "Frankenstein, the True Story; or, Rousseau Judges Jean-Jacques." In *Frankenstein*, by Mary Shelley, ed. Paul Hunter, 313–32. New York: Norton.

Moers, Ellen. 1996. "'Female Gothic': The Monster's Mother." In *Frankenstein*, by Mary Shelley, ed. Paul Hunter, 214–24. New York: Norton.

Mulvey, Laura. 1989. "Visual Pleasure and Narrative Cinema." In *Visual and Other Pleasures*, 14–26. Bloomington: Indiana University Press.

Picart, Caroline Joan. 2002. *The Cinematic Rebirths of Frankenstein: Universal, Hammer, and Beyond*. Westport, CT: Praeger.

Poovey, Mary. 1996. "'My Hideous Progeny': The Lady and the Monster." In *Frankenstein*, by Mary Shelley, ed. Paul Hunter, 251–61. New York: Norton.

Shelley, Mary. 1992. *Frankenstein*. Ed. Johanna M. Smith. New York: Bedford / St. Martin's.

Smith, Johanna. 1992a. "A Critical History of Frankenstein." In *Frankenstein*, by Mary Shelley, ed. Johanna M. Smith, 189–215. New York: Bedford / St. Martin's.

———. 1992b. Introduction to *Frankenstein*, by Mary Shelley, ed. Johanna M. Smith, 3–18. New York: Bedford / St.Martin's.

Sterrenburg, Lee. 1974. "Mary Shelley's Monster: Politcis and Psyche in *Frankenstein*." In *The Endurance of "Frankenstein": Essays on Mary Shelley's Novel*, ed. George Levine and U. C. Knoepflmacher, 143–71. Berkeley: University of California Press.

Woolf, Virginia. 1957. *A Room of One's Own*. New York: HBJ.

Kitsch and Camp and Things That Go Bump in the Night; or, Sontag and Adorno at the (Horror) Movies

David MacGregor Johnston

> Many examples of Camp are things which, from a "serious" point of view, are either bad art or kitsch. Not all, though. Not only is Camp not necessarily bad art, but some art which can be approached as Camp ... merits the most serious admiration and study.
> —Susan Sontag, "Notes on 'Camp'"

At a very young age I was simultaneously introduced to kitsch and to camp and to classic horror films by "your friendly neighborhood vampire," Sir Graves Ghastly, the Saturday afternoon movie host on Detroit's local CBS affiliate, WJBK-TV Channel 2.[1] With a ghoulish cackle Sir Graves began each show by bidding viewers to "turn out the lights, pull down the shades, draw the drapes, cuddle up in your favorite spot by the tele, and glue your little eyes to your TV screens for today's tale of terror." Viewers were treated to the full range of monster movies, science fiction adventures, and tales of the supernatural from 1930s classics to 1960s schlock. Sir Graves was as likely to introduce *Frankenstein* (1931) or *The Mystery of Edwin Drood* (1935) as he was to show *The Slime People* (1963) or *The Crawling Hand* (1963). It was the films that were my introduction to kitsch, but it was the characters who populated Sir Graves's cemetery set that exhibited camp.

Sir Graves was the creation of Lawson J. Deming, as were all the other oddball characters on the *Sir Graves Ghastly Presents* show. As a vampire Sir Graves was anything but frightening. In fact he seemed more like a supportive uncle or sympathetic grandfather as he praised young viewers' drawings that were displayed during the show's "Art Ghoulery" segment, Sir Graves's equivalent of the family refrigerator.[2] Sir Graves was dressed in the traditional dark suit and red-lined cape, his signature look completed by an obviously fake moustache and goatee and slicked-down hair with a big swirl in the center of his forehead. The movies themselves were "dug up" by the diminutive Reel McCoy, the foot-tall cemetery caretaker, and immediately preceded by Sir Graves's cousin, the German-accented Baron Boogaloff, who would point at the viewers and declare, "You vill vatch the movie und you vill enjoy it! Zat is an order!" A common sketch paired Sir Graves with the Voice of Doom, a mechanical skull with long red hair, to tell corny jokes sent in by viewers.

Other characters would usually appear as random interruptions to lip-synch songs by the likes of Spike Jones, Gene Moss, Tom Lehrer, and the incomparable Mrs. Miller. Deming dressed in drag to perform the castle scullery maid and "gorgeous cookie" Tilly Trollhouse, flipped his cape and lost the facial hair and pomade for Sir Graves's slightly effeminate "alter ego" Walter, and donned wraparound sunglasses for the disembodied head of the beatnik Cool Ghoul. But my and my friends' favorite was the Glob, a bizarre facial apparition that would appear on the full moon above Sir Graves's cemetery. The Glob was created by painting a reversed nose and eyes on Sir Graves's chin: his moustache became the Glob's beard and his goatee became its hair. With the limited special effects capability of the time, Deming actually had to lie upside down for the extreme close-up shots of his lip-synching songs such as "Ghoul Days," "The King Kong Stomp," and "I Want to Bite Your Hand," a parody of the Beatles' "I Want to Hold Your Hand."

Yes, the *Sir Graves Ghastly Presents* show was pure camp, as Susan Sontag defines the term. It was an intentionally tongue-in-cheek portrayal of the standard monster movie fare. In other words, Deming exaggerated aspects of one genre of kitsch, the formulaic horror film, to take them over the top. The familiar stereotypes and hackneyed characters of horror movies were perversely celebrated in Sir Graves's ghoulishly twisted world.

Tales from the Kitsch

The horror genre has been popular with filmmakers almost since the invention of movies themselves. Georges Méliès, the French master of early special effects, is generally credited with making the first horror film, *Le manoir du diable,* in 1896, and Thomas Edison produced a version of *Frankenstein* in 1910. The German expressionist movement brought some of the earliest feature-length horror films, such as *The Golem* (1915 and 1920), *The Cabinet of Dr. Caligari* (1920), and *Nosferatu* (1922). About the same time in Hollywood, Lon Chaney, known as "the Man of a Thousand Faces" for his skill with makeup, became the first American horror movie star for his portrayals of the title roles in *The Hunchback of Notre Dame* (1923) and *The Phantom of the Opera* (1925).

With the advent of sound, Universal Pictures began production of a series of successful monster movies that not only launched the careers of Boris Karloff and Bela Lugosi but also generated a new genre of American cinema, often referred to as Universal Horror. With films such as *Dracula* and *Frankenstein* in 1931, *The Mummy* in 1932, *The Invisible Man* in 1933, and *Bride of Frankenstein* in 1935, Carl Laemmle Jr., son of the studio's founder, helped create some of the genre's trademarks, such as creaking staircases, cobwebbed castles, and mobs of torch-bearing angry peasants. When Laemmle lost control of the studio after several mainstream flops, the monsters took a hiatus from production, but the smashing success of the rereleased original monster movies convinced the new studio executives to green-light *Son of Frankenstein* in 1939. Universal had found a formula. Throughout the 1940s the studio brought us returns, ghosts, or revenges of all of their classic creatures and gathered them together in *Frankenstein Meets the Wolf Man* (1943), *House of Frankenstein* (1944), and *House of Dracula* (1945). Universal even teamed the monsters with their hit comedy duo Abbott and Costello for a series of films, but the golden age of Universal Horror came to a close soon after the 1954 release of *Creature from the Black Lagoon* in 3-D and its sequels in 1955 and 1956.

While the original monster movies are rightly considered classics, the subsequent sequels and spin-offs, not to mention lesser works such as *Night Monster* (1942) or *The Mole People* (1956), are clear examples of kitsch, a word believed to have originated in the Munich art markets of the 1860s and 1870s and used to describe the cheap, marketable paintings and sketches that appealed to the newly moneyed bourgeoisie. "To fill the demand of the new market, a new commodity was devised: ersatz culture, kitsch, destined for those who, insensible to the values of genuine culture, are hungry nevertheless for the diversion that only culture of some sort can provide."[3] Now generally understood to refer to an aesthetically impoverished work of shoddy production, the term was popularized beginning in the late 1930s by theorists such as Clement Greenberg, who contrasted avant-garde and kitsch, arguing that the latter is a threat to culture. More precisely, the mass culture associated with kitsch is a threat to the creative spirit and enlightenment enriched through the development of genuine artistic expressions and the commensurate aesthetic sensibilities. When given a choice between "the bad, up-to-date old and the genuinely new," mass culture mistakenly inclines people toward the former.[4]

In 1939 Greenberg published "Avant-garde and Kitsch," in which he argued that avant-garde and modern art was a way to combat the dumbing-down of culture through consumerism, that is, through the perfunctory art he called kitsch. Modern art explored the circumstances of our experience and understanding of the world, while kitsch turned art into something learnable and easily expressible through clear rules and standard formulations: "Kitsch, using for raw material the debased and academicized simulacra of genuine culture, welcomes and cultivates this insensibility. Kitsch is mechanical and operates by formulas. Kitsch is vicarious experience and faked sensations. Kitsch changes according to style, but remains always the same. Kitsch is the epitome of all that is spurious in the life of our times. Kitsch pretends to demand nothing of its customers except their money—not even their time."[5] Kitsch is both directly and indirectly a result of the industrial revolution. Not only did the "methods of industrialism displace the handicrafts," but consumers now have both the personal inclination and the financial ability to pretend to acquire the tastes and trappings of true culture.

Faced with an inundation of kitsch in the form of Norman Rockwell illustrations (or Anne Geddes baby photographs and "Hang in There" inspirational cat posters, for more contemporary examples) and even the *New Yorker* magazine, "which is fundamentally high-class kitsch for the luxury trade," Greenberg turned toward the avant-garde to defend aesthetic standards and to rescue society from the decline of taste promoted by the consumer culture. "Hence it developed that the true and most important function of the avant-garde was not to 'experiment,' but to find a path along which it would be possible to keep culture *moving* in the midst of ideological confusion and violence."[6] Since kitsch is nothing more than a simplistic rehashing of hackneyed art, it stagnates society. On the other hand, the avant-garde must be encountered on its own new terms and so enriches the aesthetic sensibilities of those enlightened individuals who take the time and make the effort needed to enjoy it.

The Kitsch from Another World

Theodor Adorno called the production of kitsch the "culture industry," a term used in a chapter title in *Dialectic of Enlightenment,* a book cowritten with his Frankfurt School colleague Max Horkheimer. With the development of the culture industry comes a change, such that art's commodity character is deliberately acknowledged and art "abjures its autonomy." Instead of art being valued in its purposelessness, that is, art for art's sake, the value of art comes from its marketability. Instead of a genuine use value based on the mere enjoyment of art, products mediated by the culture industry have only an exchange value in the marketplace. "Everything has value only in so far as it can be exchanged, not in so far as it is something in itself."[7] Art that is autonomous, "something in itself," challenges the viewer and promotes his or her critical tendencies and potential.

The culture industry, on the other hand, manipulates the population by producing art that is nonchallenging and that serves to distract people from the oppressiveness of the power structure. "The isolated moments of enjoyment prove incompatible with the immanent constitution of the work of art, and whatever in the work goes beyond them to an essential perception is sacrificed to them. They are not bad in themselves but in their diversionary function."[8] The culture industry turns people into passive consumers who are content with the false needs created and satisfied by capitalism. The easy pleasures available through the consumption of popular culture obscure the true needs of freedom, creativity, and genuine happiness: "The commercial character of culture causes the difference between culture and practical life to disappear. Aesthetic semblance (Schein) turns into the sheen which commercial advertising lends to the commodities which absorb it in turn. But that moment of independence which philosophy specifically grasped under the idea of aesthetic semblance is lost in the process. On all sides the borderline between culture and empirical reality becomes more and more indistinct."[9] The culture industry blurs the line between true and false needs and does not allow the emergence of enough challenging material to disturb the status quo. Instead the culture industry produces works of art that appear different in their surface details, but that are in reality merely variations on the same theme.

Thus kitsch does not engage culture but repackages and stylizes it in a way that reinforces established conventions and appeals to the masses. As Thomas Kulka wrote, "The painter [of kitsch] should avoid all unpleasant or disturbing features of reality, leaving us only with those we can easily cope with and identify with. Kitsch comes to support our basic sentiments and beliefs, not to disturb or question them." Of course, what seems most to bother contemporary critics of kitsch is precisely its reliance on sentimentality and cuteness. Kulka continues, "It works best when our attitude toward its object is patronizing. Puppies work better than dogs, kittens better than cats."[10] Kitsch is in opposition to the elevated consciousness generated by high art because it provokes superficial, unsophisticated, excessive, or immature expressions of emotion. In this context sentimentality and immorality seem to go together, if only because kitsch manipulates our emotions through cultural iconography guaranteed to elicit an instantaneous and predictable response.

In *The Unbearable Lightness of Being*, Milan Kundera suggests that kitsch is based on the universality of the emotions it provokes:

> Kitsch causes two tears to flow in quick succession. The first tear says: How nice to see children running on the grass!
>
> The second tear says: How nice to be moved, together with all mankind, by children running on the grass!
>
> It is the second tear that makes kitsch kitsch.[11]

People who take pleasure in kitsch do so not only because of the spontaneity of the emotion but also because they know they are moved in the same way as everyone else. Thus kitsch relies on a familiar subject matter imbued with a clear emotional charge.

Still, not every depiction of that subject will count as kitsch. The subject must be instantly and effortlessly identifiable. "Kitsch never ventures into the avant-garde, or into styles not yet universally accepted. It can jump on the bandwagon only after the novelty wears off and becomes commonplace. . . . This is why kitsch is likely to be unexciting or even boring, from the artistic point of view." A style that challenges the accepted representational framework can never be kitsch. Likewise, a work that transforms and intensifies our experience, no matter how identifiably representational, is not kitsch. "Our [kitsch] artist should strive for a stereotype. The subject matter should be presented in the most standard and schematic manner, without any individual features . . . no ambiguities, no hidden meanings."[12]

Perhaps this last consideration explains why horror films so easily fall into the realm of kitsch. Rarely do we find a horror film (Adorno would say any film) that is not a stereotype: that is, not a simple variation on a familiar theme. Although John Carpenter's *Halloween* (1978) is generally credited as the first modern slasher film, the genre is more accurately traced to Bob Clark's *Black Christmas* (1974). In any case a new genre was born, with *Friday the 13th* (1980) and *A Nightmare on Elm Street* (1984) soon to follow. To be sure, the many sequels in these film franchises are kitsch, as is the pairing of the villains in *Freddie vs. Jason* (2003), perhaps a throwback to Universal's successful groupings of its monsters. Certainly, none of these later films has added anything to our experience of slasher films, of films generally, or of the worlds they represent. As Adorno reminds us, "This selection [that has nothing to do with quality] reproduces itself in a fatal circle: the most familiar is the most successful and is therefore played again and again and made still more familiar."¹³ When *Child's Play* (1988) turned the monster into an evil doll, it added nothing to the genre. Chucky is just a reformulation of the now familiar stereotype, and the story merely repeats the standard slasher plot with minor variations.

When Steven Spielberg made *Jaws* in 1975, it was merely a variation on the standard Universal monster movie, albeit an excellent one. Instead of the monster's terrorizing a small European town, the shark terrorizes the bucolic Amity Island. Instead of an angry mob with torches and pitchforks chasing the monster through the countryside, islanders and other fortune seekers take to their boats to hunt the shark with shotguns and dynamite. Instead of being trapped on the moors with no possibility of escape, our heroes are trapped at sea with no land in sight. *Jaws* even relies on the expert scientist to help the early believer kill the monster, this time with a gun and oxygen tank instead of a wooden stake or a silver bullet. Spielberg himself admits that *Jaws* is just a variation on his own feature-length directorial debut, the 1971 made-for-television movie *Duel,* in which the leviathan stalking our hero is a seemingly supernatural semitrailer truck.

But beyond the rehashing of familiar themes, *Jaws* or *Friday the 13th* or any other familiar horror film is kitsch because of the emotions it provokes and because of the ease of its consumption. While such films are not cute or cuddly, as is the standard work of kitsch, they still appeal to our baser emotions. Instead of appealing to sappy sentimentality, horror films are frightening, but generally they are frightening in ways that do not challenge us to question these films, our responses to them, or the worlds they represent. "In the end the peasant will go back to kitsch when he feels like looking at pictures, for he can enjoy kitsch without effort."¹⁴ In this respect, even the first Universal Pictures creature features are kitsch, as is the original *Halloween.* We are not challenged when we watch these films. We are frightened in relatively familiar ways.

Revenge of the Camp

Still, several theorists suggest the possibility of rescuing kitsch. As Greenberg writes, "Nor is every single item of kitsch altogether worthless. Now and then it produces something of merit, something that has authentic folk flavor."¹⁵ For Adorno, that something of merit would cause the consumer to question the dominant beliefs and oppressive ideologies of his or her society. Consider John Carpenter's 1998 release *They Live,* starring the professional wrestler "Rowdy" Roddy Piper as Nada, a down-on-his-luck construction worker. After police destroy the tent community of homeless people he now calls home, Nada decides to investigate the neighboring church, where he has noticed some suspicious activity. In the church's storage room he finds a cache of seemingly ordinary sunglasses. Much to his dismay the glasses reveal the true state of the world: members of an alien race hold all the positions of authority in society and maintain a hypnotic control over their human underlings. With the aid of the glasses Nada sees both the genuine skeletonlike faces of the aliens and the subliminal messages of billboards, magazine covers, and the like, in which the somnambulistic masses are ordered to "consume," "reproduce," and "obey." Normally only high art interrogates the world outside of the work, but *They Live* is a film that clearly intends to shock its viewers out of their acquiescence to the alienation that the culture industry promotes.

Robert Solomon directly criticizes the assumptions on which the usual negative assessment of kitsch is based. "Granted, kitsch may be bad art. Granted, it may show poor taste. But my question here is why it is the sentimentality of kitsch that should be condemned, why it is thought to be an ethical defect and a danger to society." He suggests that instead of being based on a genuine aesthetic judgment of the work in question, the dominant attitude toward kitsch is a learned behavior based on a particular social and cultural bias: "One cannot understand the attack on kitsch, I propose, without a sociological-historical hypothesis about the fact that the 'high' class of many societies associate themselves with emotional control and reject sentimentality as an expression of inferior, ill-bred beings, and male society has long used such a view to demean the 'emotionality' of women. . . . Indeed, much of the contempt for kitsch, I would suggest, is not the product of personal or cultivated taste at all but rather the 'superficial' criterion that teaches us that kitsch—immediately recognizable by its play on the tender sentiments—is unacceptable."[16] These comments suggest that we need to learn to engage kitsch on its own terms. To be sure, we must at least accept kitsch's continued presence in the art world. As Kundera writes, "For none among us is superman enough to escape kitsch completely. No matter how we scorn it, kitsch is an integral part of the human condition."[17] But if we can come to recognize a difference between good and bad kitsch, we may be able to move beyond mere acceptance and come to embrace kitsch.

One way to embrace kitsch is through the concept of camp, "that category of cultural taste, which, more than anything else, shaped, defined, and negotiated the way in which 1960s intellectuals were able to 'pass' as subscribers to the throwaway Pop aesthetic, and thus as patrons to the attractive world of immediacy and disposability created by the culture industries."[18] Although the term can be traced to the late seventeenth century,[19] it was popularized as an aesthetic category by Susan Sontag in her landmark 1964 essay "Notes on 'Camp.'" In response to the standard attitude toward the relation between kitsch and high art, Sontag writes, "But there are other creative sensibilities besides the seriousness (both tragic and comic) of high culture and of the high style of evaluating people. And one cheats oneself, as a human being, if one has respect only for the style of high culture, whatever else one may do or feel on the sly." Instead, the camp taste, or "sensibility" as she calls it, provides a way to appreciate and to take pleasure in some examples of kitsch (if not also high art) precisely because of the work's artifice, excessiveness, theatricality, playfulness, and exaggeration. As such, the camp sensibility emphasizes style over content. "Camp sees everything in quotation marks. It's not a lamp, but a 'lamp'; not a woman, but a 'woman.' To perceive Camp in objects and persons is to understand Being-as-Playing-a-Role. It is the farthest extension, in sensibility, of the metaphor of life as theater."[20] What the camp sensibility prizes above all else is a work that is over the top.

Thus, while there is a close connection between kitsch and camp, only kitsch that is "bad to the point of being enjoyable" is appreciated as camp. To be sure, kitsch takes itself seriously, too seriously, in relation to high art. The camp sensibility appreciates that seriousness when it fails—or, more precisely, because of how it fails. "The experiences of Camp are based on the great discovery that the sensibility of high culture has no monopoly upon refinement. Camp asserts that good taste is not simply good taste; that there exists, indeed, a good taste of bad taste."[21] As such, camp taste is a particular way of seeing things. It is a refined aesthetic taste for the vulgar.

This elevation of kitsch can be found in several distinct but interrelated areas of inquiry. Sontag points to the "peculiar relation between Camp taste and homosexuality," and many other theorists point to drag shows as the epitome of camp. The key to drag as camp is the intentional excessiveness and theatricality of performing the opposite gender. Drag performers are not impersonators: there is no attempt to deceive the spectator. In fact, the heart of the drag show is "a relish for the exaggeration of sexual characteristics and personality mannerisms."[22] Returning to my childhood horror movie host, one could say that Lawson Deming performed vampire drag as Sir Graves Ghastly. While not exaggerating sexual characteristics, Sir Graves exaggerated the characteristics, personality, and mannerisms of the stereotypical vampire.

Sontag also distinguishes between deliberate and naive, or pure, camp. The former intentionally fails to be serious (whether it is a comedy or a drama), while the latter does so only by accident. *Sir Graves Ghastly Presents* is intentionally campy, but it is based on Deming's love of horror movies. "You can't camp about something you don't take seriously. You're not making fun of it; you're making fun out of it. You're expressing what's basically serious to you in terms of fun and artifice and elegance."[23] Deming was making fun out of being a vampire. Alternately, one can discover camp in an otherwise worthless work. Ed Wood's shoddily produced *Plan 9 from Outer Space* (1959) is campy only by accident, and perhaps only in retrospect. When *Plan 9* was released it was just a bad film, but as time passed the film was rescued through a camp sensibility and transformed into a cult classic. That is, we the viewers can make fun out of the bad film. "Not only is there a Camp vision, a Camp way of looking at things. Camp is as well a quality discoverable in objects and the behavior of persons. . . . True, the Camp eye has the power to transform experience. But not everything can be seen as Camp. It's not *all* in the eye of the beholder."[24] Kitsch that can be rescued by the camp sensibility must exhibit a certain originality and creative talent in a work that is obviously ridiculous or garish.

Thus the camp sensibility shares a concern with a lack of seriousness and a simultaneous attention to the quality of execution. "The whole point of Camp is to dethrone the serious. Camp is playful, anti-serious. More precisely, Camp involves a new, more complex relation to 'the serious.' One can be serious about the frivolous, frivolous about the serious." We can view *Plan 9* seriously as a candidate for the worst movie ever made, and we can watch *Sir Graves* as a frivolous romp through the horror genre. In each case we affirm "the ultimate Camp statement: it's good because it's awful."[25] And we can understand the relation among deliberate camp, naive camp, and mere kitsch in terms of Isherwood's distinction between making fun of and making fun out of something. With deliberate camp the creator of the work makes fun out of whatever it references. With naive camp the viewer makes fun out of the work itself. With mere kitsch the best we can do is make fun of it.

Attack of the Killer What?

Given the redemptive quality of the camp sensibility, "anything, given the right circumstances, could, in principle, be redeemed by camp." When we watch the best or the worst of the Universal Horror genre, we can enjoy them because "camp is a rediscovery of history's waste. Camp irreverently retrieves not only that which had been excluded from the serious high-cultural 'tradition,' but also the more unsalvageable material that has been picked over and found wanting by purveyors of the 'antique.'"[26] In a literal sense, these films are awfully good. The infamous *Plan 9* is perhaps the greatest example of a bad film rescued by the camp sensibility, but almost all 1950s sci-fi films are now viewed as camp. The camp sensibility is attracted to these films because we can now view them from a position divorced from their original social contexts and ramifications. "Camp is art that proposes itself seriously, but cannot be taken altogether seriously because it is 'too much.'"[27] When immersed in the cultural concerns of the 1950s, films such as *The Day the Earth Stood Still* (1951) or *Invasion of the Body Snatchers* (1956) appear all too serious. When we view them from the perspective of the twenty-first century, they become obviously "too much."

Examples of intentionally campy horror films are less common but, understandably, more obviously "too much." Perhaps the earliest example of deliberate camp horror occurs in Woody Allen's 1972 film *Everything You Always Wanted to Know about Sex* but Were Afraid to Ask,* in which a giant human female breast terrorizes the countryside by squirting toxic milk. Mel Brooks's deliberately campy *Young Frankenstein* (1974) is a clear homage to the Universal Horror films (Brooks even went so far as to procure the original laboratory set from the 1931 *Frankenstein*), but the historical reference may be overshadowed by the monster and young Dr. Franken-stein, each dressed in top hat, white tie, and tails, performing "Puttin' on the Ritz" before a scientific audience. *Ghost Busters* (1984) has "the proper mixture of the exaggerated, the fantastic, the passionate, and the naïve"[28] to be camp, especially when the world faces destruction in the form of the Stay Puft Marshmallow Man.

Attack of the Killer Tomatoes (1978) clearly and intentionally makes fun out of 1950s sci-fi and 1960s schlock, and may be the best deliberate example of a horror film that is "good because it's awful." Whether by dubbing the Japanese American scientist's voice into English, by including a slow-speed car chase, or by simply reversing the film to show a tomato climb out of a sink for the first attack, the film is way over the top. *Killer Klowns from Outer Space* (1988) features grotesque parodies of circus clowns who shoot popcorn from ray guns, toss toxic cream pies, and wrap their victims in cotton candy cocoons as a source of sustenance. Perhaps the greatest example of a deliberately campy horror movie is *The Rocky Horror Picture Show* (1975). Of course there are the obvious drag elements and a general frivolous reverence for the horror stereotypes, but the film also relishes minor details such as Dr. Frank-N-Furter's carving the formal dinner's roast with a cheap electric knife.

For a more detailed analysis of the relation among deliberate camp, naive camp, and mere kitsch, consider three more recent closely related films: *Scream* (1996), *I Know What You Did Last Summer* (1997), and *Scary Movie* (2000). In the first case, the filmmakers make fun out of the slasher genre. Furthermore, *Scream* challenges its viewers to interrogate the slasher genre, their responses to such films, and the roles such films play in their lives. As such, it can claim the status of an autonomous work of cinematic art. Although *I Know What You Did Last Summer* is kitsch to the extent that it reinforces the established conventions of the slasher genre and appeals to mass tastes, the camp sensibility can rescue it as viewers make fun out of the slasher film in question. In *Scary Movie,* the filmmakers merely make fun of the other two films. It does not challenge the viewers; it only requires us to join the fun and laugh at the jokes. Understood in this context, *Scream* is deliberate camp, *I Know What You Did Last Summer* is naive camp, and *Scary Movie* is mere kitsch.

When Wes Craven was tapped to direct *Scream,* the master of horror in the 1970s and 1980s had made several recent critical and commercial flops. In fact, he even at first turned down the opportunity to try his hand at another gory picture because he thought *Scream* was too violent. To be sure, the film's screenwriter, Kevin Williamson, was steeped in the history of the slasher genre, and he brought a frivolous reverence for that history to his script. But within that script the characters are deadly serious about the frivolity of horror movies. While the basic plot of *Scream* does little to move beyond the standard slasher scenario, the film presents itself as a "clever, knowing, and ironic reworking of the slasher movie"[29] that challenges viewers to rethink such films and the roles they play in their own lives. It has numerous subtle and not-so-subtle references to earlier horror films; characters watch horror films and comment on them and the genre; and, thanks to a covert attempt by a TV reporter to get a scoop, characters even watch the masked killer stalk other characters on a closed-circuit television monitor.

In this last situation, Randy (played by Jamie Kennedy) is alone in the house watching *Halloween* on TV and calls out for Jamie (Lee Curtis) to turn around to see the killer behind her, as we want to call out to Jamie (Kennedy) to turn around to see the killer behind him, and as the characters watching the monitor call out to Randy for the same reason. Of course, each of us is impotent in our attempt to warn the prey. Perhaps the most over-the-top moment that makes fun out of making a slasher film comes in a throw-away scene in which the high school principal greets Fred the custodian, actually Craven himself dressed as Freddy Krueger, the killer in Craven's own *A Nightmare on Elm Street.* Of course, the fact that the killer in *Scream* is dressed in a semicomic ghost mask reminiscent of Edvard Munch's painting *The Scream,* an image that itself has entered the camp pantheon, cannot be discounted.

Although Kevin Williamson also wrote the screenplay for *I Know What You Did Last Summer,* it was adapted from a novel, whereas *Scream* was an original work. Certainly, Williamson is adept at realizing a taut slasher story, but *I Know What You Did Last Summer* lacks the intentional "spirit of extravagance" and "theatricalization of experience" that were the hallmark of *Scream.* Perhaps it is a result of relying too closely on the source material. Perhaps it is the result of having a less accomplished director who was not as versed in the slasher genre. In any case, *I Know What You Did Last Summer* comes off from an idle screening as mere kitsch. It takes itself seriously as a standard slasher film, but viewed with a camp sensibility, we can appreciate how it fails to be serious. In the same way that 1950s sci-fi films become campy when in retrospect we view them as "pure artifice," we can enjoy *I Know What You Did Last Summer* as a stereotype of the genre. "Camp is a certain mode of aestheticism. It is one way of seeing the world as an aesthetic phenomenon. That way, the way of Camp, is not in terms of beauty, but in terms of the degree of artifice, of stylization."[30] *I Know What You Did Last Summer* can be rescued by the camp sensibility precisely because it is a well-executed serious failure, because it is awfully good. In that way the viewers can question the slasher genre and their responses to such films.

The Wayans brothers' *Scary Movie,* on the other hand, cannot be similarly rescued. It does not challenge our notions of horror or of comedy. It places no demand on the viewer other than effortlessly to consume its coarse humor. It is not "too much" in a way that counts as camp. "When something is just bad (rather than Camp), it's often because it is too mediocre in its ambition. The artist hasn't attempted to do anything really outlandish."[31] While *Scary Movie* is not bad as a comedy, it is kitsch. The film is genuinely funny and effectively satirizes both *Scream* and *I Know What You Did Last Summer,* but it doesn't go over the top. It doesn't attempt anything really outlandish. Certainly, there are kooky sight gags such as the ghost mask's contorting when the killer gets stoned, but the bits generally rely on a strong familiarity with the films they spoof. There are plenty of references to homosexuality, but those gags lean more toward homophobia than toward a celebration of the camp sensibility.

The key point is that *Scary Movie* exhibits no reverence for the slasher genre. It is not clear that the Wayans brothers take seriously the films they parody. They make fun of those specific films, rather than making fun out of them. "What is extravagant in an inconsistent or an unpassionate way is not Camp. Neither can anything be Camp that does not seem to spring from an irrepressible, a virtually uncontrolled sensibility. Without passion, one gets pseudo-Camp—what is merely decorative, safe, in a word, chic."[32] In the final analysis, *Scary Movie* is not a scary movie, and it does not pretend to be one. But neither is it camp. It is a film that seriously intends to be a comedy and that succeeds in that attempt. It is safe. It is easy to consume. *Scary Movie* plays to our base emotions through vulgarity and predictability. In a word, it is kitsch.

Were Lawson Deming to join the ranks of the undead and resurrect *Sir Graves Ghastly Presents,* I would expect Reel McCoy to dig up *Scream* and *I Know What You Did Last Summer,* but I would be surprised to find *Scary Movie* in their dungeon's film vault. Aside from the fact that it is not a horror film, *Scary Movie* is not awfully good enough to be camp. "Camp is a vision of the world in terms of style—but a particular kind of style. It is the love of the exaggerated, the 'off,' of things-being-what-they-are-not."[33] Sir Graves, or more precisely Deming, shared that vision and that love. He never made fun of the films he showed, but he always made fun out of them. More important, Deming let us viewers in on the fun he made out of his television program. I end this essay as he closed each show and bid you Happy Haunting.

Notes

My epigraph is taken from Susan Sontag, "Notes on 'Camp,'" in *Against Interpretation and Other Essays* (New York: Farrar, Straus, & Giroux, 1966), 278.

1. More famous examples of similar shows include *Mystery Science Theater 3000* and *Elvira, Mistress of the Dark.*

2. For an entire family of campy TV characters, consider *The Munsters* or *The Addams Family.*

3. Clement Greenberg, "Avant-garde and Kitsch," in *Art and Culture: Critical Essays* (Boston: Beacon, 1961), 10.

4. Ibid., 13.

5. Ibid., 10

6. Ibid., 11, 5.

7. Max Horkheimer and Theodor W. Adorno, *Dialectic of Enlightenment: Philosophical Fragments,* ed. G. S. Noerr, trans. E. Jephcott (Stanford, CA: Stanford University Press, 2002), 128.

8. Theodor W. Adorno, "On the Fetish Character in Music and the Regression of Listening," in *The Culture Industry,* ed. J. M. Bernstein (New York: Routledge, 1991), 32–33.

9. Theodor W. Adorno, "The Schema of Mass Culture," in *The Culture Industry,* ed. J. M. Bernstein (New York: Routledge, 1991), 61.

10. Thomas Kulka, *Kitsch and Art* (University Park: Pennsylvania State University Press, 1996), 27.

11. Milan Kundera, *The Unbearable Lightness of Being,* trans. Michael Henry Heim (New York: Harper & Row, 1984), 251.

12. Ibid., 33, 37.

13. Adorno, "Fetish Character in Music," 36.

14. Greenberg, "Avant-garde and Kitsch," 18.

15. Ibid., 11.

16. Robert Solomon, "Kitsch," in *Aesthetics: A Reader in Philosophy of the Arts,* ed. David Goldblatt and Lee B. Brown (Upper Saddle River, NJ: Prentice Hall, 1997), 450, 453.

17. Kundera, *Unbearable Lightness of Being,* 256.

18. Andrew Ross, "Uses of Camp," in *Camp: Queer Aesthetics and the Performing Subject: A Reader* (Ann Arbor: University of Michigan Press, 1999), 309.

19. Although of uncertain origin, the concept of camp is generally traced back to *se camper,* used in Molière's 1671 play *Les fourberies de Scapin* and believed to refer to the large, ornate military tents of satin and silk, highlighted with jewels, tapestries, and gold banners, that were typically used by France's King Louis XIV and his courtiers when on maneuvers.

20. Sontag, "Notes on 'Camp,'" 286–87, 280.

21. Ibid., 284, 291.

22. Ibid., 290, 279.

23. Christopher Isherwood, *The World in the Evening* (New York: Random House, 1954), 214.

24. Sontag, "Notes on 'Camp,'" 277.

25. Ibid., 288, 292.

26. Ross, "Uses of Camp," 321, 320.

27. Sontag, "Notes on 'Camp,'" 284.

28. Ibid., 283.

29. Mark Jancovich, general introduction to *Horror: The Film Reader,* ed. Mark Jancovich (London: Routledge, 2002), 5.

30. Sontag, "Notes on 'Camp,'" 283, 286, 277.

31. Ibid., 283.

32. Ibid., 284.

33. Ibid., 279.

Contributors

PAUL A. CANTOR is Clifton Waller Barrett Professor of English at the University of Virginia. He has taught at Harvard University in both the English and the government departments, and served on the National Council on the Humanities from 1992 to 1997. His *Gilligan Unbound: Pop Culture in the Age of Globalization* was named one of the best nonfiction books of 2001 by the *Los Angeles Times*. His award-winning essay on *The Simpsons* has been widely anthologized and has been translated into Russian and Spanish. He has published frequently on popular culture in scholarly journals and books as well as newspapers and magazines.

SUSANN COKAL is associate professor of English at Virginia Commonwealth University and author of the novels *Mirabilis* and *Breath and Bones*. She has published articles on authors such as Jeanette Winterson, Marianne Wiggins, and Georges Bataille, and on pop culture subjects such as supermodels and Mary Poppins.

THOMAS FAHY is associate professor of English and director of the American Studies Program at Long Island University, C. W. Post. He also writes horror novels for adults and teens. He has published eleven books, including *Freak Shows and the Modern American Imagination, Gabriel García Márquez's* Love in the Time of Cholera: *A Reader's Guide;* three horror novels, *Sleepless, The Unspoken,* and *Night Visions;* and several edited collections on theater, film, and television—*Considering David Chase, Considering Alan Ball, Considering Aaron Sorkin, Captive Audience: Prison and Captivity in Contemporary Theater,* and *Peering behind the Curtain: Disability, Illness, and the Extraordinary Body in Contemporary Theater.*

ROBERT F. GROSS holds a PhD in comparative literature from the University of North Carolina, Chapel Hill, and teaches theater at Hobart and William Smith Colleges, where he has directed more than fifty productions. He has published books and articles on a wide range of plays, from *Rosmersholm* and *Fuhrmann Henschel* to *The Red Devil Battery Sign* and *The Houseguests,* as well as movies (*Sabrina, Malice*) and television series (*The Rockford Files, Six Feet Under*).

ANN C. HALL is professor of English at Ohio Dominican University and president of the Harold Pinter Society. She has published *Phantom Variations: The Adaptations of Gaston Leroux's* Phantom of the Opera, *1925 to Present;* coedited *Mommy Angst: Motherhood in American Culture;* edited *Making the Stage: Essays on the Changing Concept of Theatre, Drama, and Performance;* coedited *Pop-Porn: Pornography in American Culture;* and is working on a book about playwright and screenwriter Ronald Harwood.

DAVID MACGREGOR JOHNSTON teaches philosophy and film studies at Lyndon State College. His primary research interests include aesthetics, existentialism, and phenomenology.

AMY KIND is associate professor of philosophy at Claremont McKenna College. Her philosophical research, which primarily concerns issues in the philosophy of mind relating to the problem of consciousness, has been published in such journals as *Philosophy and Phenomenological Research, Philosophical Studies,* and the *Philosophical Quarterly.* Her work on philosophy and popular culture has previously appeared in volumes such as *"Battlestar Galactica" and Philosophy: Mission Accomplished or Mission Frakked Up?* and *"Star Trek" and Philosophy: The Wrath of Kant.*

JOHN LUTZ was a visiting professor of philosophy at Long Island University for nine years. He is currently assistant professor in the English department and teaches philosophy and literature, Marxist theory, and postcolonial literature. His published work, much of it dealing with commodity fetishism in the twentieth-century novel, has appeared in journals such as *Conradiana, Research in African Literatures, Texas Studies in Literature and Language, Mississippi Quarterly,* and *Rethinking Marxism.*

JEREMY MORRIS received his PhD from the University of Miami and is visiting assistant professor of philosophy at Ohio University. His areas of specialization include epistemology and the philosophy of language. He has published articles in *Logique et analyse* and *Argumentation.*

PHILIP J. NICKEL is assistant professor of philosophy and ethics at Eindhoven University of Technology in the Netherlands. He writes about epistemology, moral philosophy, and applied ethics, and is currently writing a book about the philosophy of trust.

JESSICA O'HARA earned her PhD in English at the University of North Carolina, Chapel Hill. She is associate director of Writing across the Curriculum for the Center for Excellence in Writing at Penn State, where she teaches Irish literature, literary theory, and composition courses. She is also pretty afraid of ghosts.

LORENA RUSSELL is associate professor at the University of North Carolina, Asheville, where she teaches in the Department of Literature and Language. Her essays have appeared in *Considering Alan Ball, Straight Writ Queer, Horror Film: Creating and Marketing Film,* and *Gothic Studies.* Current projects include an article on queer intimacies and family violence in *The Deep End* and *In the Bedroom,* and a book project on Angela Carter, Jeanette Winterson, and Fay Weldon.

PHILIP TALLON received his PhD in theology at the University of St. Andrews, where he is a part of the Institute for Theology, Imagination and the Arts. He has taught in a variety of university settings, including Asbury College and the University of St. Andrews, in philosophy and theology. He is currently adjunct faculty member at Asbury Theological Seminary. Among his recent publications are "The Problem of Evil in *Psycho*: Hitchcock and Horrendous Evil," in *Hitchcock and Philosophy;* "Evil and the Cosmic Dance: C. S. Lewis on Beauty's Place in Theodicy," in *C. S. Lewis as Philosopher;* "Why Not Live in the Holodeck? Virtual Reality and the Problem of Pain," in *"Star Trek" and Philosophy* (cowritten with Jerry L. Walls); and "Superman and *Kingdom Come:* The Surprise of Philosophical Theology," in *Superheroes and Philosophy* (cowritten with Jerry L. Walls).

Index

HORROR MONSTERS

- Zombie (28 Days Later, Train to Busan, Dawn of the Dead, REC)

- Ghost/Spirit (The Grudge, Insidious, Mama, The Ring)

- Mutant (Hills Have Eyes, I Am Legend, Wrong Turn)

- Robot

- Witch

- Vampire

- Serial Killer/Human (Halloween, Nightmare on Elm Street, Friday the 13th, Psycho, Human Centipede,

- Demon/Occult (Verónica, Exorcist, Evil Dead, Hell Raiser)

- Savage/Cult (Green Inferno, Cannibal Holocaust, Texas Chansaw mass.)

- Cryptid/Creature (The Mist, Cloverfield, Alien,

- Curse
- Disease (Cabin Fever, Carriers, The Crazies,
- Conspiracy (Cabin in the Woods, Suspiria,

HORROR CATEGORIES draft
(Nickel)

1 - Death/dead people
2 - Technology run amok
3 - deterioration of body/manipulation of body
4 - collapse of the human mind
   5 - uncertainty of the human mind

<u>GHOSTS</u>

- 13 ghosts
- Mama
- Devil's backbone
- the others
- the grudge
- the ring
- Babadook
- Insidious
- conjuring

1. Death + the dead

- Ghosts
- Zombies
- mummies

2. Technology

- sci-fi
- robots
- war/political conflict
  → Mutants?

3. Deterioration/manipulation of body

- zombies
- disease
- witchcraft
- body horror/torture porn

4. Collapse of the human mind

- Ghosts/hauntings
- serial killers
- asylums
- cults

5. uncertainty of the human mind

- Exorcisms

PARANOIA → 6th sense, the others, Jacob's ladder, session 9